HOLLYWOOD ENLISTS!

FILM AND HISTORY
Series Editor: Cynthia J. Miller

HOLLYWOOD ENLISTS!

Propaganda Films of World War II

Ralph Donald

ROWMAN & LITTLEFIELD
Lanham • Boulder • New York • London

Published by Rowman & Littlefield
A wholly owned subsidary of The Rowman & Littlefield Publishing Group,
Inc.
4501 Forbes Boulevard, Suite 200, Lanham, Maryland 20706
www.rowman.com

Unit A, Whitacre Mews, 26-34 Stannary Street, London SE11 4AB

British Library Cataloguing in Publication Information Available

Library of Congress Cataloging-in-Publication Data

Names: Donald, Ralph, author.
Title: Hollywood enlists! : propaganda films of World War II / Ralph Donald.
Description: Lanham : Rowman & Littlefield, [2017] | Series: Film and history | Includes biblio-
     graphical references and index. | Includes annotated filmography.
Identifiers: LCCN 2016039956 (print) | LCCN 2016057266 (ebook) | ISBN 9781442277267
     (cloth : alk. paper) | ISBN 9781442277274 (electronic)
Subjects: LCSH: World War, 1939-1945—Motion pictures and the war. | Motion pictures in
     propaganda—United States—History. | War films—United States—History and criticism. |
     Motion pictures—United States—History.
Classification: LCC D743.23 D66 2017 (print) | LCC D743.23 (ebook) | DDC 303.3/75—dc23
LC record available at https://lccn.loc.gov/2016039956

♾ ™ The paper used in this publication meets the minimum requirements of
American National Standard for Information Sciences Permanence of Paper
for Printed Library Materials, ANSI/NISO Z39.48-1992.

Printed in the United States of America

To journalist, author, and editor Elizabeth Donald, my daughter, who kindly gave this manuscript a highly skilled second look

CONTENTS

INTRODUCTION

American Propaganda

To many Americans, propaganda is a dirty word.

Because of common usage, the word evokes visions of an artless, tasteless, untruthful practice used only by totalitarian countries to achieve thought control over their populations.

The popular belief is that Americans are not propagandists, and have not engaged in its use. But that's far from the truth.

Those few Americans who have seen the 1938 Nazi hate documentary *The Eternal Jew* would undoubtedly call it propaganda. That insidious film was designed to prepare the German people to accept the Nazis' eventual slaughter of six million Jews. Most Americans would be comfortable describing a North Korean newscast as propaganda, as we believe the citizens of that country receive only their government's altered version of the facts. The reality has been filtered and edited through their closed media system to serve the interests of Supreme Leader Kim Jong-un. Basically, most Americans believe that propaganda is only practiced by evil people bent on circulating anti-American thought. And because it's anti-American, such messages are also assumed to be a pack of lies.

But these very attitudes might well have been learned through what can be called "American propaganda."

Much of the world certainly thinks so. When they are inundated with the flood of intentional and unintentional messages about

In the climax of *Casablanca* (1942), Rick's plan to get Victor and Ilsa safely out of Casablanca depends on whether Maj. Renault is more loyal to France and his friend, Rick, than to the Nazis.

American culture, thought, and values in the media products that America exports to them, folks in other countries have a name for this phenomenon: they call it "cultural imperialism." Because the United States is by far the world's biggest exporter of media, Americanism penetrates and affects most media markets around the world. Even in countries like Iran where consumption of American media is officially discouraged, bootleg American films, TV shows, and music find their way to the people. Add to that ongoing Voice of America broadcasts into Iran telling the American story in their native Farsi. Third-world nations in particular have good reason to fear that the huge amount of US media that they import could result in the "Americanization" of their countries.

So what about this American propaganda? If Americans do engage in propaganda, how did this obviously decent, acceptable American practice earn such a bad name for itself?

A HORTICULTURAL METAPHOR

Originally, the term propaganda carried no negative connotation. The horticultural verb "to propagate" means to cause something to grow, expand, or to reproduce by sexual or asexual means. The Roman Catholic Church, which centuries ago created their Society for the Propagation of the Faith as its evangelistic arm, is responsible for one of the first uses of the term in the marketplace of ideas.

Most propaganda scholars agree that the basic term has a value-neutral definition. Propaganda is, simply put, persuasion via mass communication that keys on two important goals: first, forming new or adjusted attitudes in the minds of audiences, and second, urging them to action, to do something about these newly acquired attitudes. Albert Bandura's work on modeling demonstrated how the media to which individuals are exposed can persuade them to mimic the behaviors seen on the screen. Regular American commercial advertising believed in Bandura's ideas to the tune of $171 billion worth of propaganda in 2013 (eMarketer). Especially in an election year, American political ads overwhelm media, and the entertainment programs we listen to or watch certainly contain wholesome and not-so-wholesome American values for worldwide audiences to adopt as models for their behavior. At least $3.67 billion was spent on the 2014 midterm elections, an increase over the last four years of $40 million (Center for Responsive Politics). Someone in America believes in modeling and propaganda and puts up big money to get it working for them.

PROPAGANDA AND PERSUASION

There are only a few insignificant differences between the much-maligned term "propaganda," and the venerable and respected word "rhetoric," used to describe persuasive discourse. Kenneth Burke said that rhetoric "refers to the use of language in such a way as to produce a desired impression upon the reader or hearer" (1952, 265). Propaganda and rhetoric are essentially the same, but propaganda transcends it, in that propaganda is always mass communicated. Also, propaganda most often contains at least an implicit call for the audience to respond with some sort of action. With such similarities to rhetoric, a socially accepted form of communication, why should rhetoric be dubbed a "god-term" while propaganda is singled out to be the corresponding "devil-term" (Weaver, 212, 222)?

The answer is probably the same reason that "god and devil terms" develop in a culture, that is, through the gradual shifting of contemporary values and images of a word. So today, when an entity whose beliefs and/or actions we disapprove practices a form of mass persuasion, they are denounced as practicing propaganda, pronounced with solemnity and furrowed brow as if the word itself should be spat out, not gently intoned. However, when American mass media and the Voice of America use the same persuasive techniques, their propaganda messages are described as "the free flow of information" or "education." When the author practiced propaganda for the US Air Force during the Vietnam War, the Air Force referred to the practice as "public information." Usage defines the term, recoins the phrase, and gives it new meaning within the frame of reference of a culture.

Movies as Propaganda

"We are now in the midst of a war, not for conquest, not for vengeance, but for a world in which this nation and all that this nation represents will be safe for our children."
—Franklin D. Roosevelt (FDR), fireside chat, December 9, 1941

"And a lot more 'Mikes' are going to die until we wipe out a system that puts daggers in the hands of five-year-old children—that's what Mike died for—more roller skates in this world—and even some for the next generation of Japanese kids."
—Cary Grant, as a submarine captain addressing his crew, in
Destination Tokyo, 1944

Armed with a better understanding of the meaning of propaganda, let us consider these quotes from President Roosevelt and actor Cary Grant (via screenwriters Delmer Daves and Albert Maltz). Perhaps we can now accept the likelihood that in the opinion of America and the world, Franklin D. Roosevelt's speech, one of his famous "fireside chats," was an example of a highly effective propaganda message on radio, the then dominant medium of American mass communication. But in examining Cary Grant's speech, was this merely a line of dialogue from a movie, pure entertainment and escapism peppered with a bit of flag-waving? Not according to documentary film historian Paul Rotha. He said that all movies, American and otherwise, political-social to fantasy, contain propaganda (57–59).

At this point, readers may be willing to accept the notion that some American films might communicate elements of propaganda. But in all cases? What about something as innocent and apolitical as a children's fable such as Walt Disney's animated film, *Snow White* (1937)? Can a simple fairy tale be laden with propaganda messages?

Certainly *Snow White* can be judged on a superficial level. But doesn't such surface analysis ignore *Snow White* as veiled praise for an organized and inspired proletariat that finally rises up in revolt against an evil, patrician oppressor? And what about *Snow White* as a morality tale demonstrating the folly resulting from the sins of pride and envy? Considering its 1937 vintage (and, therefore, its "unliberated" mentality) the film might simply be meant to reinforce the great rewards in store for a woman willing to give up her own independence and career (as a live-in maid) in exchange for the greater domestic joys of being Mrs. Prince Charming.

It is likely that there is no such thing as a film that fails to communicate some kind of ideas and values. Skillfully presented, ideas and values are quite capable of persuasion.

Writers on the subject assert that propaganda is communicated in both explicit and implicit ways, by blatantly obvious statements as well as through subtle background stimuli. For example, a film such as *Rambo: First Blood, Part Two* (1985) exhibits moments when the message is as obvious as the jags on Stallone's killing knife. When the Vietnam veteran, asked to return to Southeast Asia on a mission, asks if "they will let us win this time," America's nationalistic Vietnam guilt and anger is there for all to see and hear. But in the 1970 anti-war film *M*A*S*H*, Robert Altman subtly communicates much more than the explicit, shocking hospital blood and gore that is the product of such armed conflict. For example, while principal action goes merrily on at the 4077th MASH, the audience hears in the background a bored enlisted man announcing the evening's Dow Jones averages and other financial news over the camp loudspeaker. What news? The huge profits accumulated by corporations profiting from the war, such as Remington Arms and Dow Chemical. *M*A*S*H* wasn't really about the Korean

War: it was Altman's way in 1970 to get a film made that criticized the Vietnam War and the military industrial complex.

But the purpose of all this introductory commentating about propaganda is not to discuss the status of modern American films, although there is much to see in that direction. Instead, its intent is to prepare the reader for considering and accepting another dimension of reality with respect to the American film: that in the 1940s, US war films not only served the war effort and made buckets of money for Hollywood studios, but also had a profound influence on that era's generation and subsequently on their posterity.

It is hoped that these pages will provide the reader with an informative and often nostalgic guided tour through World War II as seen through Hollywood's chauvinistic cyclops eye. Written and edited to propagandize as well as to entertain, films made during World War II accomplished their objectives so well that they helped to forge an entire generation into one of the most ideologically unified, singularly minded populations in the history of the world. This was certainly a praiseworthy aim, considering the perilous world situation at that time. But physicists tell us that every action has a reaction, every movement a consequence. This residual effect is also true regarding the consequences of human persuasion. And in this instance, Hollywood and Washington saw fit to alter the attitudes of American citizenry with blindly nationalistic, unrealistic, savagely ethnocentric, and racist propaganda messages. Consequently, a population jubilant in victory, finding itself the dominant force in the postwar world, began to believe in its own exaggerated importance, its own racial and cultural superiority, and in a role for America in world affairs in which the United States lives out its manifest destiny as the planet's omnipotent and all-wise peacekeeper.

And then came Korea and Vietnam, and more recently, Iraq, Afghanistan, and ongoing operations against the Islamic State/ISIL throughout the Middle East.

This book, then, is a critical chronicle of the war propaganda that has had such a profound and lasting effect on our nation.

THE PODIUM AND HEARTS AND MINDS

To do more than simply serve up a random sampling of aural and visual invective hurled by American filmmakers against the Axis powers, we will examine these films with a certain organization and orientation. This begins with examining what will hereafter be called war rhetoric, and then applying what we learn to the propaganda messages found in American films produced during World War II.

> "Such is the spectacle of injuries and indignities which have been heaped on our country, and such the crisis which its unexampled forbearance and conciliatory efforts have not been able to avert."
> —James Madison, war message to Congress, 1811

> "Our motive will not be revenge or the victorious assertion of the physical might of the nation, but only the vindication of right, of human right, of which we are only a single champion."
> —Woodrow Wilson, war message to Congress, April 2, 1917

> "This is not a jungle war, but a struggle for freedom on every front of human activity."
> —Lyndon Johnson, special message to Congress regarding the Vietnam War, August 5, 1964

These speeches and many more throughout the history of the United States possess one common goal: to persuade one's countrymen to agree with and support the speakers' contentions that armed conflict against other nations were the requisite and only remaining course of action to be taken. It's assumed that war was rarely in the best personal interests of the majority of these presidents' constituencies. So it became necessary to resort to persuasive discourse (rhetoric) to convince large groups of people that the defense of their country required them to temporarily give up their homes, their jobs, their personal safety, and perhaps their lives for the cause of truth, right, and justice. Furthermore, American leaders had to convince citizens that they were required to take up arms to kill a fellow man with whom they had no particular personal antipathy. In every one of America's wars, regardless of how justified or unjustified they were, speakers have risen to provide that impetus.

In this century, scholars studying the speeches of many influential Americans have discovered an amazing similarity in the appeals used to sway their audiences. Although their lives were separated by as much as two centuries, and their personalities varied from phlegmatic to bombastic, men as diverse as Presidents Madison, Wilson, and Johnson had surprisingly much in common when it came to their notions of effective mass persuasion.

But since the advent of the motion picture and especially television, the public podium no longer shares with the printed word the distinction of being the two primary means leaders use to persuade a nation to go to war. Nearly since its inception in the late 1800s, film's ability to convincingly communicate to the American people has surpassed the public podium or even the printed page. And television, the electronic child of the motion picture, now brings that persuasive power directly and effortlessly into America's living rooms.

Research in war rhetoric has not devoted itself to investigate how these particular oratorical appeals have been used in war films. That is what this book is intended to do: to explore how these historical pleas to solidarity and action in the face of a belligerent enemy have been thoughtfully or unwittingly translated from the podium to the motion picture screen during World War II, and then to discuss the impact and influence of this campaign on subsequent world events.

Since no critical study of political communication in any historical period can be properly conducted in a vacuum, groundwork will first be laid by investigating the political and economic times in which these films were made. Once the relationships between the Roosevelt Administration and the motion picture industry are known, their motives for producing 375 films, which can only be classified as war rhetoric, in four years will be better understood. In investigating these relationships, evidence will demonstrate that the motion picture industry not only enthusiastically provided a persuasive medium for the war appeals of the Roosevelt Administration, but did so with a not-so-hidden agenda of objectives which transcended both nationalism and patriotism. As the facts seem to indicate, the goal of this agenda may simply have been the unfettered continuation of movie industry profits during a national emergency that—had they not acted—had the potential to reduce that income.

FOCUS ON NARRATIVE FEATURE FILMS

To focus this book further, we'll only discuss feature-length, narrative motion pictures produced by the American film industry during the period of America's direct involvement in the war, 1941–1945. This relegates the study of pre and postwar narrative films, wartime documentaries, short subjects, animated films, and other movie fare to another occasion.

As well, it would be impossible for one volume to house a historical/critical analysis of every genre of film produced in Hollywood during the war. So this book's contents are limited to a category of feature motion pictures slightly larger than a single genre, but which possesses certain identifiable characteristics. This category will simply be referred to as the "war films" of this period, defined as motion pictures in which the principal story pertains to, and centers on, the conflict between the Axis powers and the Allies which began with Hitler's invasion of Poland in 1939 and concluded on Victory over Japan (V-J) Day in 1945. This includes stories portraying the actual combat, the occupation of subjugated countries, the "home fronts" of the belligerents, and tales of war-related espionage.

HISTORY AND THEORY

As previously mentioned, chapter 2 contains an investigation of the relationship between Hollywood and Washington during World War II, using books, articles, diaries and autobiographies, period publications, etc. Then, the main body of this book details the conscious or unconscious adaptation of the appeals found in American war rhetoric to the feature-length war films Hollywood made during the war.

Robert Ivie once wrote that war rhetoric "begins with the premise that metaphor is at the base of rhetorical invention" (1987). As we will discover, using the highly effective propaganda tactic known as "name calling," Ivie maintains that a subject becomes so closely identified with a name that it "is imagined to be that very thing which it only resembles." For example, in a subsequent chapter we will see how the term "monkey," or "ape" (via the tactic of name-calling) is used effectively in Hollywood's racist portrayals of countless Japanese soldiers. Sufficient repetition of this helps convince audiences of the subhuman nature of the enemy.

Ivie also provides us with a series of logical steps toward "identifying key metaphors" in rhetoric. He writes that one first familiarizes oneself with the speaker's milieu, his or her "text and context." The following chapters provide that orientation. Secondly, "representative texts are selected," which the analysis chapters of this book examine. Next, Ivie's method calls for the grouping of these metaphors into conceptual units, followed by citing their occurrences. Finally, an examination of the interrelatedness of these units completes this systematic approach. This book's analyses follow Ivie's pattern of inquiry, albeit adapting it from the podium to the larger-than-life movie screen, and noting the use of cinematic techniques (e.g., film editing or the use of music to emphasize a point) to achieve persuasive objectives.

MAJOR WAR PROPAGANDA APPEALS

Prussian general and military strategist Karl von Clausewitz once said that war is the result of the failure of conventional diplomacy (78). As a rule, wars do not spring suddenly upon two countries; neither do the reasons their leaders cite for commencing hostile actions. War rhetoric often begins with a history lesson in which a series of indignities or aggressive actions perpetrated by the enemy leave one's peace-loving nation with no honorable alternative besides armed conflict. Both history and theories combine to create our historical-critical model for analysis of filmed war rhetoric, the archetypical heritage for which is found in the 200-year-old history of American war oratory.

Five General Categories of Appeals

Although literally dozens of war rhetorical messages are found in World War II films, we can summarize them under five general categories of appeals. One of the earliest and best of America's war propaganda scholars, Harold Lasswell, found three main appeals in his analysis of the persuasive messages used to urge people to action during World War I ([1927], 1971). The first appeal he named "Guilt," defined as clearly establishing the blame for the present conflict on the enemy.

The second he gave the unusual and somewhat misleading name of "Satanism," which is rhetoric designed to polarize. The third Lasswell called "the Illusion of Victory," which stresses that the sacrifice of life, money, and time that the conflict requires will inevitably result in our ultimate triumph (47, 77, 102).

In the 1980s, American historian and war rhetoric scholar Ronald Reid identified two allied (and therefore combined) appeals based on the Christian Bible that comprise our fourth major appeal. He named them "Apocalypticism" and "Typology" (1983). Apocalypticism is based on the ultimate clash between good and evil as found in the Biblical books of Revelations and Daniel. For the purposes of this volume, I will call such appeals "Apocalyptic." Reid's reference to "Typology" or "Biblical Typologies," which I will refer to as "Biblical," deal with scriptural analogies. Among others, Reid's writings and those of anthropologist Robert Ardrey make the case for a fifth appeal category, "Territoriality," the human instinct to protect one's own. In this volume, I will refer to these appeals as "Territorial."

Guilt

Lasswell wrote that Guilt is the concept of laying the blame for the war squarely on the enemy. It is based on the truism that no one in his right mind desires war, and that anyone who precipitates such a conflict is automatically in the wrong. Therefore, Guilt stresses the fact that the speaker's peace-loving nation would never, of its own, covet its neighbor's holdings or desire to rule its population. The Guilt appeal asserts that the currently deteriorated state of affairs is always due, in one way or another, to the less-than-legitimate desires and actions of the enemy. Even Hitler's blitz on Poland, which started World War II, was characterized by Nazi propaganda chief Joseph Goebbels as a necessary move to protect ethnic Germans living in Poland from persecution and discrimination.

The concept of Guilt is certainly not a modern invention. US President James Madison's speeches prior to the War of 1812 place the blame for the conflict firmly on England, explaining that our peaceful country had been attacked without provocation by a belligerent England: "We behold, in fine, on the side of Great Britain a state of war against the United States, and on the side of the United States a state of peace toward Great Britain" (Meyers, 290).

In a speech to the Virginia convention on March 23, 1775, Patrick Henry provides us with another example of Guilt. "Our petitions have been slighted; our remonstrances have produced additional violence and insult . . . if we wish to be free, we must fight! An appeal to arms and to the God of Hosts is all that is left us!" (Tyler, 142–43).

And on December 9, 1941, thirty-six hours following the attack on Pearl Harbor, President Franklin D. Roosevelt spoke these words on radio in a fireside chat to the nation:

> I can say with utmost confidence that no Americans, today or a thousand years hence, need feel anything but pride in our patience and in our efforts through all the years toward achieving a peace in the Pacific . . . and no honest person, today or a thousand years hence, will be able to suppress a sense of indignation and horror at the treachery committed by the military dictators of Japan, under the very shadow of the flag of peace borne by their special envoys in our midst. (523)

Guilt, then, firmly establishes in the minds and hearts of our citizenry that our country is in the right, is innocent of any warlike intent, and that we have tried with all our resources to avoid war, but that the enemy has thrust the present conflict upon us, giving us no choice but to take up arms.

Satanism

Satanism, or as academics often say, "god and devil terms," refers to oratory meant to polarize. Lasswell says that when using the major appeal category of Satanism, the enemy is pictured as barbaric and totalitarian, unmindful of any rule of law or decency, while Americans and their allies are contrastingly characterized as being civilized and democratic. Cultural and racial differences between belligerents and allies are often highly exaggerated. The notion is that the more different the enemy, the greater threat he is to us and our way of life, and the easier it is to motivate a soldier to exterminate him. Describing ethnocentricism, one of Satanism's many culturally related tactics, Reid wrote:

> Both world wars, for example, were depicted as battles between
> Democracy and Totalitarianism; and [World War I] atrocity stories,
> such as those about the Germans chopping off the hands of Belgian
> children, were used widely, if not always truthfully. . . . Ethnocentric
> appeals emphasize the threat of the barbarians to one's superior
> culture. (*Communication Monographs*)

Because it is the easiest and most simplistic of appeals, Satanism is the
most frequently used war propaganda appeal. Also, perhaps Satanism's
popularity is due to the fact that, due to the sneak attack on Pearl
Harbor, World War II was for Americans a war of emotion, of righteous
anger over a dastardly deed. Among the Satanism appeals of the films of
this era were the racial and cultural disparities between the Axis powers
and Americans; the distaste of the enemy for our way of life; our character and courage versus their lack of those virtues; our intelligence versus
their stupidity or rigidity of thought; and many other contrasting assertions.

There is little subtlety in either filmed or spoken appeals in this
category. For example, in his war message to Congress, Woodrow Wilson characterized Americans as peace-loving humanitarians. But in describing Germany's announcement of submarine warfare "unrestricted
by rule of law and decency," Wilson said that the German Navy had
"thrown aside all considerations of humanity and is running amuck"
(Congressional Record, 102–103).

In the fireside chat previously mentioned, FDR spared few devil
terms in characterizing the Axis powers:

> The sudden criminal attacks perpetrated by the Japanese in the Pa-
> cific provide the climax of a decade of international immorality. Pow-
> erful and resourceful gangsters have banded together to make war
> upon the whole human race. Their challenge has now been flung at
> the United States of America. (522)

Similarly, in a news conference in July of 1965, President Lyndon Johnson stated:

> Thousands of [South Vietnamese] have died. Thousands more have
> been crippled and scarred by war. We just cannot now dishonor our
> word, or abandon our commitment, or leave those who believed us

and who trusted us to the terror and repression and murder that
would follow. (Johnson, 795)

Writing about the same theme, US Secretary of State Dean Rusk characterized the Viet Cong thusly: "He can destroy, but he cannot build; he
can assassinate schoolteachers and health workers, but he cannot serve
people" (US State Department, 1964).

As well, as Reid points out, "Prowar spokesmen often urge the nation to protect other countries who are weak but who share the nation's
basic values, on the grounds that God and Destiny have given it the
duty to perform such a noble mission" (1976). For example, as FDR
said during his fireside chat to the nation on December 29, 1940, "If
Great Britain goes down, the Axis powers will control the continents of
Europe, Asia, Africa, Australasia, and the high seas—and they will be in
a position to bring enormous military and naval resources against this
hemisphere."

In Harry Truman's special message to Congress on the situation in
Korea on July 19, 1950, the president said, "We are determined to
maintain our democratic institutions so that Americans now and in the
future can enjoy personal 'liberty, economic opportunity, and personal
equality' . . . but we know that our future is inseparately joined with the
future of other free peoples" (Truman, 536).

So Satanism in war messages clearly isolates the enemy's culture,
race, religion, and method of government, using every possible avenue
of polarization, from that of our own.

Scapegoating Reinforces Guilt and Satanism

The concept of "scapegoating" is helpful to understand both Lasswell's
Guilt and Satanism categories. Burke says that in primitive societies,
someone or something was often endowed with most of a culture's
unwanted evils. This served the purpose of both purifying the people
and directing any feelings of group inadequacy from the group to the
scapegoat (1973). "Making him an offender against legal and moral
justice, so that he 'deserves' what he gets," was a helpful method Burke
cited for creating an even more effective scapegoat. Later in the same
volume, Burke uses Hitler's own characterization of the Jews as an
international devil to explain just how effective scapegoating can be

(194). As Lasswell's categories of Guilt and Satanism point to the perpetrators of our country's current misfortune and to the evil and foreign nature of the enemy, Burke explains Hitler's use of the same techniques in terms of scapegoating: "Hence, if one can hand over his infirmities to a vessel, or 'cause' outside the self, one can battle an external enemy instead of battling an enemy within" (203).

In speeches eerily similar to today's divisive rhetoric against immigrants in the United States and Europe, Hitler often criticized "Jewish finance," "Jewish Bolshevism" (in themselves, oxymoronic claims), and "Jewish arrogance." In rant after rant, Hitler recounted the purported sins of the race of people he selected to be Germany's scapegoat. And attempting to separate and distinguish the Jewish race from the rest of Germany's *herrenvolk*, Hitler created the polarities necessary to galvanize the German people into support of his illusory notion of the "master race." Finally, Hitler insisted that Germans were tasked with the duty of obliterating the Jewish menace (208). Burke wrote, "The projective device of the scapegoat, coupled with the Hitlerite doctrine of inborn racial superiority, provides its followers with a positive view of life. They again can get the feeling of moving, forward, towards a goal" (203).

The Illusion of Victory

Lasswell's notion of the Illusion of Victory is the third propaganda appeal category. To establish the Illusion of Victory, the propagandist must convince his audience that the defeat of the enemy is not only possible, but is the most likely outcome of the current conflict. No political constituency is likely to give its wholehearted support to a conflict that appears doomed to defeat at the outset. Therefore, it is vital that the population be secure in the belief that ultimate victory is inevitable.

In his inaugural address as president of the Confederate States of America, Jefferson Davis knew how important it was to make a case to the people of the South that this new government could survive:

> [Although] the tide for the moment is against us, the final result in our favor is not doubtful. The period is near at hand when our foes must sink under the immense load of debt which they have incurred,

a debt which in their effort to subjugate us has already attained such fearful dimensions as will subject them to burdens which must continue to oppress them for generations to come. (201)

In his emotional oration to Congress requesting a declaration of war against Japan on December 8, 1941, President Roosevelt predicted total victory: "With confidence in our armed forces—with the unbounded determination of our people—we will gain the inevitable triumph—so help us God" (515).

Often Illusion of Victory statements are prefaced by some kind of qualifier, asserting that if Americans persist in some task or meet a certain objective, victory is assured. This can refer to personal sacrifice, tenacity, doing one's job well, or any number of wholesome American virtues, as detailed later. Contrariwise, the Illusion of Victory asserts that we will be victorious because of the great number of deficiencies attributed to our enemies. This can include the enemy's moral shortcomings, lack of courage, inability to think independently and solve problems or—as depicted often—not being able to shoot straight.

Apocalyptic and Biblical Appeals

Reid writes that Apocalypticism creates a shift from reality to metaphor. In this shift, the two warring countries cease being themselves and instead are described as representatives of the forces of good and evil in the final conflict between light and darkness as foretold in the Bible. As such, Apocalypticism sometimes is articulated in a way that uses the god/devil-terms outlined earlier. But the difference between Apocalypticism and Lasswell's concept of Satanism is that Apocalypticism strictly refers to happenings predicted in the Revelation of John and the Book of Daniel. Therefore, the polarities of good vs. evil and light vs. darkness are discussed, along with the concept of false gods vs. the Lamb, the sheep vs. the goats and the Antichrist. Contrastingly, Satanism is Lasswell's catch-word for the many polarities not found in the Bible. These range from "we are human and the enemy is more like an animal," to "important civilizing aspects of our culture are missing from our enemy's culture."

Reid explains Apocalypticism this way: As found in the books of Revelations and Daniel, human history has been interpreted as a long struggle between the forces of God and Satan, Christ and Antichrist. Early Christians (as well as some today) were living in the prophetic "dark days," but Christ will soon return. The Antichrist would be destroyed in an apocalyptic struggle, and Christ's early kingdom would last for a millennium, after which another struggle would take place, and the world would end. (1983, 232)

In war rhetoric, the orator's country is portrayed as the godly people, the faithful, and the enemy is, by default or by explicit definition, the Antichrist. Using the Satanism and Illusion of Victory appeals to create slurs against the enemy, this contrast can be amplified. As will be demonstrated often throughout this book, major appeal categories are often used in combinations.

Oftentimes, the declaration is made that since the American people are agents of the Creator, God is on our side. Therefore, by association, Americans become the children of light and the eventual beneficiaries of the millennium. Logical deduction tells us whom the enemy is supposed to represent.

In a radio address on May 27, 1941, Roosevelt said:

Today the whole world is divided between human slavery and human freedom—between pagan brutality and the Christian ideal. We choose human freedom which is the Christian ideal. . . . We reassert our abiding faith in the vitality of our constitutional Republic as a perpetual home of freedom, of tolerance, and of devotion to the word of God. (192)

Reid's concept of Biblical typologies extends only to appeals drawing analogous relationships between Biblical characters and present day individuals. But I argue that Biblical appeals in these films can exist that portray similarities between the types of situations and actions found in the Bible and in World War II. This approach expands Reid's concept to include any scriptural analogies that associate either positive or negative meaning to either the propagandist's community or the enemy's. References to present-day activities put in the context of Biblical events can be strong motivators for those in the audience predisposed to Christianity—the majority of Hollywood's American audience in the 1940s—especially to those who favor Christian fundamentalism.

At this point, readers may be wondering how we will differentiate between Apocalyptic and Biblical appeals. Although they are closely allied concepts, Biblical appeals involve the similarity between present-day events and biblical accounts of what has already occurred, whereas Apocalyptic appeals are concerned with prophesies that have not yet happened: "However, both involved the same exegetical method, which presumed the historicity of scriptures and interpreted them as foretelling the future" (Reid, 1983).

So Apocalyptic and Biblical appeals create and illustrate a relationship between God and America that implies or overtly expresses divine approval and support, and directly supports the Illusion of Victory.

Territorial

Territorial is our fifth and last propaganda appeal category. Robert Ardrey made the convincing case that as in lower species on this planet, man is a territorial creature who will instinctively defend his space against all comers (1966). Critics point out that this contention is predicated upon the belief that man is an animal evolved from lower species. Since virtually all the scientific world accepts that stipulation, I consider human evolution to be a fact, not just a theory. As well, with reference to all forms of war rhetoric, I will confidently settle for this proof: that American presidents and other famous orators of past ages have intuitively believed Territorial appeals to be effective, and have included them in nearly every war message ever presented.

A few examples: both Abraham Lincoln and Jefferson Davis insisted that the other's forces were out to usurp their territory, government, and institutions; Lyndon Johnson maintained throughout the Vietnam War that American freedom itself was threatened "so long as the forces of violence are allowed to pursue their wider pattern of aggressive purposes." James Madison insisted that Britain's true intention in their naval belligerence with the United States was no less than "total re-colonization" of America. In all of these, this defensive instinct, this territorial imperative, is employed to create in the minds of the audience a credible threat to our homes, families, our rights, our laws, and our democratic way of life.

Interestingly, Hitler used what Burke called a "doctrine of resignation" to create in the German people more than just a protective instinct about the fatherland: Additionally, the "struggle on behalf of the (Aryan blood) triumph" required offensive action (208). This philosophy was used as a premise for Germany to invade the territory of others, armed with the knowledge that spreading the "culture-creating" Aryan influence around Europe was a defensive act.

Reid supports Lasswell's propaganda categories, saying that nations are more than willing to go to war when they "are persuaded that (1) their territory, especially the center of their territory, is endangered, (2) the enemy is a barbarian who threatens their basic values, and (3) the prospects for victory are good" (1976).

Reid also maintains that since the War of 1812, the concept of American territoriality has extended to US possessions on the high seas. Great Britain's acts of impressing sailors and confiscating ships were among the offenses that President Madison cited were grounds for declaring war. Lyndon Johnson's speeches in August of 1964 show how this same portrayal is accomplished in the latter twentieth century. In a radio and television report to the American people following what he characterized as the "renewed aggression in the Gulf of Tonkin," August 4, 1964, Johnson said:

> In the larger sense, this new act of aggression, aimed directly at our own forces, again brings home to all of us in the United States the importance of the struggle for peace and security in Southeast Asia. Aggression by terror against the peaceful villagers of South Vietnam has now been joined by open aggression on the high seas against the United States of America. (498)

In a speech the next day at Syracuse University, the president assured his audience that "Peace is the only purpose of the course that America pursues," and that "Aggression . . . has unmasked its face to the entire world. The world remembers—the world must never forget—that aggression unchallenged is aggression unleashed" (498).

ANALYZING PROPAGANDA FILMS

As previously mentioned, the primary source materials for this study are World War II era narrative films. In the analysis chapters, each appeal category is treated, illustrated, and enlarged upon with multiple examples found in these films.

Although, strictly speaking, this is not a study of film form, it is important to restate the uniqueness of cinematic technique in communicating these propaganda messages. Only in film or video can the audience be taken into the scene in the close-up, led to understand metaphoric relationships by the use of film editing techniques (montage), or simply shown detail that the director wishes to emphasize to make a point. Lacking cinematic tools, an orator on a podium, a newspaper writer, or even an actor on a stage cannot match the multifaceted power of the motion picture or a similar television presentation. Yet the orator, writer, actor, and many others combine to create cinematic communication. A shot-by-shot analysis of film's communication techniques in these movies would fill many volumes. So occasionally during the analysis, examples of a cinematic nature are mentioned as provocative illustrations.

Since Guilt, Satanism, the Illusion of Victory, Apocalyptic/Biblical, and Territorial appeals rarely exist independently, in many instances in a medium such as film, one scene—or even a single shot—may contain a combination of words, sound effects, music, visuals, actions, editing, and *mise-en-scene* that are simultaneously at work. But before analyzing these World War II filmed propaganda appeals, individually or in tandem, it will be helpful to examine the history of the era and the personalities and predilections of the key participants in Hollywood feature film production. Their situations, motivations, and character are all important in laying a foundation of understanding for the analysis of their propaganda films.

I

HOLLYWOOD AND WASHINGTON

During World War I the medium of film was not an infant, but was certainly no more than a toddler. Motion pictures were silent, so early filmmakers intent on propaganda messages were missing an important tool later used by their counterparts in World War II. Lacking sustained dialogue, film propagandists of World War I were not able to fully adapt all the subtleties found in the appeals of war rhetoric discussed in the previous chapter. Relying almost entirely on the visual, film pioneers such as America's D. W. Griffith and France's Abel Gance were nonetheless able to pile on heavy doses of Guilt and Satanism into their wartime melodramas.

Typical among these early efforts at filmed propaganda was Griffith's 1918 *Hearts of The World*, in which the father of modern motion picture technique gave an auteur performance as writer, producer, and director. Depicting scenes of Prussian depravity and brutality in occupied France, the film featured the stereotypical Griffith climax: the helpless heroine is saved from a fate worse than death at the hands of the bestial Hun.

Despite Griffith's polarizing but simplistic approach, his efforts were restrained and diplomatic compared to a little Fox Company epic in 1918 called *Why America Will Win*. Ostensibly it was to be a biography of the commander of US forces in Europe, General John Pershing. However, any similarity to the facts was purely coincidental. At one point, Pershing leads a triumphant march into Berlin and tells off the Kaiser, who is then struck by lightning.

Figure 1.1.   While a wounded Nazi pilot menacingly holds a gun on her, Kay Miniver bravely debates bombing helpless civilian populations in the six-Oscar-winning MGM production of *Mrs. Miniver* (1942).

Abel Gance's *J'Accuse* was somewhat similar to Griffith's, in that it placed regular folks in the crucible of war to show war's suffering and needless waste of life. But rather than an anti-German melodrama, *J'Accuse* is considered by film scholars to be the first feature length anti-war film.

WAR IS HECK VS. WAR IS HELL

During the first half of the twentieth century, nearly all American films produced while a war was still underway tended to glorify America and the American soldier. Such films also stress the sacrifice that these actions entail, glorifying and immortalizing deeds of valor average Americans performed while at great personal risk. This lionizing approach to war might be called the "war is heck" approach. However, in the years following the ending of one of the United States' conflicts, more of a "war is hell" outlook emerges. These more realistic postwar treatments emphasize that surviving the war is a soldier's main objective, and that ordinary men often find themselves trapped in the insanity of war. It seems that after a given war, it is no longer necessary to be chauvinistic about one's country or its cause: the elation of victory subsides and is replaced by postwar disillusion. As usual, art mirrors life.

After World War I, licking their collective wounds and mourning their dead, disillusioned Americans became isolationist, vowing to be much more cynical about "foreign entanglements." Economically, massive unemployment and the Great Depression followed World War I. This also contributed to viewing the conflict with prejudice. *What Price Glory* (1926) and especially *All Quiet on the Western Front* (1930) typify this postwar disillusionment, stating in no uncertain terms that "war is hell." Rather than memorialize men's sacrifices or make any kind of positive propaganda statement, these kinds of films decry the waste of life and limb, soundly condemning national leaders who start the wars and those who profit from them.

However, in the late 1930s, correctly foreseeing the horrors Hitler had in store for Europe, the leaders of the motion picture industry in Hollywood set upon the task of erasing the memory of "war is hell" films from the collective consciousness of American audiences, convincing them instead that war was just "heck" after all. Films in war and action genres once again interjected high adventure, comradeship and heroism as dominant themes. Among these were *Beau Geste* (1939), *Gunga Din* (1939), and *They Died with Their Boots On* (1941), this last film a whitewash of the bloody career of George A. Custer which gave new meaning to the term "white lie." Another example that can't be overlooked when discussing the films of this period is *Only Angels Have Wings* (1939), a "fly the airmail over hazardous mountains" picture that was, for all intents and purposes, later remade, lock, stock, and sacrifice in 1942 into the World War II propaganda film, *The Flying Tigers*.

But as the threat in Europe gave way to a war in Europe, another kind of picture began to appear in America's theaters. This was the beginning salvo in Hollywood's anti-Nazi, anti-isolationist barrage that would finally explode on the screen as the openly propagandistic post-Pearl Harbor war film. But not everyone in America was pleased with this new wave of anti-Axis filmmaking.

TRIAL BY GOVERNMENT

In 1938, isolationist US senators obtained passage of a resolution authorizing them to set up a committee to investigate what they correctly labeled as Hollywood's opening propaganda salvo of World War II. Misguided as they were, the senators were also accurate when they said that the intent of these films, besides selling tickets to the Bijou, was to persuade America to join England and France in their struggle against Nazi Germany. The official congressional mandate obtained by these senators was to "investigate moving picture and radio propaganda."

Republican Senator Gerald P. Nye of North Dakota, cosponsor of the resolution, opened the hearings with a broadside against these movies, saying that they were "the most vicious propaganda that has ever been unloosed against a civilized people" (US Congress, 1942). Of course, these men had no idea how really vicious a propaganda film could be. Nye would never have given America's first, timid attempts at mass persuasion such a label if he had viewed some of Hitler's hate "documentaries" such as *The Eternal Jew* (1938) or *Campaign in Poland* (1940). By comparison, these infamous motion pictures, made under the supervision of Hitler's propaganda chief Joseph Goebbels and German film industry head Fritz Hippler, make Hollywood's prewar efforts at propaganda seem amateurish.

In *The Movies in Our Midst,* Gerald Mast writes:

> The official question that provoked the hearings was, why did Hollywood films one-sidedly support the Allied cause in the European war? The odor of anti-Semitism attached itself to the hearings even before they had begun. The motion picture industry came through this first trial by government with renewed unity and strength [as they would not a half-decade later]: The Hollywood spokesmen were so fervently sincere and committed to their beliefs, the motives of their accusers so suspicious, public and press opinion was as one-sided on the hearings as was the content of the movies on the war in Europe. Within three months, the question that had provoked the hearings had become moot. (476)

Condemning the Nye committee hearings, *Fortune* magazine used the MGM film *Escape* (1940) as an example of a double standard.

Quoting film industry spokesman Wendell Willkie's testimony, *Fortune*, in an article titled "Hollywood in Uniform," said:

> Did anybody say anything when the *Saturday Evening Post* ran *Escape* as a serial? Did anybody complain when Little, Brown published the book? Did they crack down on Harry Scherman when the Book-of-the-Month Club selected it? No. Of course not. But the minute we make a picture out of it, then it's propaganda. (50)

But the Nye committee was not alone in its condemnation of Hollywood. In his autobiography, Will Hays wrote:

> The matter had been brewing in the minds of one or more senators for several months. Early that year Senator Burton K. Wheeler of Montana repeatedly accused the films of stirring up a demand for war. On one occasion he was reported in the *New York Times* to have told the America First group in Utah that movies were "designed to incite the public," and that they were the "Benedict Arnold of 1941." . . . In justice it must be said that the burden of the speech, as reported, was isolationism. Specifically, the senator was quoted at one point as saying, "They [motion pictures] are cleverly directed for passion-rousing effect, and to bring an overwhelming call for convoys. And convoys, as any clear-thinking American will know, means entrance of the United States into the European conflict." (538)

Between the last quarter of 1938 and Pearl Harbor (December 7, 1941), Hollywood produced over a thousand feature films. But it is significant to note that of those, over fifty pictures released by the film industry of an officially neutral country were blatantly anti-Nazi in theme. Although Hollywood ventured deeper and deeper into pro-interventionist, anti-Axis themes from 1938 onward, Bernard Dick recalls that as early as 1933, Hollywood had begun to warn the nation and the world about the threat of fascism (41). Mild messages such as *Gabriel Over the White House* (1933), in which a conservative protagonist becomes a New Dealer, eventually gave way to the reactionary Cecil B. DeMille's *This Day and Age* (1933), in which Americanism is defended by youthful vigilantes, who appear both like Minutemen and Hitler Youth.

Dick writes that German refugee Fritz Lang's *Fury* (1936) is more to the point, "emphasizing a feature of dictatorships that is often overlooked: their self-proclaimed infallibility" (43). In 1937, Republic's "Three Mesquiteers" (Bob Livingston, Ray Corrigan, and Syd Saylor) take down black-shirted *Schutzstaffel* (SS) look-alikes in *Range Defenders*. In *Pals of The Saddle*, made a year later, the Mesquiteers foil the plans of enemy agents trying to make off with a poison gas formula.

As the war widened, and many European and Asian markets for the export of American films dried up in 1938, Hollywood's anti-Nazi propaganda became even more strident. Film industry spokesmen such as 20th Century Fox Chief Darryl F. Zanuck often spoke out in favor of American intervention, and especially for support of the British. He once told an American Legion convention, "If [the isolationists] charge us with being anti-Nazi, they're right. And if they accuse us of producing films in the interest of preparedness and national defense, again they are right" (Gussow, 104).

A PUNCH IN THE NOSE FOR ADOLPH

Warner Bros.' *Confessions of a Nazi Spy* (1939) was a notable example of the films made at the outset of the war in Europe. The picture, an exposé of the subversive activities of Nazi party members in America, resulted in the German–American Bund filing an unsuccessful libel suit against the studio. Here are some excerpts from a less-than-kind Frank S. Nugent review in the *New York Times* on May 24, 1939:

> Hitler won't like it; neither will Goebbels; Frankly, we were not too favorably impressed either, although for a different reason. We can endure just so much hissing, even when *Der Fuehrer* and the Gestapo are its victims. The Warners had courage in making the picture, but we should have preferred to see them pitch their battle on a higher plane . . . Membership in the National Socialist Party cannot be reserved entirely to the rat-faced, brute-browed, the sinister. We don't believe Nazis let their mouths twitch evilly whenever they mention our Constitution or Bill of Rights. . . . (2:13)

Finally, in the furor created by the first feature film produced by Louis de Rochemont's *March of Time*, we get a feeling for the "split personality" that was America's political and social climate in the days before Pearl Harbor. The 1940 picture, *The Ramparts We Watch*, is supposedly set in "middle America" during the period 1914–1918. Although the townspeople are provincial and isolationist at first, they are depicted in their growing concern for the turn of foreign events, such as the Germans' unrestricted submarine warfare, causing them eventually to change their minds. They finally become staunch supporters of the US entry into World War I. To make this allegory current, fifteen minutes' worth of selected segments of a Nazi terror propaganda film, *Baptism of Fire*, were spliced onto the end of the picture. As well, de Rochemont, taking a lesson from the Nazi propagandists, adjusted reality to suit his objectives. He removed the original German narration, and replaced it with his own, in English, tinged, for effect, with a threatening Teutonic accent. Far from a literal translation, this new ending's narration and shocking visuals of the Nazi blitz in action reinforced the growing American image of the Germans as a serious threat to America. These were among the mixed reviews:

> Bosley Crowther—*New York Times*, September 20, 1940: There has never been a motion picture just like this one. . . . A nation which eight months ago felt comparatively secure and aloof from the echo of an old war abroad is today most alarmedly aware of a new and unpredictable menace. (1:27)

> Margaret Frakes—*The Christian Century*, October 16, 1940: *The Ramparts We Watch* is "to convince the American people that the German menace threatens today even more than in 1917, and that our only recourse is to plunge into a gigantic armament program to get ready for a battle with our future foes." (1277)

Finally, Frakes turns the tables on de Rochemont: She writes that films such as *The Ramparts We Watch* . . . are not so much anti-Fascist as a presentation of a sort of *America uber alles*, a picture of Americans as a people destined to protect the wealth of the Indies and the future of the entire Western hemisphere. As such, would we not become what we seek to overcome?

Then there was the case of *Sergeant York*. This film was one of the most important contributions to the reorienting of a new generation from "war is hell" back to the "war is heck" mentality. Released in 1941, *Sergeant York* took careful but gentle aim at pacifists. In the wake of the last war, this was a significant constituency. In league with the isolationists, pacifists could make many lucid arguments in favor of sitting out this war in Europe. *Sergeant York* is the story of another pacifist, a true-life conscientious objector, who nonetheless set down the plowshare and picked up the sword in defense of his comrades in World War I. The story of this recipient of the Medal of Honor is a simple yet eloquent argument that says pacifism is a wonderful philosophy, but that there are circumstances that warrant setting it aside.

THE WAR BEGINS

It is not surprising that over 375 films released between 1942 and 1944 were clearly propagandistic. After Pearl Harbor, Hollywood "took off the gloves" regarding its characterizations of the enemy. These films idealized American boys and using the power of the medium to its fullest, set about the task of prosecuting an ideological war with no holds barred. To Hollywood press agents, this was public relations heaven: subject matter that made the film capital appear to be the most patriotic city in America, and, simultaneously, box-office dynamite.

By then, releasing pictures in Europe was a thing of the past, so even the most selfish of Hollywood producers ceased considering the effect of anti-Axis messages on film profits in Germany, its allies, or even neutrals. After the Day of Infamy, producers also discarded any fear of alienating any sizable US pacifist or isolationist audience. US war propaganda at the movies was good business, and Hollywood was full of good businessmen.

Judith Crist described the way Hollywood characterized the enemy in this fashion: The German image was that of "cultured swine. . . . They could be brutal, but were intellectual about it all." She wrote that depictions of the Japanese (after the internment of Japanese-Americans in 1942, all Japanese were played by Chinese actors) were not, relatively, as polite: They were labeled "fanatics, near-savages—sneaky, dirty fighters . . ." (Morella, 6). As a matter of fact, most Asian actors in this period became box office poison, except when they portrayed the enemy. For example, although it was produced to aid the war effort, the 1944 Monogram release, *Charlie Chan in the Secret Service*, was a commercial flop. The venerable old detective's original 1930s series of profitable whodunit movies came to an abrupt end for the duration of the war, despite the fact that the Chan character (often played by Caucasians) was not even Japanese but Chinese, and the Chinese were America's allies! After this film, and one other money-loser in 1944, Charlie Chan movies were retired until 1958, then as a short-lived television series. As for films featuring the Japanese secret agent Mr. Moto, Hungarian actor Peter Lorre went back to playing shady characters and Nazi spies for Warner Brothers.

Hollywood was doing a land-office business, with many studio-owned theaters screening pictures twenty-four hours a day. It wasn't unusual to see a theater located near a defense plant crowded at 4 a.m., as workers just off late-night shifts spent some of their war dollars on the cinema.

Amazingly, despite shortages of gasoline, vehicles, and many other essential ingredients needed for filmmaking, Hollywood studios kept busy. Film stock was scarce and there were restrictions on how many release prints could be made for each new picture. But Hollywood was able to get around many of these restrictions because, besides armed services training films, the film capital made movies for virtually every branch of the federal government, from the Department of Agriculture to the Department of the Treasury. But films made in direct support of the War Department received the most publicity. General Dwight D. Eisenhower once said that Hollywood's training films were of great value because soldiers could learn many things in a relatively shorter amount of time than they could through books, demonstrations, or lectures.

As a result, the many wartime rationing restrictions that crippled other kinds of American businesses were waived because Hollywood had been designated an essential war industry.

One would think that only wartime documentaries and other non-fiction films made in support of the war effort would have merited the classification of "essential." How did Hollywood arrange for all their entertainment films to be lumped together in the same category as a "how-to" film on the flush riveting of a bomber? As we will see in the pages that follow, the film industry, through a combination of planning, political action, and clever public relations work, managed to convince the nation and the federal government that, to paraphrase Joseph Heller, what was good for Hollywood was good for America.

A SYMBIOTIC RELATIONSHIP

If he wanted to, the president could have exercised his war powers to the point of imposing total censorship over the American film industry. But that was not in Roosevelt's game plan. Joe Morella writes:

> Soon after the war began, FDR appointed Lowell Mellett to coordinate film production. Mellett was personally opposed to censorship and had hoped to avoid it, but censorship was ordered for all films that would be exported or imported, which in effect applied to every major film in production, since the studios exported to foreign markets. (57)

But in the production of combat films, almost all of which required the active assistance of some branch of the armed forces, Washington's relationship with its anxious-to-please partner on the West Coast was mutually beneficial and far from antagonistic. It's true that the Pentagon reviewed scripts before they agreed to lend assistance, and they did have a policy of not helping those that were objectionable. But after a decade of dealing with the script approval people at the Hays Office, Hollywood producers were old pros in the art of thrust-and-parry with censors. This was especially true when it came to Washington bureaucrats. Treated like visiting royalty, government-types were served all of the "sizzle" that the film capital could muster, and seldom realized that the "steak" was absent. As a result, Hollywood generally got what it wanted, including plenty of non-salaried help. Dore Schary, an MGM producer during the war, described the kind of assistance provided by the War Department:

> We got technical advisors . . . we were able to go into the Army camps to shoot the guys; we were able to get the armed forces' assistance in terms of soldiers who were portraying soldiers, and we got the use of Army, Navy, and Air Force equipment. We got very good cooperation. (58)

The editors of *Look*, in their book, *Movie Lot to Beachhead*, gave this account of government/film industry cooperation on the making of two war epics:

Winged Victory (1944)

During the filming, the Army sent no less than 14 technical advisers—all of them officers—to Hollywood. . . . The studio was given the use of facilities at seven different Army posts and air bases. At various times and places it was able to borrow—among military items—27 Liberator bombers, 55 basic trainers, six Higgins boats, 40 anti-aircraft guns, 90 oil drums, 75 trench knives, 330 cartridge cases, and such miscellany as crash trucks, ambulances, jeeps, walkie-talkies, rifles, parachutes, and power cranes. In addition, 400 inductees at one camp were held there additional days because the studio needed retakes and added scenes. More than 2,000 men paraded for the cameras.

Guadalcanal Diary (1943)

One scene was filmed on the beach at a Marine camp near San Diego, with Marines filling in on the crowd scenes, the Navy supplying the convoy and small boats, the Army Air Force the planes. Without such help, the studio could never have afforded to make the picture. It was a good investment for the services, though. The Marines set up recruiting stations near theaters where the film played and secured 12,000 recruits. (112)

The mutual admiration society that this relationship created is also seen in the style, nuances, tone, and certainly the words and ideas found on scripts produced by the studios of the period, which were "reviewed" with mostly glowing praise by Lowell Mellett's section of the Office of War Information. What follows is a more in-depth look at that relationship:

In our films we shall try to interpret the American spirit to the rest of the world, so that a coordinated and enlightened civilization can transform itself and thus ensure universal freedom and security from spiritual or material attack. The motion picture industry cannot work without freedom. And as it is the very expression of freedom, it never will give up the fight for liberty—for all men.

—Hollywood Producer Walter Wanger in *Free World* magazine,
1947 (447)

Columnist Dorothy Jones wrote in 1945, "From December 1, 1941, to Dec. 1, 1944, the industry released 1,321 feature films. The main story of three in every ten of these films revolved around the war" (October, 94). It's safe to say that Hollywood produced an abundance of war stories during the period, and that these pictures were extremely unflattering to the enemy. But to what extent were these themes simply Hollywood performing "business as usual," creating scenarios sure to be popular, and dramatizing them on the screen for profit, and how much of this was a concerted effort in the film industry's patriotic "fight for liberty?" This brief historical overview won't attempt to see beyond what we are capable of seeing: No one knows for sure what was truly in the hearts and minds of the makers of these films. Instead, we'll investigate the evidence that points to both of the above scenarios, and let the reader make his or her own judgments.

THE PARTY LINE

In attempting to connect the nation's foreign policy with the sentiments of the Hollywood film industry, one reasonable assumption can be made. It can be stipulated that the public statements of Franklin D. Roosevelt during this period of national emergency and unprecedented bipartisan cooperation accurately reflect the US government's conduct of domestic and foreign policy. So it's appropriate to review some of FDR's most famous speeches, news conferences, and "fireside chats" to discern the mood of government at the time. As well, occasionally I'll make note of how FDR's rhetoric can be categorized under the five appeals outlined in the introduction. This will be helpful later in chapter 3, when similar rhetoric is highlighted in Hollywood's wartime films.

As early as 1937, Roosevelt, speaking in Chicago, shared with his audience his "haunting fear of calamity." Referring to the Third Reich as "the present reign of terror and international lawlessness. . . . It has now reached the stage where the very foundations of civilization are seriously threatened. The landmarks and traditions which have marked the progress of civilization toward a condition of law, order and peace are being wiped away" (Vol. 1937, 407–408). Recalling the five major propaganda appeals, we see here examples of Satanism and Territoriality.

Characterizing America and the soon-to-be allied nations as "peace-loving," the president nevertheless preached against neutrality. This interventionist point of view, as we will see, was often mirrored in Hollywood's pre-Pearl Harbor films. Addressing an extraordinary joint session of Congress in 1939 to request repeal of the embargo provisions of the neutrality law, FDR said of the Nazis: "An ordering of society which relegates religion, democracy, and good faith among nations to the background can find no place within it for the Prince of Peace. The United States rejects such an ordering and retains its ancient faith. . . ." (Vol. 1939 514). Here we see examples of Satanism and Biblical appeals. Later in the same speech, Roosevelt, for the first time, uses a light vs. darkness metaphor (Apocalyptic appeal) to characterize the Allies vs. the Axis (he also uses the major propaganda appeal category of Guilt to remind his listeners that the fault for the conflict lies with others):

I should like to be able to offer the hope that the shadow over the world might swiftly pass. I cannot. The facts compel my stating, with candor, that darker periods may lie ahead. The disaster is not of our making. No act of ours engendered the forces which assault the foundations of civilization. (Vol. 1939, 522)

In his "fireside chat" on national security, the now-famous "Arsenal of Democracy" speech in 1940, the president characterized the international situation as verging on a "last-ditch war for the preservation of American independence" (Vol. 1940, 633). He then said, "The Nazi masters of Germany have made it clear that they intend to not only dominate all life and thought in their own country, but also to enslave the whole of Europe, and then to use the resources of Europe to dominate the rest of the world" (634). These are excellent examples of the Territorial propaganda appeal.

Speaking of the nations fooled into a false sense of security at Hitler's bargaining table one day, only to be invaded and overcome the next, FDR used a combination of Guilt and Satanism by saying, "The fate of these nations tells us what it means to live at the point of a Nazi gun" (637).

"The Nazis have proclaimed, time and again, that all other races are their inferiors, and therefore subject to their orders," Roosevelt continued. Using Biblical allusions and flat-out name-calling Satanism, the president called the Axis nations "an unholy alliance of power" and "a gang of outlaws." FDR said, "The history of recent years proves that shooting and chains and concentration camps are not simply the transient tools, but the very altars of modern dictatorships" (639).

Always mindful of maintaining good media relationships, in an address by radio to the Academy Awards dinner in February of 1941, FDR thanked Hollywood, especially the newsreels, for their cooperation:

> We have seen [the American motion picture] reflect our civilization throughout the rest of the world—the aims and the aspirations and the ideals of a free people, and of freedom itself. . . . For all of this, and for your splendid cooperation with all who are directing the expansion of our defense forces, I am glad to thank you. In the weeks and the months that lie ahead, we in Washington know that we shall have your continued aid and support. (Vol. 1941)

In a radio address to the nation in May of 1941, during which the president proclaimed a national emergency, FDR warned that if Britain and China were to fall, their fate would soon be ours (Territoriality). Referring to France and other nations already defeated, he said, "The masters of Germany have marked these silenced peoples and their children's children for slavery—those, at least, who have not been assassinated or escaped to free soil" (186). Here we see further examples of Satanism and Territoriality.

And, of course, on December 7, 1941, in his "Day of Infamy" speech, FDR said, "It is obvious that the attack was deliberately planned many days or even weeks ago. During the intervening time the Japanese government has deliberately sought to deceive the United States by false statements and expressions of hope for a continued peace" (514). This, too, references Guilt and Satanism.

On December 9, 1941, in a fireside chat characterizing Pearl Harbor and the attacks throughout Asia that followed as "criminal" (Satanism), FDR said:

> Powerful and resourceful gangsters have banded together to make war on the human race. . . . No honest person, today or a thousand years hence, will be able to suppress a sense of indignation and horror at the treachery committed by the military dictators of Japan,

under the very shadow of the flag of peace borne by their special envoys in our midst. (523)

These were the kind of official government sentiments that found their way, sometimes in spirit, sometimes in paraphrase, and sometimes even in actual reproduced recordings of FDR's speeches, into the very fiber of Hollywood's prewar and wartime output. With these ideas in mind, we will now turn to the motion picture industry to see how they and their celluloid products mirrored America's gradual shift from non-involvement to active participation.

HITLER VS. THE AMERICAN FILM

Contrary to public belief, it was probably not Hollywood's late 1930s anti-Nazi films, but rather the Germans themselves who fired the first ideological salvo that rallied influential members of the film community into an antagonistic stance against the Third Reich. We learned in the previous discussion that FDR was on the record as anti-isolationist in 1937, and that there is evidence that the film industry was already preparing for war at this time. Most of these early efforts, however, were devoted to the shift from the "war is hell" mentality back to a "war is heck" stance. But the very nature of the American film was a threat to Adolph Hitler. In Will Hays's autobiography, the former film industry spokesman and regulator writes that because American films depicted "the way of life of a free people, the Axis nations virtually declared war on them long before Pearl Harbor" (524).

As early as 1933, Germany's Nuremberg Laws allowed their government to censor and/or to ban all films, including American imports. Hays said, "The Nazis not only feared the effects of American films, but they also feared their influence on world opinion. They took all the measures they could to combat the release of our pictures in Latin America and the Far East as well" (524).

But one thing you don't do is tamper with Hollywood's profits. In attacking the American film industry, Hitler greatly underestimated film moguls' ire at losing markets, control of their theaters and, of course, all those overseas receipts. Gradually in the latter 1930s, Hollywood studios joined the chorus of politicians, social commentators, and journalists warning of the coming storm. Even Disney's Mickey Mouse inadvertently got into the act. Richard Schickel outlined *Der Fuehrer's* failure to defeat even an American mouse:

> By 1937, the mouse had become something of a political figure. Hitler, whose wrath had been kindled because in one of Mickey's films his animal friends appeared wearing the uniforms of German cavalrymen, thus dishonoring the nation's military tradition, banned the mouse's films. (165–166)

JACK WARNER

Warner Brothers President Jack Warner was one of the first major Hollywood moguls to take on the Nazis. In his autobiography, *My First Hundred Years in Hollywood*, Warner recalls the protests, threats, prank calls, and letters from the German-American Bund and other groups demanding that Warner Brothers not release *Confessions of a Nazi Spy*. The German consul in Los Angeles had demanded that Joe Breen, the film code administrator, ban the film. The Nazis even promised "serious reprisals by the German government." Warner writes:

> Even some of our powerful Hollywood executives were furious with me for going ahead on the film. "Look Jack," one studio owner told me, "a lot of us are still booking pictures in Germany, and taking money out of there. We're not at war with Germany, and you're going to hurt some of our own people over here."
>
> "Hurt what?" I said angrily. "Their pocketbooks? Listen, these murdering bastards killed our own man in Germany because he wouldn't heil Hitler. The Silver Shirts and the Bundists and all the rest of those hoods are marching in Los Angeles right now. There are high school kids with swastikas on their sleeves a few blocks from our studio. Is that what you want in exchange for some crummy film royalties out of Germany? I'm going to finish this picture, and Hitler and Goebbels can scream all they want. And so can guys like you!" (262)

Warner wrote that on the night of the premiere, his wife received a letter showing a detailed floor plan of their home and its grounds, with a letter which read, "The whole Warner family will be wiped out, and the theater will be bombed. . . ." Warner said, "Hitler was especially livid about [the release of] *Confessions of a Nazi Spy*, and he had me put on his extinction list" (263). This, of course, only caused the Warners to redouble their propagandistic efforts.

But were the Warners true patriots first and movie moguls second, or were they simply more astute, more conscious of changing public attitudes than the rest of the film community? Were Jack and his brother Harry the rule or the exception? Critics and historians have conjectured regarding Hollywood's true motives in their early-on celluloid pillorying of the Axis powers. During and since those years before the war, some pointed out that compared to Roosevelt and others, filmdom's foray at the enemy was late in coming, and only appeared after the popularity of the cause became financially viable. Peter Soderbergh writes that in the early and mid-1930s, Hollywood was only willing to display Germany's "annexation" of Austria, the invasion of Ethiopia by the Italians, and the conquest of China by the Japanese with the objective and therefore non-controversial eye of the newsreels:

> Hollywood belatedly shook off its catatonia and addressed itself to those developments which only the sightless could legitimately refuse to recognize. Still, the pressing question which plagued the moviemakers was not "How shall we make our tardy observations as telling as possible?" But rather, "How shall we capitalize on a 'hot' theme without destroying our foreign markets?" (14–15)

Koppes and Black, in *Hollywood Goes to War*, made a similar observation: "Hollywood's boldness [in treating war issues] was inversely proportional to the extent of its German and Italian market" (39).

In a 1941 article in *Nation*, entitled "Propaganda or History?" the unsigned author also agrees with the more venal scenario, and takes its own pro-involvement stance:

> Far from being too vigorously anti-Nazi, the movies, as long as they could, avoided making any films that might endanger their markets in Germany and Italy. Business was their first consideration. All this, in honesty, must be said before one can enter a defense of the movie industry against the preliminary investigation now being conducted by the [Nye's] Senate Interstate Commerce Committee. It is not the nobility of the movie magnates, but the context of the inquiry and the motivation of those behind the investigation which make it sus-

pect . . . [after a discussion of evidence of the Nazi threat] . . . The American people are expected to believe, after all that has happened in the past decade, that the Nazi menace is a figment of the Jewish imagination. (241)

However, an unsigned 1942 article in *Fortune* magazine, with Pearl Harbor hindsight, took the opposing view, praising Hollywood's foresight:

In advance of most of the country, some picture makers had discerned the true nature of Axis designs on the world, and were also aware of the complacency that blinded the US public to the dangers ahead of the country. More than a few producers considered it their patriotic duty to turn out films calculated to arouse audiences to the threat. (50)

Other industry spokesmen ballyhooed Hollywood's praises. In a speech before a motion picture industry War Activities Committee rally in 1941, Francis S. Harmon, executive vice-chairman of the Film Industry's War Activities Committee (WAC), on loan for the duration from Will Hays and the Motion Picture Association, said: "No bombs on Pearl Harbor were needed to galvanize the motion picture industry into action in the struggle between freedom and oppression. . . . The very month that France fell . . . leaders of our industry organized the Motion Picture Committee Cooperating for National Defense." After vilifying the Nye Committee, Harmon said, "Verbal abuse from those so blind they would not see was a small price to pay for the privilege of fulfilling our responsibilities to a vast screen audience of patriotic Americans" (6).

Historians of this period may be at odds about many aspects of Hollywood's relationship with the government during the war, but all agree about this fact: 1940 to 1945 were five years of unprecedented cooperation between government and the motion picture industry. It certainly was an arrangement in which both sides gained much more than they contributed:

Item: In 1943 congressional hearings, Colonel K. B. Lawton said, "I have never found such a group of wholehearted, willing, patriotic people trying to do something for the government." (6896)

Item: The "America Speaks" series of patriotic shorts, unlike most contract films made for wartime use, was produced and distributed by the WAC free of charge to the government. (Larson, 438)

Item: The Office of War Information (OWI) tasked by the president with reviewing films for objectionable war content, agreed to make all of their "suggestions" at the script stage, so that any changes necessary could be made as inexpensively for the studios as possible. (Larson, 440)

Item: On another occasion, Mellett said that producers were "completely free to disregard any of our views or suggestions."

Item: The above privilege was rarely exercised. (Larson, 441)

Item: OWI Motion Picture Bureau Chief Lowell Mellett made it clear that "There is nothing in any part of our operation that can possibly be construed as censorship." (Larson, 440)

Item: Warner, quadrupling its output of patriotic shorts, presented its Vitagraph Studios in New York free of charge to the Army Air Forces Motion Picture Unit for the duration of the war. Ninety-five percent of Warners' employees bought war bonds and stamps, netting Uncle Sam nearly $20,000 per week. (Warner, 269)

As stated previously, Hollywood put great effort into projecting an image of itself as the components of "an essential war industry," worthy of priority for war-rationed resources. The OWI agreed. Mellett, in a speech to an assemblage of movie moguls, said, "We are hoping that most of you and your fellow workers stay right here in Hollywood, and keep on doing what you're doing, because your motion pictures are a vital contribution to the total defense effort" (*Fortune*, 134). Roosevelt was quoted by Will Hays as saying, "Entertainment is invaluable in times of peace; it is indispensable in time of war. . . The American people will never fully appreciate the debt of gratitude they owe the motion pictures" (Hays, 535).

And motion picture makers, in return, should not forget that in a time when all Americans had to "tighten up the belt" a few notches, Hollywood became bigger and fatter. While US automobile makers could make no new passenger cars, Hollywood continued to make films at nearly the same pace as in the late 1930s.

The war was great for business.

WAR ACTIVITIES

In the prologue to the 1944 book compiling the best of Francis S. Harmon's orations on behalf of Hollywood, the WAC is described thusly:

> The War Activities of the American motion picture industry cover a wide range of services. These include the production, distribution, and exhibition of war information films; cooperation with the United States Treasury, the War Production Board, and the armed services in bond sales, scrap collections, and recruiting drives; the provision, without cost, of 16 millimeter prints of current pictures for free showing in combat areas overseas; and theatre collections for the Red Cross, the March of Dimes, and United Nations Relief. (v)

In their annual reports, published from 1942 to 1945 (the WAC was dissolved in January of 1946), the organization patted itself on the back long and often. "Perhaps [historians] will agree with two American presidents, numerous Cabinet officers, and scores of military and naval leaders in describing the industry's extraordinary service as a great contribution to our common cause" (WAC, 1945, vol. 4). Maintaining that the entire motion picture industry was "enlisted" in one way or another in the common cause, the WAC advertised itself as being divided into seven divisions: the Theaters Division marshaled the exhibition of government films in 16,486 movie houses; the Distributors Division, through 352 film exchanges in 31 key cities, handled WAC releases free of charge to the government; and the Hollywood Division was, of course, the production arm of the WAC. The Newsreel Division, composed of *The March of Time* and five newsreel companies, cooperated with both the War Department and Hollywood in documenting both the war abroad and at home; the Trade Press Division contributed articles and free advertising space for war drives; the Foreign Managers Division distributed America "informational films" (read: propaganda) and features to "United Nations countries" (although the United Nations as we know it today did not yet exist) and to US servicemen; and the Public Relations Division "dedicated promotional abilities and showmanship experience to a succession of industry projects requiring the enlistment of public support," including the publishing of their own slick, glitzy WAC annual reports (WAC, 1945, vol. 2).

In these reports, ten kinds of WAC produced films, mostly shorts, were listed:

1. Victory Films: Government appeals (rationing, materials conservation, bond drives, etc.).
2. "America Speaks" Films: Hollywood-inspired films on various wartime topics, such as *Don't Talk, Don't Waste, Let George Do It*, etc. These shorts were produced and distributed by the film industry to its theaters free of charge.
3. Films For The Fighting Man: Heretofore unheard of, 16 mm prints of feature films and shorts were distributed to servicemen. US stationed soldiers paid a small admission at their post theaters, which the WAC donated to their mess funds. Overseas servicemen viewed these films free.
4. Training Films: Made "for cost" for the government through the Motion Picture Academy's Research Council. It should be noted that in Hollywood's film industry, both then and now, many unusual, and some would say, outrageous "costs" were charged to the production of motion pictures. These and other films made for the government were no exception.
5. Orientation Films: Pictures such as Frank Capra's famous *Why We Fight* compilation documentary series of propaganda films, explaining America's reasons for being at war, whom we are fighting, and why.
6. Strategy Films: "Stock" film and the still photo departments of the major studios provided military intelligence with footage of many locations which they may soon have to assault.
7. Good Neighbor Films: Both features and documentaries designed fully, or at least in part, to foster American unity.
8. Newsreels: Domestic and foreign circulation of war-related American "news."
9. Morale Films: General Hollywood feature film production and release activities for domestic audiences.
10. United Nations Films: Promotion and distribution of films produced by the British Ministry of Information, the Canadian Film Board and Soviet films. (WAC, 1945, vol. 2)

In short, 100 percent of everything Hollywood did, whether it had a war-related purpose or not, was promoted in War Activities Committee annual reports and thousands of WAC public relations news releases as having been produced in support of the war effort. The same group of talented Tinseltown publicists responsible for the coining of the term, "Hollywood hype" were on loan to the WAC to keep the film industry's altruistic endeavors in the public (and the government's) consciousness.

Also noticeable for its apparent selflessness was Darryl Zanuck's Research Council of the Academy of Motion Picture Arts and Sciences. A committee of film producers, the Research Council petitioned Washington to award them the job of handing out the contracts to make all those government films on what they called a "rotation basis." The "carrot" they dangled in front of Washington was that these pictures would be produced "for cost," ostensibly yet another case of Hollywood "pitching in" to help with the war effort. Robert Sklar scraped away a bit of Hollywood's veneer to reveal the actual result of this arrangement:

> The seven major production companies [Hollywood studios] quickly agreed, along with Republic Studios and four independent producers—Hal Roach, Samuel Goldwyn, Disney, and Walter Wanger. During the 23-month life of the agreement, from January 1, 1941, to December 10, 1942, the Army Pictorial Division spent slightly over $1 million in Hollywood, of which $270,682 went to Paramount, $243,515 went to Zanuck's 20th Century Fox, and a little more than $100,000 each to RKO and MGM—more than 70 percent of the government's business to four major studios. The Research Council's plan had been to assign filmmaking tasks equally among the twelve participating studios in alphabetical order, but exceptions were far more common than the rule. . . . The Truman Committee suggested that the work had been distributed on the grounds of convenience so that big studios, with large overheads and staffs, could do government films in otherwise wasted slack time, while for other studios, government assignments need not interfere with feature-production schedules. (251)

Eventually other producers, specifically smaller production companies not involved in the original agreement that were therefore "frozen out" of the competitive bidding process, complained about this cozy arrangement. Finally, in 1943, following the Truman Committee's exposure of the way the arrangement was actually working, the government cancelled its agreement with the Research Committee. Afterward, jobs were bid and contracts issued on a cost-plus basis.

At this time and in later years, Hollywood continued to pat itself on the back for its contribution to the war effort. The WAC's 1945 report summarized these "Filmland Facts and Figures." Below are some of the more interesting notes:

- 76,406 16 mm prints of features and shorts delivered to servicemen.
- Estimated value of gift film, based on stock costs and a hypothetical charge of 5 cents per man, $38.5 million.
- 6,810 film artists made 55,286 appearances at home and abroad, including 150 hospital tours, 256 USO camp show trips and 122 overseas tours.
- Hollywood inspired theater audiences contributed $36,857,282.03 (yes, they listed the 3 cents) during the war years to several charitable endeavors. These included the Red Cross, the March of Dimes, United Nations Week, Army-Navy Emergency Relief, the USO, and Greek War Relief.
- Hollywood's own war charity contributions totaled $1,876,887.67. (WAC, 1945, vol. 4)

In an ironic turn of events, Harry Truman, former chairman of a wartime committee head-hunting in Hollywood for war profiteering, found himself in the awkward position of praising that industry in 1945, thanks to some brilliant WAC press agentry that, as usual, had a passing regard for the truth. Truman, who had by that time succeeded FDR to the presidency, as a courtesy had issued a letter on White House stationery, addressed to the director of the Office of War Mobilization and Reconversion, who was soon to make a speech to a film industry gathering. After the WAC boys got hold of it, it read:

> I wish you would express my *gratitude* to the industry for the *extraordinary service* they rendered the government during the period we were preparing for war and during the war itself. This gratitude is shared by every responsible agency of the government that needed to obtain the attention and understanding of the American people in those difficult times. We are aware that without the *assistance* of the

screen we never could have presented our problem to the people as
fully as was *necessary* in order to assure a united national effort.
(WAC, 1945, vol. 4)

Amazingly, the words above that are italicized were not done so by
Truman, but by the WAC publicists in reprinting a copy of the letter in
their 1945 annual report. In that publication, this innocuous White
House letter is artfully framed as one would set off a diploma, with a
battle ribbon superimposed on the top! Above the battle ribbon was
placed the misleading headline, "Presidential Citation." Hollywood
could always be counted on for a happy ending.

STUDIO BRASS

One sure indicator of Hollywood's commitment to US war aims would
be the actions of the heads of the major studios, the "brass," as they
were called. This was an era in the history of film in which a few
executives possessed immense power. No picture was made at Warner
Bros. without Jack Warner's personal imprimatur; at MGM the same
was true of Louis B. Mayer, and so forth. In contrast to the twenty-first
century, the age of the independent producer, in wartime Hollywood a
relatively few immensely powerful individuals singlehandedly determined which films were made, which were not, and what content went
into them.

During World War II, studio heads and top independent producers
were issued senior officer commissions as if they were stock certificates,
directors and producers became overnight captains and majors, while
many famous actors enlisted as common soldiers. Actresses and overage
actors made guest appearances at canteens, instigated bond drives, and
went on long tours to entertain the troops. Actors over forty and those
with physical impairments that relegated them to 4–F, such as John
Wayne, still led attacks against the enemy . . . on the silver screen.

Some studio executives were personal friends of President Roosevelt. Jack and Harry Warner and Walter Wanger, an independent producer and president of the Motion Picture Academy, went so far as to
campaign for FDR's reelection. Others who were Republicans set aside

their political differences, begrudgingly remaining loyal and even obe-
dient to the president's wishes until the war was over (Jones, 4).

Studio brass, whether or not they spent any time in uniform, were
routinely given head-of-state treatment by crack civilian-turned-soldier
public-relations men like Army Bureau of Public Relations Chief Colonel Curtis Mitchell. Taken on junkets with Army brass for guides, these
powerful movie executives' allegiances were clear: one photo (shot,
printed, and donated by the Army, of course) proudly reproduced in
the WAC's 1945 report, shows a dozen executives and producers, including the likes of Universal's Clifford Work, Warner Brothers' Jack
Warner, Harry Cohn of Columbia Pictures, and 20th Century Fox's
chief Darryl F. Zanuck. They all are posed, uniformed, for a "group
shot" on a Washington air base flight line with Army P.R. and OWI
officials before boarding a plane for a whirlwind junket around Europe
(WAC, 1945, vol. 4).

HAM AND EGGS

This is not to say that all studio heads' contributions were equal: All
were "involved," but some, additionally, were committed. There is an
old saying that helps to explain the difference between involvement and
commitment: "ham and eggs." In the preparation of this dish, the chick-
en was involved, but the pig was committed. So it was with studio
heads. Below, briefly are listed some of the wartime activities of the
most influential moguls of the period: Darryl Zanuck, Jack and Harry
Warner, David O. Selznick, Walter Wanger, Walt Disney, Louis B.
Mayer, Y. Frank Freeman, and Harry Cohn.

The Militant Mogul

One of those who appears to have been truly committed to the war
effort was the legendary, cigar-chomping Darryl F. Zanuck, himself a
veteran of World War I. A year before Pearl Harbor, while simultaneously running 20th Century Fox, Zanuck was commissioned as an Army
Signal Corps lieutenant colonel. A fervent and early advocate of
American lend-lease to the embattled British, he delivered many
speeches on the subject, including the comments to the national con-

vention of his fellow American Legionnaires in September of 1941 mentioned earlier in this chapter.

In the last quarter of 1941 (pictures mostly distributed in 1942), the tireless Zanuck made, among others, *Secret Agent of Japan*, *To The Shores of Tripoli*, *This Above All*, *The Pied Piper*, *Berlin Correspondent*, *Manila Calling*, *Thunder Birds*, *China Girl*, *The Immortal Sergeant*, and *They Came to Blow Up America*, none of which, as you can imagine, had anything pleasant to say about the Axis powers. Then he took a leave of absence to produce films fulltime for the signal corps. In doing so, Zanuck and his crew members often were found in combat situations (Gussow, 109).

A favorite with Army Signal Corps GIs, Zanuck drank (heavily and often) with the troops, but was known as a "tough SOB." Robert Sklar reports of Zanuck making a blanket statement about his men's chances for postwar employment at Fox. He said, "I don't want any of you guys coming to me for jobs after the war. The reason is that they're still coming to me from the last war and the studio can support only so many wars" (252).

Zanuck finally returned to Hollywood in 1944 (some say that his taking leave of active service was due to the shortage of cigars at the front). Upon his return, he produced (with Alfred Hitchcock directing) the allegorical *Lifeboat* (1944). He also produced and wrote pseudonymously the scenario for the bitterly propagandistic *The Purple Heart* (1944), perhaps the most melodramatic of the many savage depictions of the Japanese in any World War movie.

Zanuck also was a close friend of Roosevelt, and visited the president informally at the White House numerous times.

Filmdom's Intellectual Spokesman

Independent producer Walter Wanger fought as an officer in World War I. His term of duty as president of the Motion Picture Academy spanned all the war years, from 1939 until 1945. Not in uniform during World War II, Wanger nonetheless was a committed participant in nearly every phase of Hollywood's war activities. Making propaganda pictures such as *Eagle Squadron* (1942), *Foreign Correspondent* (1940), and *Gung Ho* (1943), Wanger (to paraphrase a line from *It's a Wonderful Life*) "fought the battle of the home front." An intellectual and a prolific writer, his comments found their way not only onto the screen, but also into a number of periodicals, in which he defended and promoted the film industry's unique role in the war, often comparing our system of free expression with that of the Nazis. In an article in the magazine *Saturday Review*, Wanger wrote, "Hitler, who started his career as a propagandist and never won a military campaign except when propaganda weakened his enemy first, has spread his thought-poison even in those countries he has brutally occupied."

As well, Wanger preached long and hard about the superiority of the Hollywood-made, Hollywood-supervised film product:

> Herr Goebbels ordered his moribund motion picture industry to produce a "perfect picture" to convince the Alsatians and Lorrainers that they lived, under Schickelgruber, in the best of all possible worlds. The picture was made. Presumably, it pleased Goebbels. Unhappily, there turned out to be only one way to make the desired audiences sit through the film. The audiences had to be herded in, then, the doors locked. (Wanger, 101)

In another edition of the *Saturday Review of Literature*, Wanger defended American propaganda on film:

> Every nation at war seeks to instill in its people two things: Unity of purpose and strength of purpose. It seeks general accord as to the objectives of the war and as to the methods used in the conduct of the war. It seeks sufficient strength of purpose to endure with fortitude and understanding reverses and sacrifices necessary to the winning of the ultimate victory. We in the field of mass communications—press, radio and motion pictures—are seriously concerned with bringing about this ideal public state of mind. (March 1942, 12)

And exhibiting Hollywood's willingness to submit, ultimately, to government participation in the editing process, he wrote:

> As for censorship—any American gladly yields to a censorship of information that may give aid or comfort to the enemy. But the process of weeding out of pictures those elements which make for confusion, disunity, or misunderstanding is one in which every movie maker must participate. If a picture be based on truth and artistic

honesty, it is doubtful whether more than a few objectionable elements will have to be removed.

However, as both a producer and as the industry's elected spokesman/watchdog, Wanger was vocal in his criticism of the Office of War Information, especially of "amateurs" attempting to dabble in the picture-making business. Some say Wanger was instrumental in the OWI's later loss of congressional funding. After making *Eagle Squadron* (1942), intended to show that Americans and British are "blood kin," Wanger bitterly reported in *Public Opinion Quarterly* that shortly after he received this urgent OWI directive: "Would you, as quickly as possible, put your mind on producing a short subject designed to show that Americans and English are fundamentally alike?" This, after narrator Quentin Reynolds affirmed in *Eagle Squadron*, "The British are our kind of people" (105).

Eventually, Washington agreed that the "amateurs" Wanger objected to should step aside to let the enthusiastic Hollywood professionals do their job: Congress slashed the OWI's 1943 Domestic Branch budget from $7.6 million to $2.1 million, nearly a 75 percent cut. The OWI was forced to lay off eight hundred employees, and Hollywood breathed a sigh of relief. A hobbled Office of War Information was no major threat. All that remained was Ulric Bell's Overseas Branch, which decided what films were in the country's interest to export. Since foreign distribution often made the difference between just covering negative costs and turning a profit, much deal-making and outright feuding between studio heads and the government continued for the duration of the war. But American audiences now saw films free of OWI's script review before they went before the cameras. As Cedric Larson wrote in *Hollywood Quarterly*:

> With Mr. [Lowell] Mellett and his bureau—the *bete noire* of the motion picture industry of 1942—safely shorn of power by the congressional economy axe, the Hollywood producers were left to handle propaganda on the silver screen unhampered by officialdom in Washington. . . . (443)

Warner's War

Higham and Greenberg write that Warner Brothers "was indeed, *the* war propaganda film studio, its output exceeding all others in quantity, and (on a craftsmanship basis) quality" (97).

Higham also provides us with an excellent example of how cooperative the Warner Brothers were with Washington. In it, the OWI suggested that Warners and other Hollywood studios make war films in six general categories: The Enemy, Our Allies, the Armed Forces, the Production Front, the Home Front, and the Issues.

> As it happened, *Captains of The Clouds* (1942), dealing with the Royal Canadian Air Force; *Across The Pacific* (1942), which dealt with Japanese activities in the Pacific [many guilt appeals]; *Wings for the Eagle* (1942), which showed the efficiency of the Lockheed plant; and the patriotic musical, a biography of George M. Cohan titled *Yankee Doodle Dandy* (1942), had all been planned before Pearl Harbor. In the category of the Enemy, *Edge of Darkness* (1943) [a tour de force of Satanism appeals], together with a reworked version of *The Desert Song* (1943), in which German activity in North Africa was shown. For the Armed Services, Warners produced Howard Hawks' *Air Force* (1943), based on the adventures of the crew of the flying fortress, "Mary Ann." For the Production Front, Warners produced *Action In The North Atlantic* (1943), about Merchant Marine convoys to Murmansk [to resupply the Russians]; for the Home Front they made *This Is The Army* (1943); for the Issues, Warners produced *Watch On The Rhine* (1943), about a German refugee family. . . . *Air Force* was made at the recommendation of General H. H. "Hap" Arnold, commander of the US Air Forces, a close friend of Jack Warner, who placed at the disposal of the director, Howard Hawks, Drew Field in Florida and several aircraft for the production. (148)

Jack Warner referred to Joseph Goebbels as "Adolph Hitler's minister of the big lie." He writes that he was proud of the fact that his *Confessions of a Nazi Spy* "would hurt Herr Goebbels far more than Bugsy Siegel's chopper" (261).

On one occasion, with no advance notice and with a day's worth of the studio's dailies to process, the Warners turned over the entire resources of their studio film labs to the FBI overnight so that they could speedily duplicate some Axis films the G-men had taken from a freighter in LA Harbor. Performing this favor caused a log-jam in their labs that resulted in a twenty-four-hour delay in processing for the many current Warner productions.

In 1942, Jack Warner requested that he be commissioned, and, befitting his Hollywood rank, requested that Roosevelt start him off in the Army as a brigadier general. Roosevelt told Warner that general officer commissions must be approved by Congress, and that some legislators could be counted on to take a dim view of such action. Although Jack wrote that he "would have settled for buck private," he accepted the rank of lieutenant colonel. During his stint in the service, Jack "traveled a good deal, visiting Air Force bases, commuting to Washington, checking our scattered companies on location, and planning major productions with war stories or settings" (284). In other words, Warner had the US government's subsidy to do all the things and visit all the places that he, as a studio executive, had been doing on his own nickel prior to being commissioned.

This stint "in the service" resulted in, among other projects, *Flying Fortress* (1942); the 1943 films *Air Force, Casablanca, Action in the North Atlantic, Watch on the Rhine*; *Destination Tokyo* (1944); and 1945 films *Objective Burma, Hotel Berlin, Pride of the Marines*, and *God Is My Co-Pilot.*

Never one to hide his light under a barrel, Warner proudly wrote: "We had taken on Hitler, Mussolini, Hirohito, Tojo and the rest of the totalitarian mob in one gutty picture after another. . . . Our hundreds of wartime films had only one purpose—to give our people the facts" (292).

Yet despite leaving their special mark on all these patriotic projects, the brothers Warner were soundly thrashed in the press for making the pro-Soviet film, *Mission to Moscow*. Right-wing columnists such as Westbrook Pegler vilified Warner Bros. for the film, and philosopher John Dewey described *Mission* as "the first instance in our country of totalitarian propaganda for mass consumption." In his autobiography, Warner states that he would never have made *Mission to Moscow* had it not been for "orders from the president." He relates this conversation:

FDR: Jack, this picture must be made, and I am asking you to make it.

Warner: I'll do it. You have my word. (290)

Jack's brother, Harry, equally committed to FDR and the war effort, was one of the Hollywood spokesmen in the 1941 Nye committee hearings, and made his views abundantly clear. Here are excerpts:

> Shortly after Hitler came to power in Germany, I became convinced that Hitlerism was an evil force designed to destroy free people, whether they were Catholics, Protestants, or Jews. I claim no credit as a prophet. Many appraised the Nazis in their true role, from the very day of Hitler's rise to power. I have always been in accord with President Roosevelt's foreign policy. In September 1939, when the Second World War began, I believed, and I believe today, that the world struggle for freedom was in its final stage. . . . I am unequivocally in favor of giving England and her allies all supplies which our country can spare. I also support the President's doctrine of freedom of the seas. . . . Frankly, I am not certain whether or not this country should enter the war in its own defense at the present time. The President knows the world situation and our country's problems better than any other man. I would follow his recommendation concerning a declaration of war. (Mast, 486)

Yet Bernard Dick maintains that this most patriotic of studios never really made a propaganda film "in the usual sense":

> If propaganda is manipulation by word or image, then the Warners did not as much manipulate audiences as confirm what audiences already believed but could not articulate, thus affecting a coinciding—rather than an imposing—of visions. By dramatizing the mass convictions of a people, Warners enabled moviegoers to project their feelings onto the same screen on which the studio projected its own. (65)

Lazarsfeld and Merton call this kind of reinforcement of an already accepted propaganda message "canalization": The Warners' articulation of the national attitude provided public approval for the not-yet-articulated national attitude.

Memos to Washington

Although independent producer David O. Selznick personally produced only two films designed to support the war effort, *Since You
Went Away* and *I'll Be Seeing You*, he stated—in his usual overblown
manner—that he was ultimately willing to sacrifice his career for the
war effort.

At first, Selznick offered his services to the War Department, but
refused a major's commission, in part because of his reluctance to "take
what had not been earned," but mostly because the job they wanted
him to do—run a radio program—was not agreeable. Later, however,
Undersecretary of the Navy James V. Forrestal requested that Selznick
take on the job of coordinating the Navy's motion picture activities and
to create a new bureau of photography. In a memo to Forrestal, Selznick detailed his plans to liquidate his studio holdings before enlisting.
But, as Rudy Behlmer notes,

> Selznick followed up this letter the next day with a 12-page tentative
> plan to establish a bureau of photography for the Navy Department
> (for purposes of extending combat intelligence as well as making
> recruiting, training, and promotional films). Neither this plan nor
> subsequent efforts by Selznick to involve himself personally in the
> war effort materialized. Nevertheless, he continued to send sugges-
> tions of various kinds to all the branches of the Armed Forces, the
> State Department, and the President. (324)

The Mouse That Warred

Walt Disney may have been the only major producer in Hollywood to
lose money during the war. *In Free World* magazine, Walter Wanger
wrote:

> Every American should go through Walt Disney's studio. He would
> come out of it with a new admiration for his country. There is noth-
> ing comparable to it in all the world, more experts, and technicians
> operate under Disney's roofs than in any other one organization in
> the world. Out of that amazing place come films on meteorology, on
> countless types of technical subjects for the Army, for the prevention
> and cure of malaria, on every subject that might be, and is, useful in
> time of war. (445)

Disney's failure to come out of the conflict a richer man than in 1939 was in large part due to Walt's well-known obsession with perfection. Although for most of the war, he was not being reimbursed on a cost-plus basis by the government, Disney fussed and reshot many war projects until most ended up costing him more than he bid for the job. Richard Schickel writes in his book, *The Disney Version,* that "[Walt] kept pushing beyond the cost estimates on which contract terms were based" (271).

In 1943, Thornton Delahanty wrote that "studio production records show that Disney is now devoting virtually 90 percent of [Disney Studio's] output to films for the Army, Navy, and such other governmental agencies as the Department of Agriculture, the Treasury Department, and the Coordinator of Inter-American Affairs" (31). This resulted in Disney's canceling or postponing plans for his own projects, further contributing to his studio's wartime losses.

In films as diverse as explaining methods of flush riveting (a project Walt personally sold to the War Department as necessary to make) to encouraging Americans to pay their taxes, Disney used his own particular talents in his country's service and worried about the bills later. For example, a special five-artist Disney crew worked full-time providing Allied fighting units, especially flyers, with their own cartoon insignia for their aircraft and other vehicles, free of charge.

Not satisfied to simply do war contract work, Disney drafted Mickey Mouse, Goofy, and Donald Duck and his nephews into the war effort. Walt even won an Oscar for the anti-Nazi Donald Duck nightmare cartoon, *Der Fuehrer's Face.* Interestingly, after its initial distribution in 1942 and for many years after the war, this cartoon was hidden away in the Disney film vault. No one at Disney would say exactly why, but this researcher, who in 1985 contacted Disney Studios about seeing it for the first time, was told that I was welcome to come to Burbank for a private screening, but that no recording of the film was available to rent or purchase. I can only speculate that while Disney aggressively marketed VHS and eventually DVD home video recordings of virtually all of its productions, someone at the studio was still ashamed of the blatantly propagandistic cartoon, featuring Donald Duck forced to work as a slave on a Nazi assembly line. By 2004, Disney's policy must have changed, because *Der Fuehrer's Face* was included along with dozens of other wartime cartoons on a DVD from the "Walt Disney Treasures"

collection, entitled "Walt Disney on the Front Lines: the War Years."
New management?

The Lion's Roar

Louis B. Mayer was responsible for perhaps one of the greatest films to
emerge from World War II, *Mrs. Miniver* (1942). He was also involved
in many WAC activities. At the outset of the war, Loew's, MGM's
parent corporation, endured the confiscation of all their theaters in
Nazi-occupied Europe. But this was to be expected of Hitler, since
Mayer had released anti-Nazi films such as *The Mortal Storm* (1940). It
must have especially galled the MGM chief to know that his theaters in
Europe were being used by Joseph Goebbels to spread lies about Jewish people.

Before *Mrs. Miniver* was to be released, the MGM distribution people planned a huge publicity campaign for the film. But President
Roosevelt, after seeing an advance screening, requested that Loew's
release it right away (Crowther, 276). Mayer complied, and on its own
merits the film was a huge commercial success. It won six Oscars, including Best Picture of 1942.

Holding Down the Fort

Another involved studio head was Y. Frank Freeman, vice president in
charge of production at Paramount Pictures. Freeman, an archconser-
vative banker and theater owner from Georgia, was both suspicious and
critical of federal government meddling with his studio. Although he
served during the war years as president of the Association of Motion
Picture Producers and Hollywood chairman of the War Activities Committee of the Motion Picture Industry, Freeman did not lend much aid
and comfort to the OWI, submitting few scripts for preproduction in-
spection. Koppes and Black characterized Freeman as an old-fashioned
Southern racist, committed to assuring that African-Americans came
into little contact with whites in Paramount films (101). As well, in
defiance of OWI wishes, Freeman's studio made films that were among
the most racially insulting to the Japanese.

Freeman was a heavy contributor to the Hollywood Canteen, a Tinseltown night spot "for GIs only, where movie stars and studio enter-

tainers did their bit for armed forces' morale." Nonetheless, Freeman stood with Wanger in opposition to giving one inch to the government's wishes. As a matter of fact, legend has it that it was Freeman who called on Georgia's US Senators Walter George and Richard Russell to help him in the eventual budgetary assassination of the OWI's Domestic Branch.

Under Freeman's supervision, Paramount released many, if not very good, propaganda feature films during the war. Among them were *Five Graves to Cairo* (1943), *So Proudly We Hail* (1943), *The Hitler Gang* (1944), *The Story of Dr. Wassell* (1944), and *Wake Island* (1942).

King Cohn

President and production head Harry Cohn's Columbia Pictures contributions to wartime propaganda included the highly polemical *Sahara* (1943), one of the best propaganda efforts of the war. Also, Columbia produced *Submarine Zone* (aka *Escape to Glory*, 1943), *Atlantic Convoy* (1942), *Counter-Espionage* (1942), *Enemy Agents Meet Ellery Queen* (1942), *Appointment in Berlin* (1943), and *Commandos Strike at Dawn* (1942). But Cohn himself was perhaps the least altruistic, most unwilling to become involved of all the studio heads. Bob Thomas' biography of the irascible mogul recalls this legendary incident:

> Cohn was suspicious and difficult to reach for wartime charities. Once he received a delegation of film executives' wives who were raising funds for the entertainment of soldiers. Each of the major studios had agreed to contribute an important film to be premiered for the benefit of the fund. Cohn was asked if he would do so. "No," he replied flatly. The women were crestfallen. "Why not?" one of them asked. "Because I am responsible to the stockholders of Columbia Pictures," he replied, "and they are entitled to every cent of revenue derived from our films." His visitors, some of them indignant over his reply, prepared to leave. "Wait a minute," Cohn said. "How much money do you expect to realize from one of these premieres?" "Six thousand dollars," he was told. Cohn wrote out a personal check for $6,000 and gave it to the women, adding, "If you ever tell anyone I gave you this money, I'll deny it." (230)

Every studio was assigned a "night" on which they were responsible for entertainment at the Hollywood Canteen. Cohn had never once made an appearance, although it was customary for studio heads to do so. When he was asked why, Cohn said that he had never been properly thanked for his huge donation of phonograph records. Once mollified, Cohn made the obligatory appearances.

And so, in various ways and at quite different levels of involvement and/or commitment, Hollywood's elite corps of film generals added their particular personalities and talents to America's war activities.

What conclusions can be drawn from all this? One's first response might be to dismiss any patriotic notions and simply maintain that Hollywood did what it has always done best: exploit the public's taste and interests while carefully feathering its own nest, that it did what was needed to protect a highly profitable "business as usual," and managed to look good to America while doing it. However, that condemnatory surface judgment cannot take into account the people involved in making those decisions. It can be viewed as quite natural for a studio head to protect and care for his business and attempt to assure that it will show a profit for the stockholders, even in such difficult times. That's the American way, after all. And since some studio heads of the time were Jewish, it's no surprise that there was great concern for the Nazis' vicious anti-Semitism. Had these producers known the depth and depravity of Hitler's plans for "the final solution to the Jewish problem in Europe," Hollywood would certainly have been a lot more vocal even sooner.

And one can explain much of the self-praise Hollywood lavished on the work of its War Activities Committee as simply the industry's way of dealing with the always-present danger of the introduction of government regulation or censorship, rather than an attempt to make earning huge profits look patriotic. Plus, one cannot paint an entire industry with the same brush: One can say that at least Walt Disney showed moments of genuine disregard for profit, and the Warners were willing to make potentially controversial and even unpopular pictures just because the president asked them.

2

THE GUILT APPEAL

Who Started It

While each of the five varieties of propaganda—Guilt, Satanism, the Illusion of Victory, Apocalyptic/Biblical, and Territorial—function independently, multiple appeals are often found combined in one scene. For example, practically all of them could be included in a hypothetical scene in which a bespectacled, ugly Japanese soldier speaking Pidgin English mistreats a prisoner of war while gloating about the surprise attack on Pearl Harbor. Then he bows in the general direction of Tokyo to honor his emperor-god just before an Allied air attack destroys his headquarters. (Except for the gloating, all this happens during the climax of the 1943 film *Bombardier*.)

Because motion pictures communicate in both explicit and implicit ways, I have translated these appeals from the various dialects of film language (e.g., verbally, visually, musically, or via film editing) into simple topic statements. Regardless of how they are expressed, these statements combine to communicate their creators' propaganda messages. These messages may be expressed in a line of dialogue or narration, visible in either signage or action on a shot on the screen, alluded to in musical accompaniment, or shown in the conceptual relationship created by the editing together of different pieces of film. So, by various cinematic means, the following statements, grouped under the appropriate major propaganda appeal categories, are found in Hollywood's World War II films:

Figure 2.1. In *Five Graves to Cairo* (1943), Field Marshal Rommel spends a lot of time demonstrating his treatment of conquered populations and gloating about how Germans secretly prepared arms and supplies caches in the desert after World War I in preparation for the next war.

- Guilt:

    1. They, not we, are the aggressor.
    2. Axis imperialism was planned for many years.
    3. Pearl Harbor was not only an attack, but a premeditated deception.
    4. Remember Pearl Harbor.
    5. Revenge!
    6. We can't stand by and let the enemy do those horrible things.

- Satanism:

    1. The enemy is not human: he is an animal or an insect.
    2. The enemy is not human: he is a machine, or nearly at the inanimate level.

3. The Japanese race is ugly and diminutive.
4. The Japanese language and lifestyle are laughable and barbaric.
5. The enemy is a "Kraut, Jerry, Jap, Nip," and infinite variations of name-calling.
6. The enemy is a savage, whose actions are cruel and barbaric.
7. The enemy preys mainly on the weak.
8. The enemy bombs indiscriminately.
9. Civilizing elements of our culture are missing from the enemy's.
10. The enemy is totalitarian.
11. The enemy is a gangster.
12. The enemy is a liar and a sneak.
13. The enemy shows disdain for Americans as a people and for its institutions.
14. The enemy's leaders are worthy of our scorn.
15. The Italians are buffoons, not worthy of serious consideration.
16. Those few American and Allied traitors do so not out of conviction, but for money and/or power.

- The Illusion of Victory:

  1. Through the leadership of FDR, we will triumph.
  2. We will win because we are confident in our eventual victory.
  3. We will win because of teamwork.
  4. We will win because the enemy is morally inferior to us.
  5. We will win because we are so much more intelligent than the enemy.
  6. We will win because enemy soldiers are inferior to us in military strategies and tactics.
  7. We will win because the enemy is a terribly poor marksman, compared to our boys, who are crack shots.
  8. We will win because the Allies are resourceful and original thinkers, while the enemy blindly obeys and cannot think as individuals.

9. We will win because our system of government does not depend on any individual.
10. We will win because America is a melting pot, containing the diversity of talents necessary to triumph.
11. We will win through Allied strength.
12. We will win because of our superior numbers.
13. We will win because the enemy underestimates our will.
14. All signs point to our winning.
15. Many Axis citizens themselves do not believe in their own cause.

- Apocalyptic/Biblical:

    1. The enemy is the Antichrist.
    2. The enemy raises up false gods against the Lord.
    3. We are the forces of light, who do battle against the forces of darkness.
    4. God is on our side.
    5. Americans put their faith and trust in God.
    6. Christian soldiers will go to heaven.
    7. The enemy will go to hell.
    8. Only a Judas betrays his country.
    9. No greater love hath a man than to give up his life for his friend.

- Territoriality

    1. The enemy threatens our democratic institutions and our way of life.
    2. The enemy threatens our loved ones.
    3. We shall turn the tables on the enemy and threaten his territory.

GUILT

Guilt possesses just a few topical statements, but they are repeated often. The first such Guilt statement is: "They are the aggressor, not we." To demonstrate how appeal categories can be used in combination, this particular Guilt statement is often followed by an Illusion of Victory statement, stipulating that although the enemy may have started the conflict, our forces will put an end to it. Typical of this kind of combination punch is the conversation in *Across the Pacific* between Humphrey Bogart's US secret agent character, Rick, and a man he calls "Joe" (Victor Sen Yung), just revealed in the film to be a Japanese saboteur and spy.

Rick: You guys been lookin' for a war, haven't ya?

Joe: That's right, Rick. That's why we're starting it.

Rick: You may start it, Joe, but we'll finish it.

Obviously, the dialogue in this appeal is not the most mature, greatly resembling the threats schoolboys on the playground make against each other.

Similarly, in *Bombardier*, old Sarge (Barton Mac Lane) is reading a pre-Pearl Harbor newspaper headline to the female lead nicknamed Burt (Anne Shirley). The headline reads, "Hitler Challenges American Navy: Fuehrer Warns U-Boats Ready to Return Fire on Ships."

Sarge: [fuming] That guy burns me up.

Burt: [amused] Don't get excited. You'll start a war.

Sarge: No, he'll start it, and the bombardiers'll finish it.

In *The Purple Heart*, Captain Ross (Dana Andrews) gives an emotional speech to a Japanese kangaroo court about to sentence him and his fellow crewmen to death for their part in the Doolittle bombing raid on Japan. In this oration, Ross clarifies the fate in store for Japan for attacking the United States, and for a film written in 1944, eerily predicts the destruction to come in the atom bombings of Hiroshima and Nagasaki a year later:

Ross: You wanted it [the war], you asked for it, you started it! And now you're going to get it, and it won't be finished until your dirty little empire is wiped off the face of the earth!

In one of the opening scenes from *Casablanca*, Vichy French Major Renault (Claude Rains) meets German SS Major Strasser (Conrad Veidt) at the airport. Renault says he hopes it is not too hot for the visiting Nazi. Strasser, in a matter-of-fact way, implies that in the business of world conquest, Nazis must make certain accommodations: "We Germans have to get used to all climates, from Russia to the Sahara."

Later in the same picture, the Guilt message is delivered with more subtlety. In addition, the implication is that the Nazis are a rampaging band of thieves, a Satanism message. Renault tells Rick's head waiter, Carl (S. Z. Sakall), to be sure that Major Strasser and his men are given the best table in the cafe. Carl replies, "I've already given them the best. Knowing they are German, they would've taken it anyway."

Since a form of appeal rarely operates independently, comments like these—in addition to a hint of Satanism—can also be considered allusions to Territoriality, in that there is an expressed threat that the Nazis plan not only to acquire other counties, but to conquer the entire world. In Julius and Philip Epstein's and Howard Koch's Oscar-winning screenplay for *Casablanca*, subtlety and verbal texture abound.

Occupation Not Temporary

Assuring that audiences were not under the assumption that the German occupation was temporary, as some early Nazi propaganda insisted, the script for *Casablanca* also provides audiences an exchange between Czech freedom fighter Victor Laszlo (Paul Henreid) and Major Strasser. Laszlo explains that he was not gracious to the Nazi when they were introduced because, "I am a Czechoslovakian." Strasser answers: "You *were* a Czechoslovakian. Now you are a subject of the German Reich." Also note the distinction Strasser makes between "citizen" and "subject," implying that people in conquered countries are of lesser status than Germans.

In *All Through the Night* (1941), Sunshine (William Demarest), discovers a painting of Hitler, stupidly hung in open sight in what is supposed to be a "secret" Manhattan Nazi saboteur headquarters. He frowns and provides us with both a Guilt and Territoriality statement: "Why don't you stay in your own back yard?" He throws an axe at the painting, ripping it.

The implied portion of any Guilt statement that "they are the aggressor, not we," is that the country of the propagandists, a peace-loving nation, did not desire war. In war rhetoric, the speaker knows that it is important to characterize his side as being the peace-lovers, the sane ones, the side of the conflict that wanted to avoid a fight. This idea is simply expressed in the conversation between two Merchant Marine seamen in *Action in the North Atlantic*, ironically a few minutes before being torpedoed by a German submarine.

Carpenter: We didn't ask for this war, none of us did . . . I know I didn't. But now, all of us are in it.

Mate: (kidding him) Sure, sure, with you in the war, we got nothin' to worry about. It's an open and shut proposition.

And then there were times directors let the enemy's actions, rather than words, subtly make Guilt statements. Such was the case in the opening scene in *The Edge of Darkness*, providing the audience with a joint message about Guilt/Territoriality. Director Lewis Milestone shows us the pilot of a Luftwaffe reconnaissance plane on a routine patrol over Nazi-occupied Norway, as the pilot begins to make an entry in his flight log. We watch as he flips through his pilot's log pages, each entry indicating countries over which he has flown while performing his duties. The pages read like a litany of Nazi conquests, as we watch him thumbing through his flights over Poland, Holland, and Belgium, on the way to his present log entry, Norway.

In *Lifeboat*, adapted from a short story by John Steinbeck, the survivors are arguing over what to do with the captain of the German U-boat which sank their passenger vessel. It seems that guns from their torpedoed ship had also managed to sink the sub, and its captain was apparently the sub's sole survivor. (Note: During World War II, many freighter and passenger vessels that crossed the Atlantic were equipped with some kind of deck gun for self-protection.) Crewman Kovac (John Hodiak) proposes a simple solution to their Nazi problem: kill him. First listening to Rittenhouse (Henry Hull) argue that having mercy on the Nazi is the "American way," Kovac replies:

Kovac: I'm an American, too. I was born in Pittsburgh, but my people are from Czechoslovakia [The implication here is to remind audiences that Czechoslovakia is among the European countries invaded and conquered by the Nazis]. I say let's throw him overboard and watch him drown, and when he does, I'll dance a jig like Hitler did when France went down!

In dialogue, William Wyler took much the same approach in the harrowing scene in *Mrs. Miniver* when the mild-mannered Kay (Greer Garson) is accosted by a wild-eyed fugitive German pilot (Helmut Dantine), whose plane was shot down over their village. Looking out the window at the beautiful English countryside, the Nazi fanatic shouts:

Pilot: We will come; we will bomb your cities, like we did Barcelona, Warsaw, Rotterdam. Rotterdam we destroy in two hours! Thirty thousand [people killed] in two hours! And we will do the same thing here!

IMPERIALISM

Similar to "they are the aggressor, not us," is our second Guilt propaganda statement: "Axis imperialism was planned for many years." This explains to the audience that no single issue, nor any single recent incident, caused the enemy to suddenly decide to go to war against us. Rather, this statement maintains that the enemy's imperialistic goals required that they make war upon us, and that in careful premeditation, they spent many years carefully planning it.

The Hitchcock-style MacGuffin (the object of the protagonist's or antagonist's efforts) in *Five Graves to Cairo* is five caches of ammunition and supplies secretly buried by the Germans in the desert during the 1930s. According to the story, five supply dumps, which a decade earlier Erwin Rommel had strategically located along the line of march he intended to take to capture Cairo, would provide the field marshal with all his necessary logistics. The hero of this Billy Wilder film, British spy Corporal Bramble (Franchot Tone), infiltrates Rommel's headquarters and spends most of the film trying to discover the locations of these caches. Rommel, portrayed in typecast Prussian martinet style by Erich Von Stroheim, thinks that Bramble is really an agent working for him. Boasting to Bramble about German preparation for conquest, Rommel says that his fellow conspirators prepared for the invasion of Europe throughout the 1930s. He explains that German couples who appeared to be tourists on holiday took a lot of "vacation pictures," but in reality, they were surreptitiously shooting intelligence photos of strategic bridges, the Maginot Line, and so forth, all across the European continent.

Other films made it clear that Japan also had an eye for their imperialistic future. Coincidentally, in *The Purple Heart* and *God Is My Co-Pilot*, two enemy villains were portrayed by Richard Loo. The Chinese actor's two characters are shown to have been secretly working toward the overthrow of America long before Pearl Harbor. In *The Purple Heart*, Loo plays a Japanese general, chief of Army Intelligence. He tells captive American flyer Dana Andrews that he lived in Santa Barbara, California, in the 1930s, and worked on a fishing boat—all the time spying, "charting every inch of water from San Diego to Seattle." In *God Is My Co-Pilot*, we learn that Loo, who in this film plays Japanese flying ace "Tokyo Joe," was sent by his government to Glendale, California, before the war to learn to fly "American-style." By inference, this Guilt statement also leads viewers to assume that it is only his American flying know-how that permits Tokyo Joe to defeat US planes in battle. Otherwise, in nearly all Satanism propaganda statements in *God Is My Co-Pilot* and *Flying Tigers*, Japanese flyers are depicted as inept, terribly predictable, and incapable of adjusting their tactics to defeat the clever Americans.

Blood on the Sun (1945) is a spy film in which the MacGuffin is a copy of the "Tanaka Memorial Plan," a semi-factual document purported to be a step-by-step design for world conquest, supposedly written in the late 1920s by Japanese Prime Minister Guichi Tanaka. Although most historians consider this plan a forgery, it was widely circulated among the Allies during the war and accepted by Americans as factual. As audiences hear in the film, this scenario calls for the conquest of China and Southeast Asia to acquire the raw materials and manpower for a sweep east to the Hawaiian Islands and on to the United States. And in *The Purple Heart*, Loo's army general character also alluded to this same master plan. Additionally, in a meeting with Tanaka in *Blood on the Sun*, we hear the famous and often-quoted and misquoted boast of Admiral Isoroku Yamamoto, commander of the Japanese Navy and architect of the Pearl Harbor attack: "I will be in the White House when Japan dictates her terms of peace."

PREMEDITATION

The third Guilt propaganda statement is "Pearl Harbor was not only an attack, but premeditated deception." In a scroll at the beginning of *Blood on the Sun*, we learn that Tanaka was "the Oriental Hitler. His plan of world conquest depended on secrecy for success." In the film *China*'s (1943) denouement, which takes place the day before the Pearl Harbor attack, a Japanese general boasts about what will be happening "in a few hours." That conversation will be revisited in chapter 6 in the Territoriality propaganda appeals.

Likewise in *China Girl*, with the month of November 1941 showing on the calendar behind his head, a Japanese Army general lies to a Yank about Japan's plans: "Japan is a friend of America: We are a peace-loving nation."

More to the point, as most Americans at that time knew, Japan's peace envoys were in Washington to begin a new round of talks with the US secretary of state, which they claimed were aimed at averting war between the two nations. Hollywood often used its films to remind audiences just how treacherous this ploy was. For example, *Black Dragons* (1942) begins with a shot of a headline that says, "Japs Bomb Honolulu During Peace Talks." In *Wake Island*, Marine and Navy officers actually wine and dine these Japanese "peace envoys," whose plane stops overnight at Wake for refueling on its way to Washington. Once again, Richard Loo, made up as another bespectacled, buck-toothed Japanese racial stereotype, plays Imperial envoy Admiral Kichisaburo Nomura. The ambassador tells American officers he's conveying "a message of peace" to President Roosevelt. Nomura solemnly swears that in the Japanese heart, FDR "will find no thought of war, but instead, wishes for a lasting peace."

"OILY GENTS"

In Howard Hawks's *Air Force*, en route to Hawaii, the crew of the B-17 bomber "Mary Ann" is listening on the radio to the December 6, 1941, evening news. The newscaster reads, "Mr. Kurusu and Admiral Nomura have assured the president that Japan's intentions are wholly peaceful." Later, when the aircrew finds out about the bombing of Pearl

Harbor, crewman Winocki (John Garfield) is livid, as we hear in this conversation with the bomber's Chief (Harry Carey):

> Winocki: They send a couple of oily gents to Washington with an olive wreath while the boys back home clobber Uncle Sam with a crowbar!

> Chief: He's a tough old gent. You just wait 'till he gets annoyed.

To drive this point home more, director Howard Hawks arranges to have the "Mary Ann's" crew listen in to a shortwave broadcast of the president's "Day of Infamy" speech to Congress. Since this is perhaps the FDR recording most often used by Hollywood in its wartime films, and since it contains so many propaganda appeals itself, I'll transcribe almost as much as Hawks chose to include:

> FDR: The attack yesterday on the Hawaiian Islands caused severe damage to American naval and military forces. I regret to tell you that many American lives were lost. But always will our nation remember the character of the onslaught against us . . . no matter how long it may take us to overcome this premeditated invasion, the American people, in their righteous might, will win through to absolute victory. We will not only defend ourselves to the uttermost, but will make it very certain that this form of treachery shall never again endanger us. Through our armed forces and in the unbounded determination of our people, we will win the inevitable triumph, so help us God. [applause is heard from Congress]

Later, the aircrew talks with Major Bagley (James Flavin), the commander of defense forces at Wake Island: "I've studied all the wars of history, but I've never come across any dirtier treachery than [Pearl Harbor]."

So emotional was this treachery issue that it came to be known by many negative colloquialisms. Hollywood, not to be left behind, borrowed from the standard terminology of the Western film genre, "shot in the back," and adapted it to the Japanese traditional affection for knives and swords. In the "Forward" narration by Quentin Reynolds at the beginning of *Eagle Squadron*, he refers to the young American flyers who joined the Royal Air Force before Pearl Harbor. He says:

"This is a story of our countrymen who didn't wait to be stabbed in the back."

Later in Reynolds's narration, he repeats the stabbed in the back reference. Although the next sequence fits better in the next chapter, I'm putting it here because of its similarity to Reynolds' "stabbed" theme. In *Destination Tokyo*, submarine captain Cassidy (Cary Grant) explains why a downed Japanese pilot whom the crew was rescuing from the water stabbed a crewman named Mike in the back:

> Captain: Mike bought his kid roller skates when the kid turned five—well, that Jap got a present when he was five: only it was a dagger. His old man gave it to him so he would know right off what he was supposed to be in life. . . . [Grant goes on to explain to his crew how Japanese kids were taught the acts of war] And by the time he's thirteen, he can put a machine gun together blindfolded. That Jap was started on the road twenty years ago to putting a knife in Mike's back. And a lot more Mikes are going to die until we wipe out a system that puts daggers in the hands of five-year-old children. That's what Mike died for—more roller skates in this world—and even some for the next generation of Japanese kids.

CUEING

In propaganda, an effective tool is to establish certain principles that the propagandist wishes to hit hard, and then repeat them. Not every film plot allowed their makers the opportunity to detail the treachery and deceit of the Pearl Harbor sneak attack. But Pearl Harbor was one story that everyone in America knew well, and Hollywood filmmakers often found ways to include it. All it took to rekindle the emotions and hatred that the memory of this deed contained was a simple code, a shorthand, if you will: "Remember Pearl Harbor." This shorthand, or "cueing" technique, has been used before in US history. It was successful in rallying support for the Mexican War and the Spanish-American War. "Remember the Alamo" and "Remember the Maine" made each war's call to action clear: righteous anger, even revenge, was justified because a Guilt statement reminds the audience of the heinous actions of an enemy "aggressor." All that was necessary was some brief reminder, a cue to make an audience recall the enemy's great sin. And sins must be punished.

As if to set in place the "Remember Pearl Harbor" cue, in *Air Force*, the bomber *Mary Ann's* captain, "Irish" Quincannon, (John Ridgely) flies over Pearl Harbor just a few hours after the attack. As Quincannon banks the plane over the devastation below so the crew can get a better look, he solemnly tells them on the intercom: "Pilot to crew. Take a good look. Maybe it's something you want to remember." Director Howard Hawks's tracking shot down the bomber's fuselage from a point of view outside the aircraft captures the faces of each of the crewmen, gazing out at the destruction of the Pacific Fleet through portholes, their faces highlighted by the fires below. And in one of the wartime foul language dispensations from the Hays Office, crewman Winocki (John Garfield) is allowed to say, angrily, as if speaking for the American people: "Damn 'em, damn 'em!"

In *Bombardier*, the entire cast sits reverently in a chapel service on December 7, when a cadet, the day room orderly, bursts in with the news that "the Japs have bombed Pearl Harbor!" Later, in the bombing school office, with his officers gathered around him, Major Chick Davis (Pat O'Brien) points to December 7 on the calendar and says: "There's a date we'll always remember—and they [the Japanese] will never forget!"

In John Ford's *They Were Expendable* (1945), the attack on Pearl Harbor is announced during a party for Navy personnel at a Philippine nightclub. After receiving the word, sailors, marines, and their officers simply take a "stiff upper lip" and immediately and quietly depart for their duty stations. But later, Ford, himself a reserve Navy captain, takes some time recalling the greatest single tragedy of December 7. The men of the patrol torpedo boat squadron are shown surveying the wreckage of their quarters following a particularly devastating Japanese air raid. "Squarehead" Larson (Harry Tenbrook), the squadron's cook, who had formerly served on board the *USS Arizona*, says he wishes "the old Arizona" would come steaming up the harbor to help them against the invading Japanese. Since as yet the men had not heard all the details of the enormous losses the fleet sustained in the attack, Larson had no way of knowing that the *Arizona* was sunk along with nearly all hands during the attack on Pearl Harbor. Officers Ryan and Brickley (John Wayne and Robert Montgomery) react to this by exchanging solemn looks, which were not lost on the Chief Boatswain's Mate Mulcahey (Ward Bond). The chief simply asks, "The *Arizona*?" Brickley bows his head and slowly shakes it.

In *Flying Tigers*, as in *Air Force*, there's a scene in which the pilots sit around a radio, listening on shortwave to President Roosevelt's "Day of Infamy" speech, itself a long-form cueing device for all the hurt and wishes for revenge that Americans felt. In both films, directors David Miller and Hawks portray the nation's horror and disbelief through close-ups of the faces of the men as they personally react to the news of the raid and to the president's call to arms.

Considerably less subtle were the references to Pearl Harbor in *Gung Ho*, although they use the same Guilt cueing tactic. The Marine Raiders' troop ship passes by the scene of the sneak attack. The men can see clearly the wreckage of the *Arizona* and other destroyed ships, as we cut from one somber Marine's face to another. But director Ray Enright felt he needed to oversell the point by adding a superfluous narrator's voice-over:

> Narrator: Pearl Harbor, five months after the day of infamy. There are men in the Second Raider Battalion who lost brothers on those ships—can we help even the score?

Earlier in the same picture, a Marine is asked why he volunteered to be a Marine Raider. With malice in his voice and a look of hate in his eyes, he says, "My brother died at Pearl Harbor." The accompanying music in the scene gets suddenly somber. "They didn't find enough of him to bury."

Not all "remember Pearl Harbor" cues were incorporated directly into dialogue or a narrator's voice-over. For example, the allusion to the sneak attack in *The Fighting Seabees* (1944) is in the Seabees' theme song, sung at the beginning and at the end of the picture, and reprised from time to time instrumentally. Composer Sam Lewis's lyrics include the line "and we promise that we'll remember the Seventh of December." Like America's cueing code for Al-Qaeda's devastating 2001 attack on the World Trade Center and the Pentagon, all one needs to say is "September 11th" or "9/11" and cueing does the rest.

REVENGE

Revenge is a strong motivator. As George C. Scott was to say twenty-five years later in his famous opening speech in *Patton* (1970), "When you put your hand into a bunch of 'goo' that a moment ago was your best friend's face, you'll know what to do . . . spill their blood! Shoot them in the belly!" In the films of World War II, the need for retribution did not end with Pearl Harbor. Actually, that's only where it began. So the fifth Guilt propaganda statement is a "revenge" statement, meant to justify the protagonists' "getting even" for any number of enemy transgressions.

The most common revenge statement deals with retribution for fallen friends. In *Action in the North Atlantic*, Captain Steve Jarvis (Raymond Massey) has just had his Merchant Marine tanker torpedoed out from under him and many of his men killed. Now he and Executive Officer Joe Rossi (Humphrey Bogart) sit with other surviving crewmen in a lifeboat. Nazis, on the bridge of their submarine, break out a film camera and begin taking home movies, which cause the survivors to shout insults and make rude gestures at the camera, including the "V for Victory" sign (probably—for the censors—a substitute for a much ruder middle-finger hand signal). Insulted, the sub rams their lifeboat, cutting it in half and killing more survivors. Still within earshot, Jarvis hears the fiends on board the U-boat laughing as they steam away. Furiously, he shouts:

Jarvis: Go on, laugh, ya apes [an anthropomorphism which will be discussed later, under Satanism]. You had your blood and fire to make ya laugh. But I swear to God our time is coming. We'll pay you back. We'll hunt you down and slice ya like a piece of cheese!

Later in the picture, sailing a new, better-armed vessel, Jarvis and Rossi find themselves again fighting off a U-boat. This time they outsmart the Nazis, and, fulfilling Jarvis's threat, ram the sub, slicing the vessel open amidships . . . like a piece of cheese.

Similarly, in *Corvette K-225* (1943), Canadian Captain MacClain (Randolph Scott) loses his ship to a U-boat torpedo. But what happens next causes him to request immediate reassignment to a sea duty combat command to even the score. He tells the admiral in a solemn, hushed voice:

MacClain: When that sub put the fish into us, she surfaced. We just got away our starboard boat, filled with men. That U-boat machine-gunned every one of those men to death. . . . That sub had a large iron cross [painted] on her conning tower. [seriously determined] We'll be looking for that.

Later in this picture, another survivor, crewman "Cricket" (Fuzzy Knight), echoes the crew's sentiments on that sub:

Cricket: I'll get the Nazis for that.

Another Crewman: We all will.

Of course, as in *Action in the North Atlantic,* in the climax of *Corvette K-225,* MacClain and his crew meet up with that sub with the big iron cross on the conning tower and send the Nazis to Davy Jones' locker.

IRONY

Similar poetic justice is shown in Hitchcock's *Lifeboat.* When the survivors discover that Willi (Walter Slezak), the German U-boat captain they rescued, had drowned their fellow survivor, Gus (William Bendix) while they all were sleeping, they all attack Willi and throw him over the side. But the German hangs on and, as in many Hitchcock films, the protagonists find that it is very difficult to kill a man: the survivors beat on him relentlessly, trying to break his grip on the boat. Finally, looking for a weapon, Rittenhouse picks up a heavy boot, and brains the German with it, which finally does the job. The boot, as it turns out, belonged to the murdered Gus. Later, when they watch an Allied warship shelling and sinking a German submarine tender, Kovac, remembering the sinking of their own vessel, simply remarks: "Well, that evens the score."

In *God Is My Co-Pilot,* Japanese ace Tokyo Joe and two other planes "gang up" on Johnny Petak's (Dane Clark's) P-40 fighter plane, killing the Flying Tiger. Later in the picture, Colonel Scott (Denis Morgan) also gets the chance to even the score: as he is diving on Tokyo Joe's tail, guns blazing, he says, "This one's for Johnny Petak."

In *Guadalcanal Diary*, Japanese troops, promising that they will all surrender, lure a platoon of Marines into an ambush at a seaside village named Matnikow and ambush them. After the lone survivor of the massacre tells the Marine commanding officer this story, the colonel resolutely says: "This time we'll go to Matnikow in force—and for blood." And they do.

At the conclusion of *Wake Island*, the voice-over narrator pronounces the post mortem on the Marines who died defending Wake from the Japanese. This became the typical kind of epilogue for war films that ended, or had the potential to end, in an Allied defeat. In such cases, Hollywood managed to turn disaster into an asset, or even a strategic victory. In this case, it was a rallying cry:

> Narrator: There are other leathernecks, other fighting Americans—forty million of them, whose blood and sweat and fury will exact a just and terrible vengeance!

In other cases, narration or actors' dialogue made it clear that the sacrifices these men or women were called upon to make had strategic value. In *Bataan* (1943), *Cry Havoc* (1943), and *Sahara*, for example, dialogue made it clear that although Allied fighting men and women may have to lay down their lives in a forlorn place, and that perhaps no one would ever know what they did there, their sacrifice would delay the enemy's advance. This would allow the Allied side to recover, regroup, and counterattack with a vengeance. There will be more on the theme of sacrifice later when we discuss Biblical appeals.

ATROCITIES ABROAD

On occasion, Hollywood used the ghastly record of Axis atrocities against the Allies' noncombatants as motivation for revenge. They usually did this by adding an ethnic member to the combat unit, or by constituting the unit out of a mix of nationalities, each with his own horror story, and/or reason for fighting.

In *Destination Tokyo*, "Tin Can" (Dane Clark), a Greek-American, tells crewmen how his uncle, a philosophy professor in Greece, was rounded up and shot, along with all the other intellectuals. Besides its propaganda value, this statement also helps viewers understand Tin

Can's all-consuming hatred for the enemy. On *Wake Island*, a Polish mechanic (Dick Morris) was asked why he joined the American Marines. His reason was that his wife and child were killed by the Nazis in Warsaw. Another Polish refugee is found among the pilots of the *Eagle Squadron*, an American group of flyers who joined the Royal Air Force to fight in the Battle of Britain before America's entry into the war. The flyer, Borowsky (Edgar Barrier), gets into the all-American squadron because he was born in the United States. When asked by Adjutant MacKinnon (Nigel Bruce) why he joined, he tells this story:

> Barowsky: My father, he take me back to old country when I was twelve. Then Nazis attack. They kill my father, my sisters, and my wife. I fight back. Me, Wadislaw Borowski, I fight and get away, back to America. Now I am come back to Europe.
>
> MacKinnon: [A Scot] Aye, and now you'll be wantin' to even the score.
>
> Barovsky: [grimly] All I want is [to] kill Nazis . . .
>
> MacKinnon: That's not a bad idea.

Explaining why he no longer worked for the French underground, "Frenchie" (Louis Mercier), one of the eclectic squad of Allied soldiers who battle a battalion of Germans in *Sahara*, said that as a Resistance member he had to stand by impotently and watch while "the white-haired mayor, the schoolteacher, and my girlfriend were all taken as hostages and shot." He explains he knew that thereafter he was not going to blend in with the townspeople without being discovered, so he left France to join the Free French in North Africa "to kill Nazis."

Dialogue wasn't the only technique filmmakers used to convey the revenge motive to their audiences. In *Destination Tokyo*, it is a few days after the stabbing of submarine crewman Mike (mentioned earlier) by the downed Japanese pilot he was trying to rescue. In this sequence, the submarine had spotted an aircraft carrier and was loading its forward tubes to take a crack at sinking her. Among the graffiti the crew wrote on one of the torpedoes was "For Mike, Torpedoman First Class. R.I.P." Likewise, one of the aircraft in the Doolittle raid in *Thirty*

Seconds Over Tokyo (1944) was nicknamed simply, "Revenger," and many bombs had unflattering messages inscribed for the Japanese.

GET OFF THE SIDELINES

"We can't stand by and let George do it" was a popular wartime saying, and is our sixth Guilt propaganda appeal. The tactics used to promote this statement run the gamut from an anti-isolationist allegory to a sermon that says that we can't avoid the fight by placating monsters.

Prior to America's entrance into the war, many in America who remembered the horrors of World War I, the "war to end all wars," supported those who clamored for the United States to stay out of "Europe's war" this time. But the Japanese "mistake at Pearl Harbor," as Admiral Yamamoto once called it, had only served to "awaken a sleeping giant" and the desire for revenge turned the United States into a united fighting machine. Like Roosevelt, American filmmakers were clamoring for American involvement in the war back the late 1930s, so it was understandable that Hollywood's wartime films might throw in an occasional "I told you so" reminder.

As well, the "conversion" theme in screenwriting, the plot convention in which a protagonist begins the story as a sinner but repents by the third act, was also perfect for an anti-isolationist allegory. Hollywood showed that it could turn even a fantasy film series hero like Tarzan into an allied soldier simply by employing the isolationist-turned-defender-of-liberty story. In *Tarzan Triumphs*, the jungle man refuses to help when a nearby African principality is occupied by Nazis who enslave its people. The reclusive Tarzan insists that if "they leave Tarzan alone, Tarzan leave them alone." But when his son, Boy, is kidnapped and sentenced to death by the Nazis, he yells, "Now, Tarzan make war!" With some help from his elephant friends and other jungle creatures, Tarzan does in the entire company of German paratroopers.

In *Casablanca*, Rick Blaine's story is a classic example of an anti-isolationist allegory. Rick was once an idealist, fighting on the loyalist side in Spain and running guns to the Ethiopians against invading Italians. Still very much anti-fascist, Rick was forced to flee Paris right before the Germans arrived. But Rick's jilting by Ilsa in Paris turned him into a cynic, an interpersonal as well as a political isolationist, who "sticks his neck out for nobody." Similarly, World War I had sobered the United States, and was the principal motivation behind America's "avoid European entanglements" attitude. But, as the well-known story goes, Rick reconciles with his former lover, Ilsa and "gets back in the fight," helping her and Czech freedom fighter Victor Laszlo escape to America. In so doing, Rick takes on German Major Strasser at the risk of his own life.

Likewise, conversions such as we see in *Casablanca* prompt protagonists in such films as *China, Air Force, China Girl, Eagle Squadron, Flying Tigers*, and *Back To Bataan* (1945) to reassess their uninvolved, often self-centered lives. In each of these cases, the good example of colleagues committed to the fight, plus a firsthand look at the evil the enemy is doing, cause protagonists to repent, join the war effort, and to fight the good fight.

In *China*, self-centered oil merchant David Jones (Alan Ladd), when faced with Japanese barbarism and Chinese suffering and bravery, converts to the cause, eventually sacrificing his life to ambush and destroy a column of Japanese Army invaders. Similarly, in *China Girl*, photojournalist Johnny Williams (George Montgomery) was "in it for what I can get out of it" until he meets a Chinese woman and her father. Their heroic example and dedication to the cause of truth and freedom cause Williams to put down the camera and pick up the submachine gun.

Those not committed to the fight for freedom are sometimes shown to be immature as well as self-centered. In *Eagle Squadron*, Chuck Brewer (Robert Stack) is a daredevil pilot and a playboy, nothing more, when on a lark he joins the Eagle Squadron of the Royal Air Force along with his friend Johnny Coe (Leif Erickson). Motivated by his desire to help Britain fight the Nazis, Coe provides Brewer with an altruistic model. As in *China* and *China Girl*, the example of others and witnessing firsthand the deaths of helpless civilians at the hands of the Axis powers matures Brewer. Coe's example, plus him seeing how the British are suffering under the German blitz, convert Brewer into a courageous and self-sacrificing hero.

Both his own immature and irresponsible actions and the examples of others cause pilot "Woody" Jason (John Carroll) in *Flying Tigers* to "straighten up and fly right," as he follows a conversion plot formula similar to Brewer in *Eagle Squadron*. Plus, to atone for his misdeeds, which caused the death of a fellow pilot, Woody takes on a suicide mission.

In *Back to Bataan* (1945), disillusioned Filipino guerilla leader Andres Bonifacio (Anthony Quinn) is amazed to see how many men, women, and children are involved in the fight to liberate their country from the Japanese. One night he witnesses the sacrifices and risks they are willing to endure in order to make that happen. Ashamed of himself, Bonifacio turns down an offer to evacuate him and his fiancée to Australia, and instead rededicates himself to the fight.

In *Air Force*, crewman Winocki is a "sorehead" because he washed out of Air Corps flight school. He wants nothing more than to serve out the few remaining weeks of his enlistment on board the bomber *Mary Ann* and then exit the service. But witnessing Pearl Harbor changes all that, and Winocki quickly becomes a willing and effective member of the bomber's "team."

A PLAY WITHIN A PLAY

In *Saboteur* (1942), director Alfred Hitchcock creates an allegory within his film the way Shakespeare's *Hamlet* features a play within a play. Bob Cummings plays Barry Kane, who in typical Hitchcock fashion, is falsely accused of the crime of wartime sabotage. Escaping from the police, Kane and his new friend, Pat (Priscilla Lane), are alone in the Arizona desert when a circus caravan drives by. Determined to find the real saboteurs and clear Kane's name, the two stow away on board the last trailer, which turns out to be a sleeper car for circus performers (freaks).

Immediately, there is a conflict among the performers regarding whether they should turn the two over to the police or hide them. The thin man, an Englishman named Bones (Pedro deCordoba), is their spokesman:

> Bones: In this situation I find a parallel for the present world predicament. We stand defeated at the outset. You, Esmeralda [a bearded woman who looks a lot like Uncle Sam], have sympathy and yet you remain passive, and are willing to let the inevitable happen. I have a belief, and yet I am tempted to let myself be overridden by force.

Most of you are ignorant of the facts and are therefore confused. Thank Heaven we're still members of a democracy. We'll put the matter to a vote.

The Major: [a nasty little dwarf with a Hitler moustache] No vote! I'm against voting!

Bones: Fascist!

All but one of the performers vote, and the tally stands even. Esmeralda, representing neutral America before entering the war, jumps "off the fence" and casts the deciding vote in favor of saving the two fugitives, because they appear to be "good people," symbolic of the affinity America feels for its allies. Nevertheless, later, when the police inspect the sleeper car, the little Major attempts to betray them. Bones and Kane ally themselves and resort to force to make the little fascist "abide by the will of the majority."

In *Lifeboat*, Hitchcock spends most of the film on yet another allegory, this time depicting the Allies, portrayed by the torpedoed ship's survivors, as being duped by Germany, represented by Willi, the shipwrecked Nazi submarine captain. Only at the end, when they realize the true nature of the Nazi beast, do the survivors set aside their class, political, and personal differences and combine to defeat their common enemy. Much of the dialogue ideologically pits a tattooed, roughneck member of the torpedoed ship's black gang, Kovac (John Hodiac)—called a "fellow traveler" and "commissar" by Connie [Tallulah Bankhead]—against spoiled, rich industrialist Rittenhouse (Henry Hull), the kind of upper-class dandy Hitler so easily deceived in Europe and, of course, in Germany. Only at the end do these dupes realize the malevolence of the Nazi and set aside their differences to ally against the German.

CHIDING PACIFISM

Rather than in allegory form, the pacifists' argument is refuted in plain talk in *Bombardier* using the ethos of Christianity. Bomb school instructors think that Cadet Paul Harris's (Russell Wade's) poor bombing scores are due to fear. About to be washed out, he confides in Chaplain

Craig (John Miljan). Harris shows his deeply religious mother's letters to the minister, letters in which she maintains that if her son continues his training, "you will be making yourself a murderer." In one of a number of times Hollywood employed clergymen to make the case for war, screenwriter John Twist has his padre encourage praising God and passing the ammunition:

Chaplain: Have you been reading the newspapers lately, Paul? [Referring to recent reports of German invasions, bombings, etc.] Harris: Yes, sir.

Chaplain: Well, my philosophy's always been to turn the other cheek, but I'm afraid we've almost run out of cheeks. I believe in peace as much as your mother and those pacifist organizations she belongs to. But peace isn't as cheap a bargain as the price those people put on it. Those people lock themselves up in a dream world. You see, there are millions of other mothers who are looking to you, and boys like you, to destroy the very forces of murder your mother mistakenly attributes to you.

Using reverse psychology, American filmmakers often communicated their ideas as the opposite of those espoused by despicable film characters. Toward the beginning of *This Land Is Mine*, George Sanders's railroad superintendent character, George Lambert, is shown to be a Nazi collaborator and a quisling who betrays his fiancée's brother to the Nazis. At this point we have already heard him tell the Nazi commandant that before the war he opposed the French forty-hour work week and unionism, and was against women refusing to have babies. So when he explains to his fiancée his "peace at any price" philosophy, it has an opposite effect on the audience, who perceive him as a selfish, evil man, and know from experience that his way is folly: "Our first duty is to stay alive, to exist . . . if no one resists [the Nazis], then we will have peace."

Prewar American greed in the same manner as Lambert's is inferentially blamed for helping equip the Japanese for aggression in *God Is My Co-Pilot*. Tokyo Joe uses the radio to taunt the Flying Tigers, calling them "gangsters." He threatens to knock them out of the sky, saying that they should "come up and get a load of that scrap metal you sold us." Likewise, in *Destination Tokyo*, the firing pin of a dud Japanese bomb the submariners defused is shown in close-up to have the words "Made in USA" stamped on it. Submarine Captain Cary Grant says that the defective fuse is the "appeasers' contribution to the war effort."

As if to learn from the mistakes of our allies, in *Eagle Squadron*, the heroine's father is a former member of Parliament, a pacifist who led the fight against British rearmament after World War I. When the war began and his son was killed in the battle against the Nazis at Tobruk, the member of Parliament resigned his post, assumed a false identity, and joined the Army as a private to make amends.

Finally, under the guise of humor, Sydney Greenstreet, playing the venal restaurant owner Ferrari in *Casablanca*, urges Rick to join him in the black market. But all Rick wants to do is run his saloon/casino and stay uninvolved. Realizing that in this day and age that's impossible and reminding America once again that they're off the fence, Ferrari remarks: "My dear Rick, when will you realize that in this world today, isolationism is no longer a practical policy?" Even the pragmatic mind of the underworld boss grasps the impossibility of a man trying to be an island during this war.

Now that we have placed the blame for the war on the enemy, let's take a look at our opponent.

3

DEFINING THE BAD GUYS

The Satanism Appeal

Satanism is war rhetoric designed to create archetypal polar opposites in the minds of the audience (Lasswell). These opposites are often referred to by rhetorical critics as "god vs. devil" terms (Weaver, 212). The Satanism appeal taps into audience's emotions more than any of the others, displaying the enemy as a monster, subhuman, barbarian, or a laughable inferior. In one way or another, the intention is for audiences to be emotionally moved by these depictions, and their feelings of alienation from the enemy should grow. On the other hand, through direct comparison or implicitly by default, America's positive attributes are portrayed as the opposite of the enemy's negatives. This is the Satanism appeal, the most popular among Hollywood filmmakers during World War II.

Convincing audiences that the enemy is not like us, that he's something lower on the evolutionary scale than we are, serves another purpose. It makes it easier for soldiers to imagine killing such a person. If the enemy is an animal, subhuman, or such a terrible monster that one would be doing the world a favor to eradicate it, it's easier to pull the trigger, drop a bomb, or order up a massacre. As previously discussed, comparing Jews to rats in the Nazi hate documentary, *The Eternal Jew*, helped pave the way in the minds of the German people for their extermination during the Holocaust.

Figure 3.1.   Some American flyers are machine-gunned while others are questioned and manhandled by their diminutive Japanese captors in *Bombardier* **(1943).**

Satanism is also the most cinematic of the five major appeal categories, since film editing is a highly effective way to display opposites and make comparisons. For example, Soviet filmmaker and propagandist Sergei Eisenstein, in his classic propaganda film, *The Battleship Potemkin* (1925), cuts from shots of the rifles of the tsar's Cossack soldiers as they fire at peaceful protesters to shots of the helpless civilians being struck by the bullets, demonstrating the Cossacks's willingness to kill innocent, harmless citizens.

Not all editing demonstrates these negative comparisons by their subjects' actions. It could be as simple as the way they look, or even comparing their looks to other images. Richard Taylor recounts a lesson by Sergei Eisenstein in his famous book on montage, *The Film Sense*, in which the famous director and film theorist uses a montage to apply a negative appeal to characterize Alexander Kerensky, an enemy of the Soviet revolution and an ally of the Tsarists:

> We see inside the Winter Palace. Kerensky climbs the stairs. . . .
> Finally . . . Kerensky reaches the tsar's apartments. His figure is
> overshadowed by a statue holding a crown. . . . [To also make the
> case that Kerensky was effeminate], we are shown his elaborate
> boots and gloves [which also demonstrates how] he is fascinated by
> the external trappings of power. [Later,] Eisenstein introduces an-
> other of his intellectual metaphors: a golden peacock, a gift from
> Tsar Nicholas II to his wife, Alexandra, preens itself. (67)

Then, editing together the images of the dandy Kerensky with a preen-
ing peacock, Eisenstein likens one to the other.

Despite many visual examples of Satanism in the films of World War
II, dialogue was the chief way the enemy was abused, and calling the
enemy names tops the list.

The tactic of name-calling itself has a name: it is referred to as the
first pillar of propaganda. In 1937, Columbia University professor Clyde
Miller and his colleagues created the Institute for Propaganda Analysis
(IPA) to study war propaganda and other kinds of persuasive mass
communication. In the second issue of the IPA's monthly bulletin,
Propaganda Analysis, in an article titled "How to Detect Propaganda,"
Miller et al. published their famous Seven Pillars of Propaganda (Jowett
& O'Donnell, 227). Name-calling, the first pillar, meant that in negative
propaganda, the propagandist would characterize a person or an idea
with a bad label so that audiences would reject it without analyzing its
true worth. In World War II and on to today's political arena, name-
calling is a popular way to slander the enemy.

The most common subcategory within name-calling, and the topic of
the first two Satanism propaganda statements we will examine, is the
anthropomorphism. The first two statements are "the enemy is not
human: he is an animal or an insect," and "the enemy is not human: he
is at the inanimate level of a foodstuff." In both, these characterizations
served a valuable purpose: they allowed draftees who had never killed a
man before and their civilian friends and relatives back home to look
upon this enemy not as a human being with the same right to life as
Americans, but as lower creatures: monkeys, rats, insects, or mad dogs
whose extermination was a service to mankind.

ANIMALS AND INSECTS

American filmmakers often used racial slurs to vilify the Japanese. The most common anthropomorphism was to label Japanese as monkeys. For example, in *God Is My Co-Pilot*, the cowardly Japanese flyer referred to as "Tokyo Joe" leads a bombing raid on a Chinese mission chapel, just missing killing helpless children hiding in a trench. An American mechanic, sharing the trench with the children, yells, "Ya dirty ring-tailed monkey!"

In *Guadalcanal Diary*, the protagonists often referred to the Japanese as monkeys. After capturing the enemy's main base on the island, Marines examined their food supplies and found caviar. Sergeant Butch (Lionel Stander) says, incredulously: "Caviar! I thought these monkeys lived on fish heads and rice!"

Later, when three ragtag Japanese prisoners, bound together, are paraded in front of a group of Marines, one jokes, "Hey, it's three monkeys on a rope. Boy, are they small." Another taunts them, saying, "Hey, Snow White: where's the rest of the seven dwarfs?"

Shortly after the beginning of *Bataan*, Corporal Jake Feingold (Thomas Mitchell), on anti-sniper guard duty, thinks he sees a Japanese sniper in the trees. He shoots. Sergeant Bill Dane (Robert Taylor) comments, "That's a monkey, Jake." Feingold says, "Well, I missed him anyway. I'd have hated to hit him by mistake for a Jap."

Later, Dane remarks to his men that from the tops of palm trees, the Japanese, sniping at his men's positions, can climb better than monkeys. Typical among dozens of other films featuring the Japanese as the antagonists, numerous comparisons of the Japanese to monkeys are found in *Guadalcanal Diary*, *The Fighting Seabees*, *Objective Burma*, *Bataan*, *Gung Ho*, *China Girl*, *Blood on the Sun*, and *Air Force*.

It wasn't just dialogue that reinforced these Satanism statements. In virtually all shots in these films that portrayed Japanese bomber and fighter pilots, the studios' costume designers "monkeyfied" the enemy. Japanese are shown wearing an authentic, but significantly different kind of leather flight cap than Americans. Americans are generally shown wearing a simple, brown, leather skullcap-type headgear. On the other hand, the Japanese wear leather flight caps trimmed up and down both sides of their faces with white fur. This gives the ugly, monkey-faced Chinese actors whom Hollywood cast as Japanese pilots the look of having white fur whiskers around their faces, common in many species of monkeys.

In *Guadalcanal Diary*, Japanese snipers shooting down on the Marines from the tops of palm trees received species promotions to the status of "apes." Additionally, in *Black Dragons*, even Nazi agent Dr. Melcher (Bela Lugosi), having been double-crossed by the Japanese, calls his supposed allies "apes." And in *Bataan*, the stereotype of the buck-toothed Japanese was undoubtedly the inspiration for referring to the enemy as "no-tailed baboons."

On the other hand, Germans were only occasionally given anthropoid classification: they are called "apes" by Raymond Massey in his rant against the Nazi submarine noted earlier. This was probably less of an anthropomorphism and more of a slang reference to large, muscled thugs employed by gangsters for killing or beating up victims.

If the Nazis could use rats to compare to Jewish people in their hate documentary, *The Eternal Jew*, so could Hollywood screenwriters. And, by virtue of this characterization, it takes very little imagination to conclude that Axis soldiers, like other vermin, should be exterminated.

In Hollywood films, this rat reference may be as simple as a backhanded insult, as in *The Purple Heart*. Captain Ross (Dana Andrews) is arguing with Japanese General Mitsubi (Richard Loo), who describes the fanaticism of his army and their willingness to fight to the death. Ross, wittily jabbing at the enemy with this mannerly insult, says, "Your figures are impressive, and from all I've heard of your soldiers, they fight like cornered rats. . . . [sarcastically] No offense, general."

In *Destination Tokyo*, the submarine's executive officer (Warner Anderson) watches the destruction of ships and shore targets caused by the Doolittle raiders. As he views cruisers and destroyers getting under way to avoid being sitting ducks for the bombers, the exec shouts: "Yipe! Our planes 're chasing the rats out of their nests!"

Also, in *Corvette K-225*, German submarines are characterized as rats, and in *All Through the Night*, German henchmen working for their saboteur boss are called "brother rats." Likewise, in *God is My Co-Pilot*, Colonel Scott calls pilot Tokyo Joe's Japanese wingmen his "brother rats." One additional variation was in *Bataan*, in which the Japanese are called "dirty, rotten rats."

In the final scene in *Bataan*, only Sergeant Dane remains alive. As he buries the last of his men and prepares for the final Japanese assault, director Tay Garnett cuts away to a dozen Japanese sneaking up on Dane's fortified position. But it is in the way these actors are directed to advance on Dane's position that makes them look like creeping rodents. The Japanese soldiers are shown crawling on all fours, scurrying on the ground, more like rats than men, more like an infestation than an enemy attack. Dane finally sees them, and the picture ends as he single-handedly takes on the enemy with his tommy gun.

"FOWL" PLAY

In the 1940s, a slang expression for an unsavory character was a "bird." It is in that context that Cadet-in-Training Connors (Robert Ryan), in a conversation with Chick Davis (Pat O'Brien) in *Bombardier*, refers to a Nazi spy trying to acquire the super-secret Norden bomb sight: "I've been thinking a lot about my oath [as a bombardier to, above all, protect the secrecy of the device], ever since that bird who wants to get his hooks on the bombsight started talking to me."

In *Lifeboat*, a film that could be called a name-callers' convention, one of the many characterizations of the enemy was as "Nazi buzzards." In *Air Force*, the Japanese are characterized as fowl in season. In one scene, the Wake Island commander, when asked what his men are going to do when the Japanese attack, says, "I've got four hundred Marines, and there'll be some Jap tail feathers flying around this island. . . ." There is another subtle bird reference later in this picture. On the intercom, one of the crewmen says, "There's a flock of Zeroes [Japanese fighter planes] ahead." In *Guadalcanal Diary*, the Marine colonel tells his men that Navy pilots took the Japanese entirely by surprise, and that "we knocked off their planes like ducks."

The Nazis are characterized as canine in three films. In *Sahara*, "Frenchie" (Louis Mercier) urges Sergeant Joe Gunn (Humphrey Bogart) to allow him to kill their Nazi prisoner. He says that Gunn and the other Allied soldiers really do not know the enemy, and that he must be exterminated for the good of all: "Zees ees a Nazi—like a mad dog." Everyone knows what must be done with mad dogs. Later in the film, as Frenchie walks back to the Allied lines under a white truce flag, the Nazis shoot him in the back. Doyle (Dan Duryea) reminds Gunn that

Frenchie was right about Nazi mendacity, and that "we really don't know the Germans."

In *Five Graves To Cairo*, the Italian general (Fortunio Bonanova) makes many disparaging remarks about the Germans, complaining about their rudeness, their lack of culture, and their disrespect and disregard for him and his troops. Finally, the general—added to the film for comic relief and additional criticism of the Germans—somewhat stoically sums up his and his country's unfortunate association with the Nazis: "Well, as they say in Milano, 'when you lie down with dogs, you wake up with fleas.'"

Additionally, in *Tarzan Triumphs*, Nazis are referred to as other canine species: "jackals" and "hyenas."

CREATIVE NAME-CALLING

Exercising their vocabularies, Hollywood's screenwriters named Axis enemies as various distasteful animals. For example, the enemies were "swine" in *The Edge of Darkness*, "polecats" in *The Fighting Seabees*, and "barnacles" in *Joan of Paris* (1943). In *The Flying Tigers*, the American pilots are listening to the Japanese propaganda radio announcer calling their American Volunteer Group force "mercenaries" because they are paid a reward by the Chinese for each enemy plane they shoot down. Pilot McIntosh (Jimmie Dodd) compares the Japanese to poisonous snakes that, like mad dogs or rats, need to be exterminated whenever they're encountered: "That's not why we're here—but it's good to know that every check you cash means a Jap has cashed in, too. Besides, back home in Texas, we kill rattlesnakes whether there's a bounty on 'em or not."

In *Lifeboat*, Kovac (John Hodiac) is arguing with Gus Smith (William Bendix) about whether or not to allow the Nazi to share their lifeboat. Kovac offers an emphatic "no," but Smith and others argue that the German appears to just be a crewman, a sailor doing his job, and is probably not a threat to any of the survivors. (This is ironic, since later in the film the Nazi—who turns out to be the sub's captain—murders Gus.) But Kovac—like McIntosh, who argues that snakes should be exterminated—can't seem to decide whether Germans are snakes or fowl:

Kovac: [It doesn't matter if the German is] a crew member or the skipper, he's German!

Smith: [whose real last name is Schmitt, of German extraction, seems defensive] A guy can't help being a German if he's born a German, can he?

Kovac: [wildly mixing his metaphors] Neither can a snake help being a rattlesnake if he's born a rattlesnake. That don't make him a nightingale. Get him outta here—throw the Nazi buzzard overboard!

Another very common practice among Hollywood screenwriters was to refer to the enemy as an insect. In *Bombardier*, the previously mentioned old Sarge is a tobacco chewer with a well-developed sense of aim when he spits out the noxious liquid. After his speech with "Burt" about finishing anything the Germans start, the Sarge spies a moth. The bug flies in front of an open window, and the Sarge nails the moth in mid-flight with an expectorated wad of tobacco juice:

Sarge: [derisively] German moth.

Burt: You're quite an entomologist.

Sarge: Nope. But I know all about bugs.

In the film's climax, we learn why the spitting scene with Sarge earlier was important to establish. He is in his tail-gunner position and has no place to spit, so he must swallow the foul juice. This shot of incidental action was added to the film to establish the fact that later the sergeant still had a wad of tobacco in his mouth when his plane was shot down over Nagoya. Captured, Sarge and Buck (Randolph Scott) are being interrogated by two surly little Japanese officers. Sarge spits tobacco juice into the face of one of the officers, allowing himself and Buck the chance to overpower the Japanese and make good their escape. The fact that Sarge spit at a "German" insect earlier in the film now extends this symbolic insult to the Japanese.

These insect comparisons continue.

In *Bataan*, Private Epps (Kenneth Spencer) is positioned at his post, on the lookout for Japanese soldiers, when Sergeant Dane makes his rounds. Dane asks, "Seen anything?" Epps answers, "No, but you can bet they're out there, all right, thicker'n fleas on a hound dog in Georgia."

In *China*, Japanese soldiers have just brutally gang-raped a young girl when Jones (Alan Ladd) bursts into the room, machine-gunning the men. Later, he tells Carolyn (Loretta Young): "I just shot three Japs, and you know, I have no more feeling for them than if they were flies on a manure heap. In fact, I kind of enjoyed it."

In *China Girl*, describing how Japanese pilots have "a nasty little habit" of strafing helpless pilots as they parachute to the ground, one Flying Tiger creates a new species of insect, calling the Japanese "cloud lice." Later, Johnny Williams (George Montgomery) gives a warning about the impending Japanese invasion. He says, "When you wake up some morning and find them crawling all over Burma like 800 million bedbugs in green pants, remember who told you."

When Captain Jim Gordon (John Wayne) returns from a mission in *Flying Tigers*, his P-40 fighter's tail is riddled with machine gun bullet holes. When his crew chief points the holes out to him, the Duke replies coolly, "Termites." Later in the film, McIntosh changes his prior characterization of the Japanese from rattlesnakes to insects. The Tigers are scheduled for night patrol, and McIntosh says he's looking forward to it, because he hears that "those Jap-os glow in the dark like bugs."

As well, in *A Walk in the Sun*, Germans are referred to as "beetles," and in *Back to Bataan* the Japanese are unspecified vermin that General Wainwright (John Miljan) says the defenders on Bataan "have to comb out of our hair." In both *Gung Ho* and *Objective Burma*, narrators use the same phrase: "Jap-infested jungle."

Finally, there is the species that even the best reptile zoologists could not identify. It is described by Johnny Petak (Dane Clark), a Flying Tiger in *God Is My Co-Pilot*, as he dives out of the sun toward a Japanese plane that had just unsuccessfully attacked him: "You missed! Now repeat after me: your mother was a turtle, your father was a snake, and you're . . . [his next few words, which we assume are curses, are obscured by the rat-tat-tat of his plane's six 50-caliber machine guns. [The enemy's plane explodes in flames]—and now, you're a good Jap [implicitly asserting that the only good one is a dead one]."

In a foxhole in *Guadalcanal Diary*, perhaps Sergeant "Hook" Malone (Lloyd Nolan) sums up this first Satanism appeal statement. He is explaining to a young Marine named "Chicken" (Richard Jaeckel) how he feels about the necessity of killing in war. Chicken asks, "How do you feel about killing people?" Sarge replies, "It's kill or be killed, ain't it? Besides that, they [the Japanese] ain't people."

THE ENEMY'S MORE LIKE A MACHINE

As proposed in Satanism appeal statement two, some films categorized the enemy as an entity lower than animal or even insect life, or not living at all. A costume cue from *Eagle Squadron* is typical of the dehumanization of the enemy: both the Royal Air Force (RAF) Spitfire pilots and Luftwaffe Messerschmitt pilots were shown wearing oxygen masks during aerial combat. The RAF pilots' masks were medium gray (in black and white, probably brown leather) masks, typical of the kind seen throughout Hollywood aviation pictures of the late 1930s. However, the German masks were black and shaped very much like the mouth area of the "Darth Vader" helmet that would become famous decades later in the *Star Wars* films. As well, they featured a robot-like, chromium tube that extended from the top bridge of the German pilot's nose down below the chin line. The effect was to make the German pilots seem robot- or even insect-like, as if they were a totally alien life form. Evidence leads us to believe that the filmmakers were deliberate in these characterizations. In *Eagle Squadron*, pilots of both sides wore masks throughout the film, whether they were flying high in the clouds or hedge-hopping—with one exception: when Chuck Brewer (Robert Stack) steals a Messerschmitt with a super-secret device on board, he flies a considerable distance over enemy territory, along the way engaging in aerial combat with three enemy planes. At no time does Brewer spoil this film's established man vs. machine visual polarity by wearing a German oxygen mask, yet the three Nazi pilots whom he battles wear them.

TAKE AN ENEMY TO LUNCH

Another characterization of the enemy as less than animate relegates Axis combatants to the status of foodstuffs. In *Destination Tokyo*, while the US submarine is waiting to rendezvous with a Navy PBY plane in the Aleutian Islands, the cook (Alan Hale) is fishing, trying to hook an Aleutian salmon. He jokes to another sailor, called "Tin Can" (Dane Clark), creating a fantasy about landing one of the big salmon and finding a little Japanese hiding inside. Laughingly, the cook says, "Fried Jap in tartar sauce!" The more serious Tin Can replies, "I'll take mine boiled in oil."

Similarly, while shooting down Zero after Zero plane in a dogfight scene from *Air Force*, B-17 waist gunner Weinberg (George Tobias) hits one, which explodes in a spectacular burst of flame. He yells, "Fried Jap going down!" In *Joan of Paris*, one member of the downed aircrew makes uncomplimentary remarks about a Messerschmitt pilot whom they have named "Yellow Spinner." The crewman, also using fish imagery, says that one of these days he is going to "have Yellow Spinner for breakfast."

Because Japanese planes were marked with a red ball on the side of the fuselage (the sign of the "rising sun"), they were often called "meatballs," including this mixed metaphor from *God Is My Co-Pilot*. Flaming a Zero, a Flying Tiger radios to his comrades using another mixed metaphor: "That's one meatball in the side pocket!"

Adding to the foodstuff motif is a quote mentioned earlier in the discussion of the Guilt category. Captain Jarvis (Raymond Massey), shouting at the German sub that has rammed his lifeboat, says that he and his colleagues will hunt the Germans down and "slice ya like a piece of cheese!"

GERMAN GERMS

On two occasions the Germans are compared to microbes that cause disease, or are assumed to be filthy enough to carry diseases. The first is a visual cue in *This Land is Mine*: the Germans have uncovered a Resistance group and arrested them. They are also confiscating the group's printing press. A large crowd of villagers has gathered, including one old man, who leans forward to get a better look. A German soldier responsible for crowd control pushes the old man back, and the man is repulsed by even having the soldier touch him. He disgustedly brushes off what he seems to think are invisible "cooties" from the spot on his coat where it came in contact with the German.

In the previously mentioned flea speech by the complaining Italian general, his litany of offenses includes the fact that he no longer even has an orderly: "He's in the hospital with measles—German measles."

In *Lifeboat*, when it appears that a German ship is not going to rescue the survivors, Rittenhouse is dumfounded at first, sputters, and then manages to say that such actions are simply "inhuman."

RACE HATRED

Hollywood exposed a tremendous amount of film stock achieving the Satanism category's third statement, "The Japanese race is ugly and diminutive." Nearly a third of the films of this era that dealt with the war in the Pacific Theater of Operations present the Japanese as what can best be described as a stereotyped Asian gargoyle. What follows is a composite stereotype from these films: his stature is usually small and skinny, as we can see clearly even without comparison to the taller Americans, because his helmet is nearly always too big for his head. His face is often darkly tanned and is poorly proportioned.

This Hollywood depiction is separated into two substereotypes: the "ferret-face" and the "pie/owl-face." A ferret-faced Japanese, who has an uncharacteristically large nose for an Asian, looks more like a rat, with an extreme set of buck teeth. Many of these ugly Asians often squint at the world from behind black, horn-rimmed, thick "Coke bottle" glasses. The ferret-face is almost always smaller in stature than the pie/owl-face. His personality tends to be sly, suspicious, and crafty. The pie/owl-face, on the other hand, has extremely rounded features. The effect can best be described as if his face was pressed against a window, like Muppet character Dr. Bunsen Honeydew. Pie/owl-face is often pockmarked and overweight.

At first, it seems ironic and even contradictory that race hatred of the Japanese is at its most vehement in films dealing with the war in China. Films such as *Flying Tigers, God is My Co-pilot, China*, and *China Girl* largely depict Japanese as unattractive to the point that some viewers decades later actually feel sorry for the truly homely looking Chinese actors "uglied up" to be stereotyped Japanese in these films.

But Hollywood had to go to these physical extremes so they could more easily make racial slurs against one Asian group while heaping glowing praise on the Japanese's Asian cousins, the Chinese. After all, one of the US State Department's priorities during the war was to differentiate between the Japanese "yellow peril" and the heroic character of our "poor, oppressed, Chinese allies." So, Hollywood simply set aside all scientific principles of physical anthropology and created two Asian races: the noble Chinese and the physically, culturally, and morally defective Japanese.

One of the most blatant examples of the use of racial stereotypes to differentiate between Chinese and Japanese is in *The Purple Heart*. Screenwriter/producer Darryl Zanuck had a problem: a Chinese man (H. T. Tsiang) had to be shown betraying his allies, a crew of American flyers, to the Japanese, as well as giving false testimony at their trial. Zanuck used the old stereotypical "Chinaman" as a toady, a collaborator who bows and scrapes before the Japanese to maintain his wealth and his position as the puppet governor of a Japanese-occupied Chinese province. This collaborator character is always seen dressed in silky, ultra-traditional Chinese garb, complete with a skullcap and scraggly "Fu Manchu" moustache. His face, rather than Chinese, looks like the Japanese stereotype: he's a "ferret-face," with tightly slit eyes, buck teeth, a phony smile, and a mincing, patronizing, "so-solly" style of speaking, complete with a high, nasal voice, which was the vocal characteristic of most of Hollywood's Japanese stereotype characters. He is portrayed as a genetic reject, more of a stereotypical Japanese than Chinese one. On the other hand, this collaborator's son dresses in an American suit with his hair cut and combed in the American style and speaks unaccented English. He is so ashamed of this betrayal of their "American friends" that he kills his father right in the middle of the courtroom. Seized immediately by the Japanese and later executed, the young Chinese man is praised by the American aircrew, and is named an "unofficial member" of their bomber crew. To draw an even stronger affinity between this young man and the Americans, Benson Fong, who played the highly Americanized "number-one son" Jimmy Chan in *Charlie Chan in the Secret Service* (also released in 1944), was cast in the role.

"SO SOLLY"

Not content with simply emphasizing an enemy's physical ugliness, Hollywood also disparaged the language and culture of its enemies, especially the Japanese. So the fourth Satanism statement is, "The Japanese language and lifestyle are laughable and barbaric."

Among the more prevalent cultural slurs was the stereotypical "so sorry, please" phrase, generally used when the Japanese speaker wished to mollify someone he was offending, but was really not sincere. These references emphasized the Japanese language having no equivalent for the sound of the letter "L," causing Japanese to pronounce "L"s as "R"s. Consequently, when the above phrase was employed, it was pronounced by both actors playing Japanese and by American actors mocking Japanese speaking English as "so sorry, prease," and at times, even the totally nonsensical "so solly, prease."

For example, in *The Purple Heart*, a Japanese officer stands at the door of the courtroom in which the American flyers are being unjustly tried. His purpose in guarding the door is to admit only members of the press who are friendly to the Axis. Neutrals or members of the press from countries sympathetic to the Allies were greeted with the following prohibition from the Japanese officer: "So sorry, prease. Credentials not in order." If the reporter protested, he was told to file a letter of complaint with "The Bureau of Enlightenment."

Pidgin English itself is a slur. When the Japanese speak English in one of these films, such as the radio propagandist character in *Bataan* or the high-pitched, nasal voice of the Japanese soldier heard from off-screen in *Cry Havoc*, these characters speak it badly. Prejudiced against them anyway, many American audiences ignored the fact that the great majority of Americans were monolingual, and instead sneered at the Japanese soldiers' poor command of our language. Unless closely scrutinized, the implicit message was that the Japanese were culturally and intellectually inferior to Americans.

In *The Purple Heart*, all the Japanese except the general—who spent prewar time as a spy in America—spoke poor, broken English. Especially interesting was the court bailiff, whose tasks included telling the court to rise when the judges entered the courtroom. "Up stand," he would always say, rather than "stand up." Needless to say, such silliness does not bear close scrutiny. In reality, the bailiff would not be speaking pidgin English in a Japanese court. He would speak Japanese. But, after all, that wasn't the point.

In *Bombardier*, the Japanese officer who captures Buck (Randolph Scott) after his plane crashes in Nagoya insists that the flyer must bow to him. The American refuses, so the soldiers force Buck's shoulders down. "Stupit," the officer says, in terrible pidgin English, guaranteed to cause the audience to put the onus of stupidity back on the Japanese, not Buck. At the conclusion of the same film, as bombers manned by the bombardiers that Buck trained are destroying factories and their Japanese Army inhabitants all over Nagoya, Chick (Pat O'Brien) looks down from his cockpit, and with the light of the flaming industrial area flickering across his face, says sarcastically, "So solly, prease." The same idea was expressed in *Destination Tokyo*: on board the carrier *Hornet*, one of Doolittle's pilots, revving his engines prior to takeoff, gestures to his ground crewman with his hand, imitating a plane diving and then climbing (to bomb and then get away), and shouts, "So solly, please."

On board the submarine in *Destination Tokyo*, torpedoes are being loaded for an attack on a Japanese aircraft carrier. Among other graffiti scrawled on the torpedoes were the following: "a Mickey Finn for the Mikado," a "so sorry" sign over a cartooned drawing of a buck-toothed, slant-eyed, bespectacled cross between Kilroy and Mr. Moto, and the notation "say 'ah,' Tojo."

NO RESPECT

In *Guadalcanal Diary*, Sergeant Malone (Lloyd Nolan) is searching a hut in a village recently liberated from the Japanese. The enemy had fled in such a hurry that their food, still warm, was left on the table. Malone smells some of it, makes a disgusted face as if it wasn't fit to eat, and kicks over the table that the food is on. Later in the same sequence, they discover a bathtub. Anthony Quinn, who plays Alvarez, the token stereotypical Mexican American in this Marine unit, says to Sergeant Malone and Chaplain Donnelly (Preston Foster):

Alvarez: Just what I need for Saturday night!

Malone: (sarcastically) I wonder what the Japs use it for.

Donnelly: (with a wry grin) That I wouldn't know.

Although there are many fewer references to German lifestyles in these films, *Lifeboat* provides a look at a typical one. When the survivors briefly think that they are about to be taken prisoner on a German submarine tender, Rittenhouse (Henry Hull) asks Connie (Tallulah Bankhead), "Do you suppose they'll have any coffee aboard?" Connie sarcastically replies, "Yes, they have some coffee, and wiener schnitzel, and pig's knuckles, and sauerkraut, and apple strudel."

In *Across the Pacific*, ethnocentrisms crossed Rick Leland's (Bogart) lips almost as often as his bourbon. He and Alberta Marlow (Mary Astor) are passengers on board a Japanese ship bound for the Panama Canal Zone a few weeks before Pearl Harbor. Despite the fact that there were a number of young, attractive young Asian men on board the vessel, Leland, flirting with Alberta, reminds her that he is lucky because "there aren't any handsome young men on board the ship" with whom he must compete. Later, Leland also remarks that the Japanese "all look alike."

In *Blood on the Sun*, journalist Nick Condon (James Cagney) has just had his daily judo session with a group of Japanese. Afterward, in the community baths, the Japanese bathe together in a common pool, but Condon chooses to bathe alone in a tub for one. Also, later in the picture, which supposedly takes place in Japan in 1929, Condon is discussing the beauty of the Japanese islands with a friend: "The scenery's great, but it's the inhabitants I object to. The higher up you go, the lower grade people you meet."

STICKS AND STONES

Since there are dozens of assorted names Americans used to characterize the enemy, I've dubbed this fifth Satanism category statement, "The enemy are the 'Krauts,' 'Jerries,' 'Japs,' 'Nips,' and infinite variations on a name-calling theme."

In *Guadalcanal Diary*, a Marine sharpshooter from the backwoods, copying Gary Cooper's "turkey shoot" business from *Sergeant York*, makes a gobbling noise. This causes a curious but really stupid Japanese soldier to raise his head high enough for the Marine to pick him off.

Transferring a bead of spittle from his thumb to the front sight of his rifle like York, he declares: "Scratch one squint-eye!" Toward the end of the picture, Coporal "Taxi" Potts (William Bendix) and his fellow Marines are soon to be relieved and shipped off the island of Guadalcanal for some well-needed rest. Potts confides in his mates that he's glad to be leaving "this gook island." In a similar reference in *Objective Burma*, Captain Nelson (Errol Flynn) refers to the Japanese as a race of "slopeheads." This is an especially selective racial slur, considering that the operation which Flynn was commanding at the time was an Allied project, including Burmese soldiers, some of whom were within earshot of his comment.

Since name-calling was a routine part of scriptwriting for any of these pictures, what follows is a brief sampling of names screenwriters called the Germans and Japanese, and a listing of at least one of the many pictures in which this very creative nomenclature can be found: The Germans are called "Heels" in *All Through The Night*; "dirty bastards" in *Action In the North Atlantic* (using the word "bastard" was still forbidden, even in the excesses of the Hays Office' wartime motion picture code's bad-word relaxation. The line, shouted by Lieutenant Rossi [Humphrey Bogart], was intentionally obscured in part by machine-gun fire, but audiences could clearly read his lips); "stupid swine" and "oxen" in *Berlin Correspondent* (oddly enough, these are names that a Nazi colonel calls his own men); "Blitzkrieg" in *Berlin Correspondent* (a derogatory nickname coined by an American about a surly head waiter in a Berlin restaurant); "Heinie" in *Captains of The Clouds* and *Corvette K-225*; "Krauts" in *A Walk in the Sun* and many others; "Huns" and "Jerries" (British slang for the enemy left over from the last war) in *Eagle Squadron*; "a nation that belches" in *Five Graves to Cairo*; (spoken by an Italian), "a crummy bunch of jokers" in *Sahara*; "brutes" in *This Land Is Mine*; "Ersatz superman" in *Lifeboat*; and various sarcastic references to "the master race" in *Lifeboat*.

The Japanese are of course called "Japs" constantly, in nearly every combat film; "Little sneakin' Nips" in *Air Force*; "dirty snipes" in *Destination Tokyo*; "Nips" in *The Fighting Seabees*; "Hong Kong Hophead" in *God Is My Co-Pilot*; "suckers" in *Bataan*; and "savages" in *China Girl*. In context, this reference is an example of the polarities that the name-calling aspects of Satanism are supposed to create. A Flying Tiger explains why he fights against the Japanese by saying, "It's savages against civilization." The Japanese are also called "stinking little savages" in *Objective Burma*.

CRUEL AND BARBARIC

The "savage" reference above, although used in *China Girl* in only one line of dialogue, was developed by Hollywood's writers into more than just name-calling. It wasn't just the enemy's identity that was savage, but also their actions. The Satanism statement used to categorize this refinement of simple name-calling is, "The enemy is a savage, whose actions are cruel and barbaric."

One of the favorite methods in Hollywood for depicting the savagery of America's foes was the enemy's total disregard for the articles of the Geneva Convention. This was exemplified by the mistreatment and torture of Allied prisoners. One of the most clearly pronounced films in this vein is *The Purple Heart*, which dealt, from beginning to end, with the illegal Japanese trial, torture, and eventual sentence of execution given to US prisoners of war. Since this film was based on the kangaroo court trial and subsequent beheading of a crew of American airmen who flew in the Doolittle Raid, the film, which has an almost fantasy flavor to it, had much credibility.

In *The Purple Heart*, these airmen are tortured, one by one, to extract information about the base from which they came. None give in. We never find out what the Japanese torturers did to Sergeant Skvoznik (Kevin O'Shea) . . . only the tough football hero's screams are heard. When he is returned to his cell, the sergeant is in a near-catatonic state. Later, they maim the hands and arms of Sergeant Canelli (Richard Conte), an artist in civilian life. Earlier, in the courtroom, Canelli is also gun-butted; Lieutenant Vincent (Don Barry) is also gun-butted and suffers a severe concussion; Sergeant Clinton (Farley Granger) is subjected to some undisclosed torture that destroys his vocal cords; and Lieutenant Bayfourth's (Charles Russell's) hands have been ravaged so severely that they do not function, and he wears black leather gloves to conceal his wounds. Finally, unable to extract the military secrets he and Japanese authorities need, the judge sentences the prisoners to death.

Similarly, in *Objective Burma*, some of Captain Nelson's (Errol Flynn's) paratroopers surrender to the Japanese. The prisoners are mutilated and flayed alive by their captors in an attempt to get them to reveal where the rest of their force was. Of course, despite this cruelty, no Allied soldier betrays his comrades. When Nelson's men find them, one soldier says to another that their bodies were "too awful to look at." The audience is not allowed to see the men, and must let their imaginations create horrors that were probably worse than those inflicted by the enemy. The only tortured soldier remaining alive begs Nelson to kill him because his pain was so intense. But before Nelson can decide what to do, the man mercifully dies.

Mark Williams (Henry Hull), a newspaperman embedded in Nelson's expedition, begins the adventure as an unbiased keeper of the record. Until this mutilation, he has refrained from even name-calling when it came to the enemy. But seeing this tortured man die in Nelson's arms, Williams is in shock. He staggers about for a moment, and then, starting rather calmly, gives an oration that concludes with the newsman bellowing like a madman: "I've been a newspaperman for thirty years, and I thought I'd seen or read about everything one man can do to another—from the torture chambers of the Middle Ages to the gang wars and lynchings of today—but this—this was different. This was done in cold blood by a people who claim to be civilized. Civilized? [He gets louder and more emotional, waving his arms.] They're degenerate moral idiots! Stinking little savages! Wipe 'em out—wipe 'em off the face of the earth!"

Japanese mistreatment and murder of prisoners after the fall of the Philippines was vividly portrayed in *Back to Bataan*, featuring real footage of the emaciated, ragged prisoners who were rescued from the Japanese prison camp at Cabanatuan. And the "death march" of Bataan is shown, in which captives who fall or falter on the march are summarily shot and/or bayoneted.

In *Bataan*, one of Sergeant Dane's (Robert Taylor's) troops, a Filipino scout named Salazar (Alex Havier), is sent to break through enemy lines and reach headquarters with a plea for reinforcements. Instead, he is captured and killed. To taunt the Americans, the Japanese string up Salazar's bloody body within view of his friends. Corporal Todd (Lloyd Nolan) says, "The Japs probably got him last night, and worked on him a long time before they strangled him and put him out of his misery."

The climax of *Bombardier* features a more melodramatic view of the mistreatment of prisoners of war. Buck, as previously mentioned, is captured by the Japanese after his plane crashes on a bombing mission over Nagoya. His parachute hung up a few feet from the ground, Buck (the six-foot-three Randolph Scott) is pulled down so that he can put his feet on the ground, surrounded by diminutive Japanese soldiers pointing bayoneted rifles at him. Later, Buck is reunited with the rest of his surviving crewmen. The Japanese bring in a wounded crewman on a stretcher. In a medium close-up of the young man, who obviously has already suffered a terrible beating, we see him plead for some water. Japanese hands reach into frame and yank him out of frame to beat him some more. When the young man's body is yanked out of frame, we can read the words stenciled on the canvas stretcher on which he has been lying: "Donated by American Red Cross for Japanese Earthquake Relief, 1923." This image is accompanied by sound effects of the Japanese beating the young man again, and a muted trumpet softly playing the "glory, glory hallelujah" chorus from the *Battle Hymn of the Republic*. Then the young man's bloody and lifeless body is flung back onto the stretcher. Later, all but Buck and his crew chief are taken out and machine-gunned.

In *Wake Island*, as the Japanese finally overrun the outnumbered Marines' headquarters, an enemy soldier finds two wounded Americans. Rather than ignore them or call for a medic, he rakes their bodies with machine-gun fire. A few scenes later, the radio operator, still at his post and unarmed, is shot by a Japanese officer. The same treatment of the wounded occurs in *Guadalcanal Diary*. After wiping out all but one of an entire platoon of Marines, the Japanese systematically bayonet the bodies of the wounded and dead Marines.

Similarly, in *Gung Ho*, a Japanese soldier comes upon a badly wounded Marine in the jungle. The Marine gasps and begs for a drink of water. Instead, the Japanese bayonets him and spits on the body.

In *God Is My Co-Pilot*, wounded Australian and American soldiers and women and children in a nearby prison camp cheer as Colonel Scott leads an air raid on Japanese positions in Hong Kong. One of the wounded Aussies points out to his comrades what is happening, and says, "God bless 'em." Hearing this, a Japanese guard gun-butts him. Later, a woman prisoner simply cries out, "they're our boys," and a Japanese officer slaps her, knocking her to the ground.

THE NAZIS, TOO

Depictions of brutality were not unique to the Japanese. In *Crash Dive*, after a German submarine sinks a freighter, the Nazis do not pick up civilian survivors, which include women and children. Instead, the sub stalks the survivors' lifeboat for days, waiting to attack whatever rescue ship should arrive. A very similar situation was previously described in *Action in the North Atlantic*, in which the sub did not rescue the survivors, but took movies of them, and when the cheeky Americans gave the Germans the "V for victory" sign and shouted insults, the sub rammed their lifeboat, sinking it and killing some of the sailors. Also, as previously mentioned, in *Corvette K-225*, the German sub first torpedoes and sinks the warship, and then comes to the surface to machine-gun any crewmen who make it to lifeboats.

The reason Hollywood hit this treatment of survivors so hard was a response to a 1942 order from no less a person than Hitler himself to Vice Admiral Karl Doenitz, commander of Germany's fleet of submarines, to direct U-boat crews not to rescue the survivors of ships they destroyed. There was further evidence—for which Doenitz served a prison term after the Nuremberg trials—that the admiral also ordered surviving crews to be killed.

REPRISALS

As evidenced above, Hollywood did not limit its portrayal of Axis violence against those in their sphere of influence to combatants only. As reprisals for acts of guerilla warfare and resistance attacks, the Japanese and the Germans took innocent civilian hostages and executed them without trial. This was a common practice, both in reality and in Hollywood's version of events. An example is the film adaptation of John Steinbeck's *The Moon Is Down* (1943). The Germans occupy a small Norwegian town and take over the town's iron mine. In reprisal for resistance attacks on German soldiers and sabotage, they arrest and hang an assortment of town leaders. In response, other civilians blow up the mine to show the Germans that reprisals will never work, and if they kill resistance leaders, others will rise to take their place.

In *Back to Bataan*, Philippine guerilla force commander Colonel Madden (John Wayne) executes four Japanese officers for the murder of the schoolmaster in the village of Balintowak. In reprisal, the Japanese randomly select forty Filipino villagers and shoot them.

The "intellectual" German commandant in *This Land Is Mine* is less arbitrary and more calculating in his selection of hostages to be shot. He selects Jews, intellectuals, and a priest, all independent-minded members of the community, to be executed in reprisal for the killing of two German soldiers by the French Resistance. A reprisal execution also occurs in *Edge of Darkness*. When the German garrison first arrives to occupy the Norwegian town of Tronus, there was some protest and some German soldiers were injured. Hostages are taken and shot, among them the owner of the town's hotel. After these murders, the Germans commandeer the hotel for their headquarters. At the climax of the film, the Germans again arrest a group of community leaders whom they suspect of leading local resistance. As the leaders are lined up in the town square and ordered to dig their own graves, the entire village rises up as one and attacks the German garrison, killing every last one.

To accent these barbaric enemy actions, Hollywood sprinkled many of these films with a number of moments designed to reinforce the idea that the enemy kills for no good reason. In *Five Graves to Cairo*, the Germans occupy a town and its hotel. The owner of the hotel is told that he is personally responsible for any "irregularities" which might occur during their stay. The Nazi (Peter van Eyck) makes the German Army's policy about innocent civilians crystal clear: "our complaints are brief: we make them against the nearest wall."

KILLING THEIR OWN

In *Sahara*, the rag-tag group of Allied soldiers led by Sergeant Gunn (Humphrey Bogart) captures two prisoners, an Italian infantryman, and a German flyer. The German is portrayed as the quintessential "mad dog" Nazi. The Italian, who finds his captors to be a group of decent men who treat prisoners fairly, refuses to help the German escape. When the Italian adds insult to injury, criticizing Der Fuehrer, the Nazi kills him.

This was symptomatic of another dastardly enemy practice that Hollywood was quick to exploit: the enemy seldom seem concerned about the lives of their own men. In *Eagle Squadron*, at a German air base where Flight Lieutenant Brewer (Robert Stack) has managed to steal a Messerschmitt, a German pilot wishing to give chase is shot trying to climb into the cockpit of his plane. The pilot, wounded, falls unconscious across the wing of the plane. Another German pilot climbs up on the wing, and, rather than see to his wounded comrade, roughly kicks the man's body off the wing.

In American submarine movies, it is standard procedure that when a crewman is left "topside" at the time of an order to submerge, every effort is made to rescue him. This practice is sometimes exercised to the point of endangering the sub, as in a scene in *Gung Ho*. In that situation, a Marine was topside when the sub began to dive to avoid a Japanese plane. Nonetheless, when they discover that one man was not yet aboard, the submarine's captain gives the order to surface long enough to retrieve him.

But according to Hollywood, this was not the way the enemy operated. In *Corvette K-225*, after a surface battle, the German sub must quickly dive. A gun crewman is wounded, and his battery mate begins to pull him toward the hatch to enter the sub when the order is given to submerge. The crewman drops his buddy and runs to the hatch, closing it behind him. The wounded man crawls to the hatch and bangs on it, pleading to be let in. At this point, the sub and the hatch are still above water. But they refuse to open the hatch and continue to submerge, and the man drowns. Justice is served a little later, when the sub is destroyed by depth charges, killing all aboard.

A similar German lack of concern for their comrades-in-arms occurs in *Lifeboat*. A German sub tender vessel has lowered a boat to pick up the survivors. However, before they can be rescued, the ship itself comes under attack from an Allied warship. Instead of retrieving the rescue party, the tender steams away, leaving the boat crew to fend for themselves. A moment later, this boat suffers a direct hit from one of the warship's artillery shells and is blown to pieces. Again, poetic justice intervenes, as director Alfred Hitchcock arranges for the tender to suffer the same fate a few moments later.

In these examples, there is some room for doubt: militarily, both instances could fall into the category of "judgment calls." But *Edge of*

Darkness leaves no doubt in the minds of the audience. A company of German soldiers arrives at the town of Tronus to find the bodies of Norwegians and Germans scattered everywhere, indicating that a great battle had just occurred. The Germans don't even see to their own fallen comrades or check to see if any are still alive, although this battle took place only a few hours earlier. When the German major in command finds the office of the commandant of the town garrison, he sees that the body of the commandant, who had taken his own life, is still seated upright in his chair. Without care or ceremony, the major twirls the chair, causing the dead officer's body to topple onto the floor. With a smirk, the major sits in the dead man's chair to compose his report of the incident.

In *Lifeboat*, William Bendix plays a German-American so ashamed of his heritage that he has changed his name from Schmitt to Smith. At one point, Smith observes the Nazi submarine captain Willi (Walter Slezak) drinking water from a flask he has hidden from the sleeping survivors. Smith, sick and suffering from a leg wound and feverish from drinking seawater, asks Willi for some of his water, but Willi kills this fellow German to shut him up.

In *Back to Bataan*, Japanese commanders are guilty of sacrificing their own men's lives recklessly. This is a trend through many films that unlike Americans, the Japanese have only one way to take a military objective: a frontal attack in which wave after wave of their soldiers are mowed down by relentless machine-gun fire until they finally overrun the Allied position, or the Allies run out of ammunition. Sometimes it's pointed out that since it's an honor for Japanese to die for their emperor, that their commanders spend the lives of their men in eighteenth- or ninteenth-century frontal attacks without any thought to tactics that might achieve the same objectives without the terrible loss of life. Early in *Back to Bataan*, Japanese soldiers are attacking in force a smaller group of dug-in Filipino scouts, commanded by Colonel Madden (John Wayne). The Americans and Filipinos are amazed at how the Japanese attack in endless waves, bridging the barbed wire with the bodies of their slain comrades.

Later in the film, Madden and his men are defending a bridge across a river, trying to deny the enemy access to the road beyond. To do this, they partially blow the bridge and score a hit on the lead Japanese tank, leaving it immobilized. At this point, although the condition of the crew inside the stricken Japanese tank is not clear, a second Japanese tank approaches. Without hesitation or any show of concern for the men inside the stricken lead tank, the second tank pushes it forward into the ditch. They use the disabled tank to fill in the span of bridge Madden and his men have destroyed, driving over it as if their comrades were not inside.

GRINNING PILOTS

A logical, Hollywood-created extension of the enemy's barbarism is the idea that he not only does heinous acts of killing because they are his nature, but that he derives a sadistic glee from doing them. This is borne out time and time again in one of the clichés of the World War II combat film genre: the sadistic enemy pilot dives to attack the Americans, grinning and sometimes laughing about the death that he is causing. In contrast, Allied pilots are mostly shown grimly or angrily attacking the enemy because they must, not because they derive pleasure out of it. An occasional exception to this is when an American pilot grins or says something to indicate that what he's doing is out of revenge for the killing of one of his comrades, for Pearl Harbor or some other similar offense.

For example, in *Captains of the Clouds*, a German fighter pilot discovers a flight of unarmed bombers being ferried from Canada to England. One-by-one, the pilot picks off the defenseless planes. This is the typical kind of scene that would follow:

1. Medium shot of a German pilot inside the cockpit of his Messerschmitt as he dives on the next bomber he intends to shoot down.
2. Medium shot of pilots MacLean (James Cagney) and Harris (Reginald Gardiner) in their cockpit, trying to spot the direction the Messerschmitt will be attacking from.
3. Point-of-view shot of the German, through his cockpit glass, as we see him dive on the ship.
4. As per no. 1.
5. Cut-in close-up of the German's gloved hand pressing the button on his stick that powers his machine guns.

6. Medium shot of the left front wing of his plane, showing his machine guns blazing.
7. As per shot no. 2. MacLean and Harris's cockpit glass shatters, struck by bullets. Debris flies for a few seconds. Harris, a sympathetic character throughout the movie, slumps over, mortally wounded. MacLean, busy looking out the cockpit window to find where the fighter has gone, does not see this, and appears to mutter some curses.
8. As per no. 1. The German pilot grins sadistically.

In *Sahara*, the Nazi pilot grins fiendishly and laughs before strafing Sergeant Gunn's tank. In *God Is My Co-Pilot*, the pilots of three Japanese Zeroes take great pleasure in diving to attack a single Flying Tiger, and in *Destination Tokyo*, two Japanese pilots dive to attack the submarine with toothy grins on their faces.

In *Air Force*, *Flying Tigers*, *China Girl*, and *Wake Island*, a nearly identical melodramatic propaganda film cliché is dramatized: the American pilot's plane has been hit, and it is going down. The pilot (or, in the case of *Air Force*, the wide-eyed, youthful Chester (Ray Montgomery), the plane's rear gunner) jumps out of the burning plane, pulls his ripcord, and thinks he will parachute to safety. Instead, grinning Japanese make pass after pass, strafing the helpless pilot in midair. And in *Air Force*, poor Chester is only wounded by these strafing passes while floating to the ground. Once Chester is on the ground, wounded too badly to take cover, he pitifully holds up his arms toward the oncoming Zero as if begging for quarter. But the laughing Japanese pilot makes two more strafing runs, killing his helpless victim . . . the equivalent of running him over, and then backing up to run him over again, twice.

Gung Ho dished up a healthy dose of poetic justice on an enemy who would strafe helpless opponents. Colonel Carlson (Randolph Scott) and his Marines have landed on Makin Island and have already taken half of it. Carlson's raiders are heavily outnumbered, but he has a plan: Carlson orders his men to paint a huge American flag on the roof of the island's hospital. Then he orders all of his troops to retreat in the direction of the hospital, then across the shallow pond beyond the hospital, and to "dig in" and hide in the jungle on the other side. Meanwhile, the Japanese are drawn in by this retreat and now occupy the hospital. Carlson has timed this retreat so that when Japanese air support arrives, they will find the hospital with a huge American flag, surrounded by soldiers. What the misguided flyers fail to realize is that the soldiers below surrounding the hospital are all Japanese.

On the ground, grinning Japanese wave to the oncoming Zeros until the planes begin their first pass. Only then do the soldiers realize that their comrades-in-arms intend to drop bombs on them. The flyers first destroy the hospital, itself an institution that should have possessed some sort of immunity from attack. But due to the lack of accuracy of their bombing, many of the Japanese near the building are killed. The panicked survivors begin to wade into the lake, trying to reach the cover of the jungle on the other side. Then come five separate shots of the laughing faces of the Japanese pilots (two medium long shots, two medium shots, and one extreme close-up), intercut with shots showing them strafing their own soldiers in the water. Finally, the Americans, secluded in the jungle on the other side of the lake, mow down the few Japanese who make it to the other side.

COWARDS AND BULLIES

The seventh Satanism category statement is, "The enemy preys mainly on the weak." By this, I mean that Hollywood pictured Axis soldiers as cowardly bullies who were at their worst when their victims were defenseless, at the mercy of the enemy.

Besides the atrocities against combatants cited earlier in this section, Hollywood depicted many Axis offenses against the defenseless, women, children, and the elderly. Beginning with mistreatment of the elderly, we see excellent examples in *Berlin Correspondent* and *Edge of Darkness*. In *Berlin Correspondent*, an old man is taken in for "questioning" by the Gestapo. Later, we see the form in which this inquiry takes place: two ugly, burly goons, stripped to the waist, beat the old man with whips. In *Edge of Darkness*, an old shopkeeper is manhandled and humiliated by a German sergeant. Later, the town schoolteacher, Sixtus Anderson (Morris Carnovsky), is told by the Germans that his house is to be occupied and turned into a blockhouse. He refuses, confronting the Nazi lieutenant, saying: "We are not animals, we are men!" The lieutenant slaps him, knocking him backward a few steps.

"Where are your courts?" Anderson replies. The Nazi slaps him again. "Your judges?" Another slap. "And your juries?" Yet another slap. Stunned, but still dignified, Anderson still resists: "Until you bring them forward, I must forbid you my house." The lieutenant, finished listening, knocks the old man down a flight of stairs, killing him, and tells his sergeant to get all the schoolteacher's books and belongings and burn them in the town square. He says, "We have no room for philosophers."

As the battered body of the old man is carried away from the town square and the books, writings, and belongings of a lifetime of scholarship are now a Nazi bonfire, director Lewis Milestone cuts to a reaction shot of two people in the crowd. Clearly visible on the wall behind these two townspeople is a Nazi propaganda poster that says, "Look up to Germany."

Women were easy prey for the enemy, especially Nazis. In *Edge of Darkness*, women and children of two Norwegian villages, fleeing gunfire, are machine-gunned by the Germans. In *Joan of Paris*, Nazis murder a little old lady. In *The Fighting Seabees*, a Japanese soldier shoots a woman, and in *Five Graves to Cairo*, the French maid is found guilty of "spreading enemy rumors." Instead of the usual Nazi "single shot from a Luger" execution, a witness said that "they beat her, and then led her out—one bullet would have been enough."

RAPE

Although rape was a motion-picture topic only rarely approved by the Hays Office, sexual assault, pillage, and plunder were commonplace occurrences in Hollywood propaganda's Satanistic depiction of the enemy. In *Edge of Darkness*, a German soldier not only rapes a woman, but to add even more shock value, the crime takes place in a church. Later, to dissuade her fiancé Gunnar (Errol Flynn) from going crazy and seeking revenge on the soldier before the townspeople are armed and ready to attack the Germans in force, Karen Stensgard (Ann Sheridan) reminds Gunnar that she's not the first to suffer: "Nazis rape women all over Europe." Karen's admonition was useless, though: her father seeks out and shoots the Nazi rapist.

In *China*, as previously mentioned, a young girl named Ton Yin is gang-raped by Japanese soldiers, who also cold-bloodedly murder her parents and even kill a baby. In *Gung Ho*, there is a veiled reference to more rapes. One Marine Raider Battalion volunteer, a Filipino, is asked by his captain why he wants to kill Japanese. He says: "My sister was caught by the Japanese in Manila. We never heard word of her, but [hatefully] we read in the newspapers what they did."

Rarely did Hollywood let such enemy villains get away with their evil deeds. Even in the fantasy film, *Tarzan Triumphs*, the African principality of Palandria is invaded and subjugated by the Nazis, turning the male population into slaves. Objecting to this, Zandra, the daughter of the king, insults a German officer. He grabs her and attempts to force his intentions on her. Her brother attempts to defend her, but the German shoots him. In the confusion, Zandra escapes and runs to Tarzan for help.

In *Five Graves to Cairo*, the attitude of the Germans toward the women of subjugated countries is slyly implied. Soon after the Germans arrive in the newly-captured town and take over the hotel, a German lieutenant dictates the conquerors' requirements to the owner (Akim Tamiroff) and the chambermaid, Moosh (Anne Baxter). Next, he orders Moosh to turn around. When she obeys, he rips the apron from around her waist, and uses it for a towel to wipe perspiration and dirt from his face. The implication is that the Nazi considers the rest of her to be similarly at his disposal.

The Axis had no respect or deference for women. In *All Through the Night, Five Graves to Cairo, Edge of Darkness*, and *God Is My Co-Pilot*, enemy soldiers strike women in their faces. In *Five Graves*, Field Marshal Rommel himself does the striking.

CRIMES AGAINST CHILDREN

Victimizing children is an appalling crime in any civilized culture, and Hollywood made sure the enemy was shown to be guilty of such crimes. In *China Girl*, the Japanese machine-gun a group of men, women, and children, who are then dumped into mass graves. The American who witnesses this mass murder is told that they were "spies." At the film's end, using pinpoint dive-bombing, Japanese planes destroy a Chinese schoolhouse, killing the schoolmaster and some of the children. Later in the same air raid, Japanese dive-bombers strafe wounded children and bomb a civilian hospital, although it was clearly marked with red crosses on the roof.

In *Eagle Squadron*, orphan children are on a beach holiday when a lone German plane attacks. The children hide underneath their truck and bravely sing songs while the German strafes them. One irritated little boy climbs to the top of the nearest hill, shaking his fists in the air, yelling, "I hate you, I hate you," at the plane, while (believe it or not) the Nazi makes a deliberate strafing pass at the child. Fortunately, he misses. The scene ends with Spitfires diving to the rescue, flaming the offending Hun.

The Flying Tigers depicts the Japanese bombing an orphan children's hospital. Not to be outdone, our *Berlin Correspondent*, an American disguised as a German psychiatrist, tours a Nazi "insane asylum," the Third Reich's euphemism for a combined political prison and extermination center for the infirm. In one cell, the American is shown a little girl with a crutch and leg brace, obviously crippled. He is told that the little girl is scheduled for a "mercy killing." The administrator of the asylum explains: "A sentimentalist might debate the point, but we have no room in Germany for their kind." The American is told that others, including the insane, the mentally disabled, dwarfs, and so forth, will also be exterminated.

Similarly, in the beginning of *Edge of Darkness*, there appears to be only one Norwegian survivor in the entire town when the Germans arrive, and he is shell-shocked, babbling nonsense. First, they gun-butt him to the ground. Next, a swine of a Nazi major looks down at him and decides that he is hopelessly insane. "Get rid of him," is the order. The soldiers stand the man up and shoot him.

In the confrontation mentioned earlier between Mrs. Miniver (Greer Garson) and the downed German pilot (Helmut Dantine), the Nazi brags about the cities the Nazis have bombed:

Mrs. Miniver: And thousands were killed, innocent . . .

German: (interrupting, shouting) Not innocent! They were against us!

Mrs. Miniver: (continuing) . . . women and children!

German: Thirty thousand in two hours! And we will do the same thing here!

Later in *Mrs. Miniver*, the Vicar of the local church (Henry Wilcoxon), speaking to the congregation, recounts the dead from the latest air raid: a young choirboy, an old man, and a young woman: "Why these? Are these our soldiers, are these our fighters? Because this is not only a war of soldiers in uniform, it is a war of the people of all the people! We shall not forget the dead. Instead, they will inspire us with an unbreakable determination to free ourselves and those who come after us from the tyranny and terror that threatens to strike us down."

A number of savage Japanese actions against noncombatants are crammed into *Cry Havoc*. Early in the film, dialogue reveals that the nurses will not be eating fish anymore, because fishermen are afraid to go out in their boats, afraid of Japanese strafing attacks. Later, the Japanese, returning from a bomb raid on Corregidor, drop their excess tonnage on the hospital on Bataan. The nurses discuss the so-called mistaken Japanese target as if it couldn't have been deliberate. But later in the film, the hospital, clearly marked on its roof with a red cross, becomes a regular target. Women and children are shown to be among the casualties.

The single worst portrayal of uncontrovertibly intentional Japanese violence against the helpless in *Cry Havoc* occurs when a Japanese fighter plane strafes three nurses as they swim in a pond. One woman is killed. One of the survivors reports to the other nurses: "He just saw us swimming, and did it for fun." Similarly, in the opening sequence of *Bataan*, Japanese planes strafe a column of civilian refugees and riddle an ambulance with bullets.

In *Corvette K-225*, this practice is extended to puppies. When the submarine crew that sank the Canadians' ship machine-guns the survivors, they take the time to riddle a dog with gunfire as the dog gamely paddles for a raft.

HELTER SKELTER

When the enemy is not pictured intentionally killing innocents, he is shown to be—unlike Americans—totally unconcerned about where his bombs fall. Thus, the eighth Satanism propaganda statement is, "The enemy bombs indiscriminately." What is interesting about this statement is the degree that filmmakers attempted to distance American bombers and their bombing tactics from those of the Axis. In most Satanism statements, it is implicit that the enemy does so-and-so, but "of course, our boys do not." In the case of indiscriminate bombing, Hollywood went to great lengths to point out the enemy's total lack of concern for civilians in or near their targets below, including hospitals and schools. But these films often stressed to the point of obsession that American bombers aimed for and hit only military targets—the fire-bombing destruction of Axis cities such as Dresden and Tokyo and the atomic bombs dropped on the civilians of Hiroshima and Nagasaki notwithstanding.

On dozens of occasions, but especially in *Bombardier*, RKO used techniques popular on Madison Avenue after the war to drum into audiences' heads that the code of the corps of American bombardiers is to "Hit the target! Hit the target! Hit the target!" And these scripts never talk about civilian cities as targets. In the action sequence at the end of *Bombardier*, dialogue includes speeches that point out that the American bombers, true to their creed, have spotted and isolated the "industrial sector" of Nagoya, implying that only industries important to the Japanese war effort were ever bombed. On the ground, as we see the bombs hit, we take note that the targets are all industrial-looking, and that there are absolutely no civilians, homes, schools, and so forth, to be seen. Every victim of the bombing is wearing a Japanese army uniform and has a gun or rifle in his hand, or is manning an anti-aircraft gun.

THE "SURGICAL STRIKE"

In *Thirty Seconds Over Tokyo*, when Captain Ted Lawson's (Van Johnson) ironically nicknamed B-25, the "Ruptured Duck," makes its bombing run over the target, it is only the last stage, the culmination of considerable preparation on the part of the bomb group. Earlier, on board the *USS Hornet*, we hear Colonel Doolittle himself (Spencer Tracy) giving the pilots their prime directive: they are to bomb only the military targets assigned to them and nothing else. Later we see Lawson's crew being briefed on the reconnaissance drawings of the area, the placement of barrage balloons, and especially the exact shape and configuration of the smoke stacks of the industrial plants that were their targets. Their secondary targets were also identified as military shipping in Tokyo Bay.

Because of this production's Oscar-winning special effects, audiences saw the "Duck" flying right down the line of intended enemy factory smokestacks, laying its "eggs" on these targets, and apparently hitting nothing else. In reality, this would have been very difficult: to avoid enemy capture of their top secret Norden bombsights if they were shot down, these highly efficient bombsights were removed from the raiders' B-25s. Doolittle's bombardiers dropped their bombs at very low altitude with just stick-like aiming devices with a fork on one end, similar to the sights on the front end of a rifle. Materials for this makeshift bombsight cost just twelve cents.

In the kangaroo court trial in *The Purple Heart*, the Japanese provide phony evidence to show that the Doolittle raiders bombed schools, temples, and civilian gathering places. Darryl Zanuck's script used neutral journalists in the courtroom to point out to each other that the photo and film evidence was doctored. When the mere mention of bombing non-military targets was first brought up at the trial, every American defendant rose to his feet, indignant at even being accused of such an "unthinkable" crime. At this point, one of the foreign journalists witnessing the trial turns to another and says "it's complete falsehood" when he sees the purported filmed damage to a temple. The reporter says he recognizes the film and the damage from newsreel footage he had seen following one of Japan's earthquakes many years earlier.

On the other hand, films like *Bombardier* made it clear how guilty the enemy was of indiscriminate bombing. In the scene between Harris and the Chaplain described earlier, after telling the young man that his mother is wrong to think of US bombardiers as murderers, the Chaplain explains, "There are millions of other mothers who are looking to you, and boys like you, to destroy the very forces of murder that your mother mistakenly attributes to you. The enemy's targets are everywhere, but yours are clear and confined. Not women and children. But [theirs] are arsenals for spreading death. That's why American bombardiers are trained to hit the target."

In *Wake Island*, the commander (Walter Abel) explains to one of his men the inept Japanese tactic called "checkerboard bombing." Apparently they are poor bombers, or have faulty intelligence information on the target area. The Japanese bomb crosswise in this checkerboard manner, so that sooner or later, by chance, they will hit something of value. However, the major says that this is also their weakness, since between air raids, the Marines simply move things that they do not wish destroyed into places that the Japanese had just bombed, knowing that the enemy would not intentionally bomb those places during the next raid.

Also, in the same film, Major Caton (Brian Donlevy) implicitly states that the Japanese bomb noncombatants. He draws the sad duty of informing one of his pilots that his wife, a civilian, was killed in the Pearl Harbor attack. *Air Force* reinforced this, in a harrowing hospital scene following the bombing of Pearl Harbor. The aircrew's officers are looking for the co-pilot's sister, wounded in the attack. They walk through the hospital ward, women and children lying everywhere, wounded and dying. For added maudlin effect, a little girl with bandages over her eyes pathetically calls out, "I can't see—why is it so dark? Why is it so dark?"

Similarly, women and especially children are the victims of indiscriminate Japanese bombings in *China, China Girl, God Is My Co-Pilot*, and *Flying Tigers*.

The Germans are equally guilty of bombing civilians in *Action in the North Atlantic*, as Rossi (Humphrey Bogart) discusses the "old days" with a Dutch captain. As an excuse for screenwriter John Howard Lawson to bring up civilian casualties caused by the Nazis, they reminisce about fine dinners in the captain's home in Rotterdam before the war. But the Dutchman says that his home and his family are gone now: the German Stukas saw to that.

Both *Eagle Squadron* and *Mrs. Miniver* displayed and discussed many instances of German bombing raids on the civilian streets of London and on quiet, country villages of no military or tactical significance. In both films, hospitals are bombed, but audiences are shown few military casualties, mostly civilian. In one poignant moment in *Eagle Squadron*, a fire-scorched rag doll is found in the rubble of a home. In *Mrs. Miniver*, as previously stated, the list of dead from the last German air raid consisted of an old man, a young woman, and a child.

DEFICIENT CULTURES

In attempting to draw the clearest possible distinction between Americans and their enemies, filmmakers attempted to amplify important concepts absent from their enemies' makeup. Therefore, the ninth Satanism propaganda statement is "civilizing elements of our culture are missing from theirs."

Both the Germans and Japanese were portrayed as lacking the usual feelings that Allied audiences possessed. In *Across the Pacific*, Alberta Marlow (Mary Astor) characterizes the Japanese as "emotionless," while in *Berlin Correspondent* the heroine, Karen (Virginia Gilmore), engaged to the Nazi colonel, is furious with him because he will not help her father, whom the Nazis have imprisoned. She criticizes his lack of human feelings, saying, "Always the official, never the man."

One of the most interesting renditions of the unscrupulous nature of the enemy appears in *Edge of Darkness*. Up until the point in the film in which the Nazi commandant discovers that the villagers are planning an uprising, his men had standing orders forbidding them to act like "normal" Nazi soldiers. Then the commandant decides that the best way to provoke the Norwegians into attacking his men before they were properly armed and organized was to provoke them to the point of foolhardiness. To do this, the commandant relaxes his standing order, thus allowing his men to act as they please.

Suddenly, the soldiers begin to commit all sorts of ghastly offenses, including the baiting and beating of an old, helpless man, rape, pillage, and plunder. The audience comes to understand that this brutal, gangster-like behavior is "normal" for the master race.

As has been mentioned in earlier Satanism category statements, the enemy was shown to be swinish in its treatment of women. Occasionally this is presented as a cultural defect. For example, over coffee in the wardroom of the sub in *Destination Tokyo*, Captain Cassidy (Cary Grant) and his officers ask Lieutenant Raymond (John Ridgely), who portrays an expert on Japan and Japanese culture, questions about the low status of Japanese women. When asked how a Japanese man can support such a large family on an average salary of $7 per week, Raymond answers, "I know [it sounds impossible]. The daughters of the poor are often sold to the factories—or worse." Then Cassidy says, "Females are useful there only to work or to have children. The Japs can't understand the love we have for our women. They don't even have a word for it in their language."

Incidents in *The Purple Heart* and *Blood on the Sun* reinforce this. In *The Purple Heart*, Japanese women are seen only once, despite the bulk of the film taking place in Tokyo. They are not shown in any position of authority, but rather are displayed as servants and sex objects for a group of Japanese generals. In *Blood on the Sun*, Baron Tanaka thinks nothing of ordering a woman to sacrifice her honor to obtain information from an American newspaperman.

In *Guadalcanal Diary*, *Gung Ho*, and *Back to Bataan*, the clash of cultures regarding the value of human life is shown. In all three pictures, the Japanese show no hesitation to fight to the death rather than surrender, and to sacrifice their lives for no particular purpose. This statement in *The Purple Heart* by General Mitsubi (Richard Loo) to Captain Ross (Dana Andrews) sums up these cultural differences, as seen through the eyes of the Japanese military, with this scary speech:

> Our people . . . are conditioned to shock. Our earthquakes have been valuable in that respect. No, Captain. Japan is united in this war through emperor worship and hate. Hate of all foreigners, white or otherwise! [The Japanese worker] wears wood fiber clothes, cardboard shoes; he cheerfully eats one-third of his usual diet. He works fourteen hours a day, seven days a week. And our soldiers—ask your troops at Bataan. We do not leave any place that we want—you must kill us. We will win this war because we are willing to sacrifice ten million lives. How many lives is the white man willing to sacrifice?

Lifeboat provides us with undeniable evidence that the "Axis brutes" do not share the same basic emotions and values as Americans. One of the female survivors becomes distraught when she finally realizes that her baby has drowned, and his body committed to the sea. A number of fellow survivors are needed to keep the shell-shocked woman from following her baby into the water. Witnessing all this, and knowing that his submarine caused all this human misery, the callous Nazi becomes bored, yawns, and stretches out for a nap.

The tenth Satanism propaganda statement is "the enemy is totalitarian." As Webster says, such a government is "based on subordination of the individual to the state, and strict control of all aspects of life and productive capacity of the nation, especially by coercive measures, including censorship and terrorism." All but one of the film examples provided here are pictures written about conditions either within occupied countries, or within the Axis countries themselves.

In the beginning of *Casablanca*, the killing of the German couriers results in a wholesale rout of the population, as the Vichy police (allies of the Germans) "round up the usual suspects." No evidence, no warrants. All inhabitants are subject to random search and arrest, and, ironically, in front of a poster touting "Liberty, Fraternity, Equality," a man whose papers have expired is shot.

JUSTICE SYSTEM COMPARISONS

"Old Howen," (Erwin Kaiser) a member of the German Resistance in *Berlin Correspondent*, is confronted by his Nazi sympathizer daughter, who warns him that he will go to prison for his activities. He retorts: "We in Germany are imprisoned by our government. There's no escape."

Later in the same film, reporter Roberts (Dana Andrews) is caught helping old Howen escape to Switzerland. When confronted by a Gestapo colonel (Martin Kosleck) who asks Roberts what he has to say for himself, the hero naively replies, "What I have to say, I'll say in court and at the trial!" The colonel replies, "Court? Trial? My dear man, this is Germany!"

The differences between the American judicial system and that of Japan's were stressed throughout *The Purple Heart*, in which American flyers, who at the beginning of the trial pointed out that they were outside Japanese civil jurisdiction, were subjected to a kangaroo court trial. Among the differences: (a) The airmen's attorney (educated in the United States, of course) is chosen for them, but works with the court, which is biased against the accused; (b) no time is given for the airmen to prepare a case, nor are they allowed time outside the courtroom to confer with their court-appointed attorney. It is clear it would not have helped them, since their counsel worked for the prosecution; (c) hearsay evidence against the Americans is accepted without question; (d) there is no right of cross-examination of witnesses (it is only allowed if the chief judge thinks they are lying; he doesn't); (e) in an inadvertent outburst, the chief judge refers to the men as guilty before the trial begins; (f) witnesses are tortured to force them to divulge information that has nothing to do with the case (as a matter of fact, the entire trial was concocted by Japanese Army Intelligence to coerce the Americans into revealing secret information about the "base" the Doolittle Raiders took off from); (g) questioning of witnesses for the prosecution is performed by the chief judge, as if he himself is the prosecutor; (h) the trial is far from public. Only Axis journalists are allowed to witness the trial and thus skew their reports to the party line. Plus, the Japanese "Bureau of Enlightenment" won't let the Swiss Red Cross get news of the trial out of the country. The credentials of all other members of the press are deemed by the officer at the door of the courtroom to be "not in order."

SUPPRESSING THE PRESS

Blood on the Sun begins with the Tokyo secret police confiscating all copies of the English language *Tokyo Chronicle*, which contains a story embarrassing to the Japanese government. Later in the film, Editor Nick Condon (James Cagney) is stopped and forced to answer questions put to him by the "thought control officer." When Condon is arrested, it's pointed out that the secret police do not allow him a traditional American "one phone call."

Joan of Paris, as the name implies, takes place in the city of light during the Nazi occupation. Paul Lavalier (Paul Henreid), a downed Free French pilot trying to escape from France, knows he cannot fall into the hands of the Gestapo because he is a famous ace who is highly successful in air combat against the Germans. Thus, Lavalier has been tried in absentia and condemned to death. When he reads the newspapers, controlled by the Nazis and used for propaganda more than news reporting, he learns he has been killed again, and says: "It's been a long time since one could believe them."

Later in this film, the Germans halt a church service and search all the worshippers. It is clear that there are no civil rights in Paris, and if the people forget, they may read the German posters, which say, "Citizens are warned that any persons harboring or assisting enemy soldiers will be shot immediately, without trial."

SLAVERY

When describing the status of those under Axis domination, American films most often called it slavery. In *Tarzan Triumphs*, the entire population of Palandria becomes literal slaves. Plus, for exercising their "free speech" (pleading with the Germans for the release of their princess, Zandra), some are shot outright, and the Nazi commander gives an order to execute every tenth man in the kingdom.

Likewise, in *Objective Burma*, a villager tells Captain Nelson (Errol Flynn) that as soon as the Japanese occupied their town, all its inhabitants were made slaves.

GANGSTERS

In both subtle and obvious ways, the eleventh Satanism statement, "the enemy is a gangster," is woven into many of the films of this era. This is especially true of World War II films that borrow heavily from the themes and icons of other genres. Included are gangster films, spy intrigue films, and the soon to become popular film noir-style films, as seen in such pictures as *Five Graves to Cairo*, *China Girl*, *Black Dragons*, *Across The Pacific*, *All Through the Night*, and *Edge of Darkness*. Themes from both the "B" Western and the gangster picture are used to help create the plot and *mise-en-scene* of *Berlin Correspondent*, and key descriptors of the 1930s newspaper film genre are used in *Blood on the Sun*.

In the silly fantasy film, *Black Dragons*, the typical gangster genre euphemism for a "double cross" is used. After mad plastic surgeon Dr. Melcher (Bela Lugosi), borrowed from the Nazis, changes Japanese agents' faces into Caucasian ones, he appears before the head of the Black Dragon Society and is told he will receive his "reward." But instead of payment or praise, Melcher is imprisoned. As they drag him away, the head of the Black Dragon Society (Stanford Jolley) says: "A little trick we learned from you Nazis: leave no evidence behind, let no sentimentality stand in your way."

Speaking of the classic double-cross, in *Berlin Correspondent*, the heroine must agree to marry the Gestapo colonel in return for the life of an American reporter, her sweetheart. The colonel agrees to arrange for his escape from the concentration camp where he is being held, but he really plans to have the journalist killed during the escape. But the colonel's own assistant and mistress, the "woman scorned" in this scenario, practices some double-crossing of her own. She helps the reporter escape her boss/lover's murder attempt and, to top it off, frames the colonel for the crime of helping a prisoner of the Reich escape. Moral of the story: don't wrong a woman, especially if she works for the Gestapo.

In most of these films, the actions of the enemy are closely identified with the actions of stereotypical villains from American gangster pictures, who, thanks to genre, have well-identified behavior patterns.

In *All Through the Night*, "Papa" Miller (Ludwig Stossel) tells Nazi agent Pepi (Peter Lorre) that his organization is made up of "murderers. I won't have any part of it!" Miller says he has decided to confess his involvement with the Nazis to the police. This, of course, was the wrong thing to say. In typical gangster style, Lorre "has the canary rubbed out."

Later, a Nazi agent called "Madame" (Judith Anderson) extorts silence and continuing service from the heroine, Leda (Kaaren Verne), by threatening to kill her father, whom Madame says the Nazis have as a hostage in a concentration camp. Of course, they have double-crossed Leda but she doesn't know it; her father has already been murdered. Later, trying to explain to his fellow hoods why they should aid him in breaking up the Nazi spy ring, "Gloves" Donahue (Humphrey Bogart) uses gangster language they all will understand: "They're no bunch of racketeers trying to muscle in on some small territory: they wanna move in wholesale, an' take over the whole country."

A note in passing: the quote above, and the context of the entire scene in which it is stated, is another example of the synergism that exists between major propaganda appeal categories. On the one hand, calling the enemy "racketeers" falls under the propaganda category of Satanism, while the notion that they intend on taking over America is certainly an example of Territoriality. The scene in which this takes place is also an allegory depicting America's prewar isolationist attitude. Initially, the hoods to whom Donahue appeals have positioned themselves as islands unto themselves. They state that they have little use for America's government and laws—in fact, they have their own gangster code. They only concern themselves with government and law when they come up against them.

Therefore, they are not immediately concerned when Gloves tells them that the Nazis are trying to "muscle in" on the United States, as they do not much care which government's laws they ignore. However, as will also be mentioned in the Territoriality chapter, Gloves explains to them the radical difference between the present government and the one the Nazis propose to enforce. This causes the gangsters to intervene in behalf of America.

Also, in *All Through the Night*, Nazi spy Ebbing (Conrad Veidt) shoots his own associate, Pepi, to facilitate his escape. This, of course, is the classical hoodlum method of dealing with fellow gangsters who wish to defect or have simply outlived their usefulness. The same scenario is found in *Blood On the Sun*, in which Tanaka's chief henchman, Oshima (John Halloran), murders Prince Tatsugi (Frank Puglia), because Tatsugi was going to defect to the American side.

THIEVERY

Besides murder, theft is portrayed as one of the principal occupations of the enemy. In *China Girl*, Williams (George Montgomery) complains to the Japanese commander that when he was arrested for questioning, his pocket was picked and his room ransacked for valuables. After a skirmish in *A Walk in the Sun* in which a German armored car is destroyed, only the bejeweled hand of a dead German protrudes from the window of the burning half-track. A GI remarks: "Nice looking ruby [on the dead man's ring]. I wonder where he stole it?"

In *Edge of Darkness*, the Nazis start their "winter confiscations," a German euphemism for stealing from the Norwegians everything that is not nailed down. While the Nazi officer carefully sees to the bookkeeping ("from Tronus, 800 tons of fish, 200 pairs of shoes . . .") Director Lewis Milestone cuts to a line of villagers' feet, so the audience can see that their own shoes are tattered, some wrapped in rags to keep warm.

Even the enemy's Axis partners are potential victims of these thieving Germans. In *Five Graves to Cairo*, an Italian general (Fortunio Bonanova) complains, "I'm getting very sick of these Germans pushing

Italian soldiers into the front lines without letting our generals even attend the staff meetings. They steal the food packages my family sends me. As we say in Milano, we are getting the end of the stick that stinks!"

More specific references to the enemy's lack of character are the substance of Satanism propaganda statement twelve: "The enemy is a liar and a sneak." Most of the "liar" references in this statement have to do with the enemy's propaganda. Shown to be of extremely low credibility, Axis media in *This Land Is Mine* are typical. German propaganda is pasted to the walls of a town in German-occupied France. These messages seem in conflict with the happenings audiences see in the streets. The new German-run newspaper in the town is called *The Voice of the People*, and even Albert (Charles Laughton), the mamby-pamby schoolmaster, labels it as "lies."

In *Mrs. Miniver*, a German propaganda broadcast is tuned in on the radio in the English village pub, but director William Wyler goes to great pains to show us that no one pays any attention. Wyler cuts to shots of men throwing darts, drinking, playing chess, anything but paying attention. Similarly, in *Destination Tokyo*, out of boredom the men are listening to a "Tokyo Rose" broadcast, apparently the only signal that plays popular music that they can receive. But then the propaganda announcer comes on and someone walks in and asks what they're listening to, Sparks (John Forsythe) replies, "Tokyo Rose, giving out with that nightly guff."

In a lull between attacks in *Back to Bataan*, guerilla fighter Andres Bonifacio (Anthony Quinn) is upset because on the Japanese side of the battle lines they have set up a loudspeaker, which nightly harangues his troops with lies about their allies, the Americans. Bonifacio is more upset about it because the announcer on the loudspeaker is his ex-fianceé. Although Colonel Madden (John Wayne) has forbidden any waste of ammunition, Madden himself, for the good of Bonifacio's morale, machine-guns the loudspeaker. All in the foxhole smile at one another.

In *God Is My Co-Pilot*, count of the kill ratio between the AVG (official name for the Flying Tigers) and the Japanese was "four hundred Jap planes downed, while Flying Tigers lost only eight." Alan Hale, who plays the missionary priest, and a friend and chaplain to the Tigers, adds, "And of the eight, the Japs claimed fifty-seven! They're the biggest liars in the world."

In *Lifeboat*, when the survivors begin to suspect that the Nazi has been deceiving them (not guiding the boat to Bermuda, as he claimed, but instead to a German submarine tender's rendezvous point), the Americans debate about confronting the Nazi. Kovac (John Hodiak) replies: "What for? We'll get nothing but lies. That's what he was brought up on!"

According to *Guadalcanal Diary*, the Japanese don't even tell their own soldiers the straight story. The Marines intercept a leaflet air-dropped to the Japanese who are holding out against the Americans. It says, "All his [the Americans'] transports have been sunk, and his choicest troops have been annihilated." The Marines laugh, and one of them jokes, "I guess we're dead and we don't know it, eh?"

Toward the end of *Bataan*, the fighting has degenerated into savage hand-to-hand combat. Amazingly, the outnumbered Americans are slaughtering the Japanese. In this allegorical scene within the fight sequence, we see America, initially deceived by the Japanese, learning from their mistake and finally winning the fight. Although a Navy bugler by training, Seaman Purckett (Robert Walker) has no trouble defeating a Japanese soldier in a bayonet duel and knocking the man to the ground. He poises his rifle with a mounted bayonet over his enemy to finish him off, but the soldier cries out and raises his hands, as if asking for quarter. Purckett lowers his rifle and his guard for a moment, and in that instant, the sneaky enemy soldier kicks his rifle away and trips him. Now the tables are turned, as the Japanese grabs Purckett's rifle and lunges with it, trying to impale the now-prone sailor. But Purckett deftly avoids the bayonet and overpowers the enemy. Having learned his lesson, this time he doesn't hesitate: he kills the Japanese.

SNEAKINESS

Enemy sneakiness and lack of honor was displayed in many ways. In *Guadalcanal Diary*, a Japanese man walks into the US camp with the story that his outfit is unarmed, starving, and ready to surrender. Believing this surrender offer is genuine, the Americans walk into an ambush.

In these films, the enemy sometimes chooses to "play dead" rather than fight. Typical of these situations, most often described in American films as acts of enemy sneakiness and/or cowardice, are the death of

Corporal Todd (Lloyd Nolan) in *Bataan*. He is killed by a Japanese soldier who plays dead, only to rise up and kill the American. In *Back to Bataan*, a Japanese soldier plays dead during an ambush. He gets up only after the American and Filipino guerrillas who staged the raid have fled into the jungle. Then, brave man that he is, the soldier captures a little boy who was working with the guerillas. He takes the child to his commanding officer, and, at the officer's order, beats the boy bloody in an attempt to extract information.

In a turn of events in *Guadalcanal Diary*, a Marine squad is overrun by the Japanese. A young Marine nicknamed Chicken (Richard Jaeckel) is shot and momentarily dazed. When he comes to his senses, he realizes that a Japanese soldier is standing over him, so he plays dead. Three enemy soldiers probe and prod the dead men with their feet and rifle barrels before passing by. Chicken waits, then gets up and machine-guns the enemy soldiers in the back. Screenwriters Richard Tregaskis and Lamar Trotti apparently were worried about this incidence of back-shooting, since in the Western genre this is considered a sneaky, cowardly act. So to remind audiences that it's the Japanese who are sneaky, they write a line for Chicken to shout to explain his deceit: "That's one you taught me, Tojo!"

THE DOUBLE STANDARD

Hollywood almost always found ways to justify the use of sneaky tactics when Americans do it, while condemning duplicity when the enemy does it. Chicken's trickery is typical, in which the young Marine claims justification for such deception because (as implied) the Japanese pulled it on his friends first, both in previous encounters on Guadalcanal and, of course, in the Japanese sneak attack on Pearl Harbor. This, then, is characterized as simply righteous vengeance. Moral fine lines, such as "two wrongs don't make a right" and similar moralistic statements have no place on the battlefield of the World War II combat film. At home, biased audiences would likely infer that the enemy used trickery in place of military ability and out of cowardice. On the other hand, American forces resorted to trickery as a valid military tactic (e.g., painting the American flag on the roof of the hospital building in *Gung Ho*), as a last resort, or to simply give the enemy a little of his own back.

Also in *Guadalcanal Diary*, Admiral Halsey's letter commending the Marines refers to the Japanese "a violent, treacherous enemy." Another example of this is found in *Gung Ho*, when two Marines spot three ragged Japanese, hands in the air, apparently willing to give up. Corporal Harberson, a minister before the war, won't allow Rube, a farm boy, to shoot them, and walks forward toward them to accept their surrender. But one of the Japanese bends forward, and we see that there is a machine gun strapped to his back. His coconspirators open fire, killing Harberson. Rube kills the Japanese.

In *China Girl*, the Japanese commandeer a church as their headquarters. Nevertheless, the Flying Tigers bomb them. This irks the Japanese commander, irritated that the AVG would bomb a sacred place, especially in light of the "extra precautions" they had taken to insure that they would not be attacked: "Can't they see the red cross we painted on the roof of this building?"

It was not only the Japanese called out for deception, but also the Germans, as in this scene from *Joan of Paris*. Gestapo prefect Funk (Laird Cregar) is interviewing downed Free French pilot Paul Lavalier (Paul Henreid). The discussion gets around to credibility:

Funk: How can we convince you Frenchmen of the Fuehrer's good intentions?

Paul: Frenchmen aren't stupid: they know the Fuehrer's intentions.

Funk: It is really so important that you should learn to trust us. After all, France and Germany are friends.

[Next we cut to a shot of Paul: feeling no need to dignify this statement with a retort, he simply reacts to Funk's suggestion with a sarcastic smirk.]

In *Sahara*, the captured Nazi (Kurt Kreuger), who sneakily pretends not to speak English, insists (in German, while someone translates) that while Sergeant Gunn (Humphrey Bogart) and his men have been out of communication with their units, Tobruk has fallen. One of the soldiers is incensed by this suggestion and reaches forward to sock the Nazi, yelling: "He's lying, just like his blasted Fuehrer!"

Perhaps the worst Nazi deception in *Sahara* is ignoring safe passage guaranteed by the white flag of truce. Early in the picture, Jimmy Doyle (Dan Duryea) tells Sergeant Gunn (Humphrey Bogart) to be careful, and to "remember that phony white flag at Berhagen," implying that when it suits them, Germans do not honor the conventions of war. Later, when Gunn and his men are defending a well in the desert from thirsty Germans, the enemy calls for a truce and a parlay in no-man's land (the area between the opponents' lines). Doyle again warns Sergeant Gunn about Germans and white flags. Two soldiers from Gunn's detachment chime in from out of frame: "You can never tell about these blighters" one shouts. The other yells, "Don't trust 'em, Joe!"

Nevertheless, Gunn agrees to the parlay. The arrogant German commander, an officer, is offended not only by Gunn being only a sergeant, but also irked when the American refuses to surrender. The German slowly begins to reach for his pistol. But when Gunn fingers his, the German realizes he can't get the upper hand and relaxes, arms at his sides. Later in the siege, "Frenchie," the Free Frenchman (Jean Leroux) in Gunn's group of mixed nationality allied soldiers, volunteers to meet with the Nazi commander. Again, instead of considering the German's terms for the Allies' surrender, "Frenchie" repeats Gunn's terms for a German surrender, "one pint of water, one gun, two pints of water, two guns," and so forth. Furious, the German turns on his heel and stomps speedily back to the lines. Before Frenchie can get back to the Allied lines, the Nazi orders his men to open fire, shooting Frenchie in the back. In retaliation, as the Allied soldiers open fire, Gunn mans a machine gun, raking bullets down the German trench, killing the treacherous officer.

THEIR DISDAIN FOR US

The thirteenth Satanism propaganda statement is "the enemy shows disdain for us as a people, and for our institutions." A typical example comes from *Black Dragons*, in which Nazi Dr. Melcher calls all democracies "archaic." Plus, his surgically altered spies seem willing to believe their own propaganda, assuming the investigations into their various acts of sabotage will die down, because Americans are "foolish and lax." Similarly, in *This Land Is Mine*, Nazi commandant Von Kellar (Walter

Slezak) maintains that "nothing can stop us from winning the world," and that America will fall because it contains many self-serving Quislings who will aid the Germans when they arrive, "just as they did in Europe:" Von Kellar's disdain of the United States and England is characterized in this line: "America is a charming cocktail of Irish and Jews. Very spectacular, but very childish. And England? A few old ladies wearing their grandfather's leather britches."

The Japanese also have high opinions of themselves, compared to their enemies. In *Bombardier*, the Japanese have just taken captured American airmen into an adjoining room and shot them. The men scream as they are killed. A ferret-faced little Japanese major turns to Buck and the Sarge, whom they have spared for the present, expecting them to reveal secret information rather than join their fellow airmen. With an air of superiority and grinning malevolently, he declares: "Japanese do not scream." Of course, in a film like this, a line like that begs an "oh, yeah?" answer. So later, when Buck and the Sarge kill their captors and Buck escapes in a flaming truck, he runs over some Japanese soldiers, each of whom screams louder and in higher-pitched voice than did the murdered Americans. This is followed by a medium close-up of Buck, who grins in satisfaction at having proven the Japanese officer a liar.

In *The Purple Heart*, after the Chinese governor gives false testimony against the American flyers and is killed by his son, the judge comments to the foreign press that the Chinese "are barbarians who will strike down their own flesh and blood, if the price is high enough." Later, two foreign correspondents discuss the Japanese hatred of all non-Japanese. One says, "To the Japanese, Portugal and Russia are neutral enemies, England and America are belligerent enemies, and Germany and her satellites are friendly enemies—they draw a very fine distinction."

Despite the fact that the Nazis consider residents of conquered countries "subjects of the Reich," they are not exempt from German disdain. In *Edge of Darkness*, the Nazi sergeant calls a Polish actress forced to accompany a German lieutenant to Norway as his mistress a "Polish sow." Of course, the woman calls the sergeant a "swine." Later in the picture, as previously mentioned, a German soldier who raped a Norwegian woman is killed by her father. The father, wishing no reprisals on his behalf, hands himself over to "justice." But the German commandant declares, "The life of one Norwegian is not worth the life of a German soldier. So ten more are to be executed. [This is] a reminder to slave populations that there must be complete submission to the master race."

In *Sahara*, a captured German pilot must be searched for weapons. But when Sergeant Gunn orders Sudanese Sergeant Tambul (Rex Ingram) to "frisk the Heinie," the Nazi (Kurt Kreuger) complains that he doesn't want to be "touched by an inferior race." This line also begs for an ironic encore. Later in the picture, it is Tambul who later ironically kills this ambassador of the master race with his bare hands. He does so somewhat symbolically by smothering the German's face into the sand.

OUR DISDAIN FOR THEM

The opposite side of this Satanism category statement, our disdain for the enemy, is one that appears frequently in these forty films. For example, the iconic symbol of the Third Reich is compared to someone's buttocks in *All Through the Night*. "Starchy" (Jackie Gleason), describing what he will do when he gets his hands on a Nazi, says that he will kick him "right in the swastika."

In *Lifeboat*, the survivors don't know how the Nazi can keep rowing the boat without tiring, since they are unaware that Willi (Walter Slezak) has concealed a flask of water and food pills. So when Mrs. Higgins (Heather Angel) asks Kovac (John Hodiak) how Willi does it, hour after hour, Kovac sarcastically quips, "The master race can do anything."

German financial institutions such as the Deutsche Bank, who were among the business organizations that supported Adolph Hitler's rise to power, are held in low esteem by Rick Blaine (Humphrey Bogart) in *Casablanca*. He will not allow one of the bank's officials to gamble in, or even enter his casino, and he tears up a check issued on that bank. Later, in reference to the two German couriers who were killed by Ugarte (Peter Lorre) to steal letters of transit, the self-described "tavern keeper" says: "They got lucky. Yesterday they were just two German clerks. Today they're the 'honored dead.'" Similarly, in the Pacific Theater, when Captain Cassidy (Cary Grant) sees bombers about to attack the Japanese in *Destination Tokyo*, he quips to his executive officer: "I hear Japs are happy to die for their emperor. A lot of 'em are going to be made very happy." As if producers Brian Foy of Fox and Jerry Wald of Warner Brothers were sharing screenwriters, in *Guadalcanal Diary*, one Marine says to another, "If the Japs are so happy to die for their emperor, I'm gonna make them very happy."

The fourteenth Satanism category propaganda statement is "Axis leaders are worthy of our scorn." Before, during, and after the war, the names of Hitler, Goebbels, Goering, Tojo, Hirohito, and Mussolini became a convenient shorthand to express American disdain for the Axis countries. In *Action in the North Atlantic*, American sailors rescued after being torpedoed by a German U-boat were asked by a radio newsman for comments. One sailor told the reporter that he had a message for Hitler personally: "My dear Adolph: [he then delivers the "Bronx Cheer," a noise made with the mouth that resembles the sound of flatulence]."

Further Fuehrer abuse included Hitler being called "Schickelgruber, the house painter" in *All Through the Night* and simply "Schickelgruber" in *Berlin Correspondent* and *Captains of the Clouds*. At the RAF aerodrome in *Mrs. Miniver*, we see a "Come to Germany" travel poster featuring a marble statue of a handsome German man, defaced with a Hitler moustache. Even the chimpanzee Cheetah in *Tarzan Triumphs* gets into the act: after the Germans have been defeated, Tarzan and company still possess the Germans' shortwave radio, which the animal has accidentally turned on. Since the transmitter was previously set at the frequency needed to contact superiors in Berlin, Cheetah accidentally reaches the German high command. A general is rushed to the radio room, expecting to communicate with Colonel Von Richter, in charge of the Palandria expedition. But when the German general listens to Cheetah's excitable ape noises, the general chides the radio operator: "Das ist not Colonel Von Reicher. Das ist der Fuehrer!"

[All in the radio room turn and "heil" the picture of Adolph on the wall, as we cut to a shot of Cheetah back in Africa, posturing like Hitler.]

There was less humor in the derisive comments about Japanese leadership, and no personal insults at all to Mussolini in these films. The Italian dictator is only briefly mentioned in *Sahara* and *A Walk in the Sun* as an inept fascist leader who misled the Italian people.

In contrast, hateful references to Tojo and Hirohito appear often in films featuring our Japanese enemies, and have been quoted in other statements prior to the present discussion. In *The Fighting Seabees* (1944), Wedge Donovan (John Wayne) refers to "Tojo and his bug-eyed monkeys"; a sailor named "Tin Can" (Dane Clark) tells a sailor named "Wolf" (John Garfield), headed for a secret mission on the Japanese mainland in *Destination Tokyo* to "give the emperor a boot for me, will ya?"; the emperor-god is simply called "little Hirohito" by David Jones (Alan Ladd) in *China*; and in *Blood On the Sun*, then Colonel Tojo (Robert Armstrong) is featured as bald, ugly, and wearing the stereotypical Japanese round, black glasses. In addition, Prince Tatsugi (Frank Puglia) refers to Tojo's imperialistic aims as "sordid."

ITALIANS NEVER TAKEN SERIOUSLY

"The Italians are buffoons, not worthy of serious consideration," is the fifteenth and last Satanism propaganda statement. Although Italy was an Axis nation in good standing for half the war, none of the films in this study suggest that Italy was ever seriously considered as an equal partner with Germany and Japan. Rather, the overall Italian stereotype was of the earthy, romantic incompetent who was bamboozled by Mussolini, betrayed by Hitler, and in way over his head.

In *Casablanca*, when Nazi Major Strasser (Conrad Veidt) arrives in the city, his plane is met by his host, Vichy French Major Renault (Claude Rains), an honor guard of German soldiers, and an Italian liaison officer, Lieutenant Casselle (George Dee). As was the custom in nearly all these films, the Italian officer is ignored. He steps in front of Strasser and Renault anyway, to attempt to force an introduction. Strasser just keeps walking and ignores the man, who doggedly falls into line behind Strasser and Renault, and begins arguing with Renault's second-in-command, a fast-talking individual. Later in the film, these two are seen again, still arguing, entering Rick's café: the Italian is still trying to get a chance to speak. Renault turns to Rick and says: "If he ever gets a word in edgewise, it will be a major Italian victory."

In *Five Graves to Cairo*, the Italian general (Fortunio Bonanova) is given the only room in the hotel with broken plumbing, and, like the officer in *Casablanca*, is barely tolerated, and, for the most part, ignored. At one point, Bramble (Franchot Tone) steals the Italian general's pistol. Later, when he discovers his weapon is missing, he complains. A sarcastic German says that the general must have lost it. But the Italian says: "I may have lost some battles, but I've never lost a gun." Later, to prove his incompetence and his preoccupation with the sensual, the Italian tries and fails to romance the maid. As well, at a dinner attended by Field Marshal Rommel (Erich von Stroheim), top German officers and high-ranking English prisoners of war, the Italian makes a fool out of himself by suggesting that war is the wrong way to settle disputes: "Why send ambassadors with ultimata [to other countries]? Send cooks, not ultimata. Send macaroni."

In *Sahara*, the men ask Sergeant Gunn (Humphrey Bogart) to share water and food with an Italian prisoner, and not to leave him in the desert. At first refusing, Gunn says that he won't take along "a load of spaghetti," but he later relents. Later in the film, the Italian, played by J. Carroll Naish, eloquently tells off the German prisoner: "Italians are not like Germans. Only the body wears the uniform, not the soul. Mussolini's not so clever like Hitler. He can dress his Italians only to look like thieves, cheats, murderers. He cannot, like Hitler, make them feel like that."

In *A Walk in the Sun*, some Italian villagers are actually portrayed as having been killing Germans all along. Also in that film, two American GIs discuss the Mediterranean, which in the days of the Roman empire was called in Latin, "*Mare Nostrum*," which means "our sea." One of them, John Ireland, remarks on the irony that today not even their country is theirs, much less the sea around them. The Italians are dismissed as a people who were "sold a bill of goods that they were going to boss the world. Now the ones who sold it to them are gone [referring to Mussolini] and they're left holding the bag, the poor suckers." Later, the company's interpreter simply views Italians as "the slap-happiest people I ever saw."

The Immortal Sergeant (1943) should be noted as the only World War II-era American film that shows Italians as an actively fighting, reasonably competent enemy: they are not prisoners, turncoats, comic characters, nor non-combatants. But not even in this film do the heirs of Caesar get respect: in one scene, two scruffy-looking Italians are on night picket (guard) duty. Not only do they fail to notice British soldiers sneaking up on their position, but they also make picking them off easy by striking a match for their cigarettes, illuminating each other for the attackers.

These are the ways Satanism is used to compare and distance the Allies, their people and culture from that of the enemy, and in doing so reduce any hesitation an audience member—especially one in uniform—might have to fight and to kill them.

4

WE WILL WIN!

The Illusion of Victory Appeal

The Illusion of Victory is a curious name for a war propaganda appeal, but essential in any war propaganda campaign is the constant reminder that the final outcome of the conflict will undoubtedly result in glorious triumph and the defeat of the enemy. A population will not support a war that they believe is sure to fail. The cooperation and commitment of all kinds and classes of people in a warring nation's population is vital to a war's success. Certainly, in the case of the greatest generation, across-the-board support for the war was given generously and mostly unselfishly. Undoubtedly, some of the credit for keeping Americans committed to the war effort was due to the Illusion of Victory statements made by US leaders, along with supporting messages created by America's media of mass communication.

The conclusion that victory can be illusory comes later, as the population of Nazi Germany found out. From the outset of hostilities, Josef Goebbels's propaganda machine, using its total control of all forms of German media, churned out optimistic, hyperbole-laden messages about the successes of the forces of the Third Reich and the glorious victory that was sure to come. Unfortunately for Germany, despite Allied invasions and bombings, these messages continued to assure Nazi victory long after it became obvious to everyone that defeat was inevitable.

Figure 4.1. Despite their size, the swift American Patrol Torpedo (PT) boats deftly avoided Japanese defenses and sank a number of enemy ships in *They Were Expendable* (1945). Here the PT boys plan their next bold attack.

In American feature films of World War II, Illusion of Victory statements—as they often are—were optimistic to the point of being silly, maintaining for various real, or sometimes baseless reasons, that victory for our side was the inevitable outcome. Although one certainly could incorporate logical arguments into this appeal category, more frequently incredible jumps of illogic were used to make assertions about America's inevitable victory. In this manner, citing some asset of the Allies and corresponding shortcoming of the Axis powers, Illusion of Victory statements pronounce or imply that this difference will tip the scales of the war in America's favor.

The first Illusion of Victory statement we will examine is, "Through the leadership of Franklin Delano Roosevelt (FDR), we will triumph." Considering the time period and the constant media demonization of Axis leaders, filmmakers did not need to be explicit about the significant differences between Allied leaders and those of the enemy. Instead, Hollywood chose to lionize FDR, and, in some films, Winston Churchill and American Chief of Staff General George C. Marshall, and didn't feel the need to engage in more detailed, point-by-point comparisons. In effect, FDR was the personification of good, even great, while Hitler, Tojo, Hirohito, and Mussolini were the symbols of the opposite. The assumption was made, in picture after picture, that FDR was our great leader and that his words were God's truth.

Many films of this era either begin or end with inspirational words from Roosevelt. These quotes take the form of title graphics, references to the president's policies or statements, and actual voice-over playbacks of FDR's speeches. When FDR's recordings are heard, Americans are portrayed as rapt, respectful, even reverent listeners. It is interesting that this reverence and awe extended beyond the war. A number of postwar 1940s and early 1950s war films included scenes of shocked and tearful Americans pausing in their operations to listen to radio reports reporting Roosevelt's death, which took place in 1945, a few months before V-J Day.

Sometimes, when Roosevelt quotes are not worked into the picture's narrative, they are inserted at the beginning or ending of the film. *Action in the North Atlantic*, about heroic deeds performed by the men of the Merchant Marine, is wrapped on both ends in FDR's words, beginning with a title roll, and ending with a voice-over. The title roll for this film says: "It is the will of the people that America shall deliver the goods. It can never be doubted that the goods will be delivered by this nation, which believes in the tradition of 'damn the torpedoes, full speed ahead.'"

During a conversation among a Merchant Marine crew early in this film, their need to go to war and their feelings of assurance that they will win the war are summed up in this line, spoken by the ship's carpenter: "I got faith—in God, President Roosevelt, and the Brooklyn Dodgers—in that order of their importance." At the end of the film, Lieutenant Rossi (Humphrey Bogart), Captain Steve Jarvis (Raymond Massey), and their long-suffering crew do indeed deliver the goods to our wartime ally, Russia, amazingly managing to destroy a German U-boat and two Luftwaffe dive-bombers in the process. The Illusion of Victory is reinforced by this concluding recording of an FDR speech: "Nothing on land, or on the sea, or in the air, or under the sea, shall prevent our complete and final victory."

As previously mentioned, in three films, *Air Force, God Is My Co-Pilot*, and *Flying Tigers*, the crew of the B-17 bomber "Mary Ann" and the AVG Flying Tigers listen by short wave to FDR's "Day of Infamy" speech, which ends with "through our armed forces and in the unbounded determination of our people, we will win the inevitable triumph, so help us God." This Illusion of Victory statement adds God as one of reasons the Allied side will win.

Similarly, in the conclusion of *Air Force*, the flyers are preparing for the first bombing mission over Japan. Audiences are given an FDR quote in the epilogue, a reminder that we are now on the offensive, and that we will not relent until the enemy has his back to the wall: "We shall carry the attack against the enemy. We shall hit him and hit him again, wherever and whenever we can reach him, for we intend to bring this battle to him, on his own home grounds."

This combination statement employs both the Illusion of Victory and Territorial appeals.

After we have witnessed two hours of Norwegian courage and heroism and the defeat of the Germans, *Edge of Darkness* concludes with a fitting voice-over by President Roosevelt, who calls the audience to follow the victorious path of these "steel-like" people: "If there is anyone who still wonders why this war is being fought, let him look to Norway; if there is anyone who has any delusions that this war could have been averted, let him look to Norway; and if there is anyone who doubts the democratic will to win, again I say, let him look to Norway."

AMERICAN (AND ALLIED) COCKINESS

The second Illusion of Victory category statement is, "We will win because we are confident in our eventual victory." As in sports, the competitor who does not have confidence in his or her ability to win rarely overcomes an opponent. Throughout the films of this period, there is an overriding optimism, almost an American arrogance, a constant reassurance that no matter how dim the immediate future looks, eventual victory will be ours.

In *Back to Bataan*, Colonel Madden (John Wayne) and his handful of guerilla fighters have been ordered to take an airfield defended by hundreds of Japanese. At first pessimistic about their chances, Madden hears about the heroism of a schoolteacher murdered by the Japanese in the village of Balintowak, and changes his mind. Madden says, "Just between us lunatics, I think we'll win."

In *The Purple Heart*, the news has arrived in Japan that Bataan has fallen, and that General MacArthur left his men (it is not mentioned that it was by presidential order) and escaped to Australia. Japanese General Mitsubi (Richard Loo) taunts Captain Ross (Dana Andrews):

Mitsubi: What do you think of your illustrious General MacArthur now? He escaped capture by running away.

Andrews: Don't be too disappointed, general. You'll see him again. [This obviously refers to MacArthur's famous quote, "I came through, and I shall return."]

This optimism also held true for our allies, especially the French. Things could not be bleaker in *This Land Is Mine*. The Germans have beaten the French on the battlefield and occupy their country. Louise (Maureen O'Hara), a schoolteacher, has been ordered to rip out pages offensive to the Nazis from her class' history books. As she instructs the children to tear out certain pages, she confidently warns the students to remove the pages neatly "because there will come a time to paste them back where they belong." In the denouement of this film, Albert (Charles Laughton), makes a brave speech in court, which characterizes not only the attitude of the undaunted French people but also of this film's director, Jean Renoir, working in Hollywood while in exile from his native France:

The aim of the occupation is to make [us] slaves. I saw ten men die [hostages shot because of Resistance sabotage in the town, led by Paul Martin] because they believed in freedom. Those ten men died because of Paul Martin, but they didn't blame him; they were proud of him. As long as we have saboteurs, the other free nations still on the battlefield will know that we are not defeated. [Although our sabotage and resultant Nazi reprisals] increase our misery, it will decrease our slavery—that's a hard choice. But they have to bring more troops into the town because of the trouble that has started, and the more German soldiers they have here, the less they have on the fighting fronts. Even an occupied town like this can be a fighting front, too. . . .

Similarly, in *Joan of Paris*, Joan (Michele Morgan) reminisces about the good old days "before France was conquered." But then Paul (Paul

Henreid) reminds her that France is not defeated, and that someday the sky will be filled with Allied planes, and Frenchmen and Englishmen will march in the streets of Paris. At the climax of the film, Joan sacrifices herself so that Paul and his air crewmen can escape Paris and the Gestapo, to once more fly bombing missions against the Nazis. Buoyed by Paul's escape, Joan boasts to the Gestapo commandant, displaying her confidence in what Paul has promised, "They have beaten you, Herr Funk, just as France will beat you!"

The same sentiment of stubborn resistance and faith in the war's final outcome is voiced by Ilsa Lund (Ingrid Bergman) in *Casablanca*. She and Rick (Bogart) were recalling their last day together, when the Germans marched into Paris. Rick recalls, "The Germans wore gray, you wore blue." Ilsa responds, "I've put that dress away. When the Germans march out, I'll wear it again." At the film's climax, Rick arranges for Ilsa and her husband, Victor (whose name means "he who conquers") Laszlo to escape Casablanca to continue leading his campaign of anti-Nazi resistance. Aware that in the past Rick has aided losing causes, such as the loyalists in Spain and the Ethiopians, Laszlo thanks him and says, "Welcome back to the fight. This time I know our side will win."

Whether or not the Allies are faced with terrible odds, Hollywood piles on the optimism. In *Sahara*, Sergeant Gunn (Humphrey Bogart) defends the sturdiness and durability of his Sherman tank, as well as predicting the outcome of the war from the vantage point of 1943: "When I go into Berlin, it'll be on that tank, with the name 'Lulubelle' written on her."

Many war propaganda films of this period, whether their stories ended in a victory or not, featured a voiceover or a scrolling graphic that reminded the audience of the ultimate victory and the peace that will follow. Typical is this scroll at the conclusion of Howard Hawks's *Air Force*: "This story has a conclusion but not an end, for its real end will be the victory that Americans on land, on the sea and in the air have fought, are fighting now, and will continue to fight until the peace is won. . . ."

In a speech that sounds part military and part football halftime pep talk, Randolph Scott as Colonel Carlson tells his *Gung Ho* Marines, "We'll fight, and endure, and win together!" The men cheer.

A TEAM SPORT

Similar to the Carlson quote, the third Illusion of Victory category statement is, "We will win because of teamwork." Allusions to the conduct of warfare as if it were a team sport abound in the majority of war films, regardless of when they were produced. And these references certainly abound in the propaganda films of World War II. All stress the necessity of subjecting one's individual needs and wants to military uniformity, cooperation, and teamwork. Many of these films, utilizing the screenwriter's standard "conversion" plot convention (a character begins the film with an incorrect attitude, but circumstances and experiences during the picture help him or her to change for the desired outcome) display a character, oftentimes representing the stubborn, individualistic American civilian, forced with having to learn (sometimes the hard way) that teamwork is essential to victory.

In *Captains of the Clouds*, veteran bush pilot Brian MacLean (James Cagney) is much too individualistic to subordinate his style of flying to the rules and regulations of the Royal Canadian Air Force. When this hardheadedness causes a near-fatal air crash, MacLean is cashiered out of the service. Only at the end of the picture does MacLean get a chance to redeem himself, using his spectacular flying skills to ram a Messerschmitt in mid-air with his plane, thereby saving the rest of his flight of bombers. This, like so many wartime scenarios, features dual appeals displaying sports teamwork (running interference—Illusion of Victory) and the ultimate sacrifice ("no greater love hath a man than to give up his life for a friend"—a Biblical appeal).

Similarly, in *A Guy Named Joe*, Pete Sandidge (Spencer Tracy) plays a skillful pilot who also refuses to follow the rules. In one breach of procedure, Sandidge causes his own death. But in this fantasy, he is allowed to return to earth as a flyer to mentor new, inexperienced pilots as a sort of "guardian angel." In performing this duty, Sandidge learns to subordinate his own wants and needs to the welfare of the pilot he is assigned to guide and protect.

In *Flying Tigers*, Woody Jason (John Carroll) plays another skillful pilot who refuses to play by the rules. Again, like Cagney's MacLean character, Jason's selfish, irresponsible actions cause damage to valuable aircraft and also the death of a fellow flyer. And as in *Captains of the Clouds*, Carroll atones for his errors by flying what amounts to a suicide mission.

In *Wake Island*, civilian Shad McClosky (Albert Dekker) dislikes all military officers, whom he calls "brass hats." Amazingly, he earns his living as a contractor for the War Department. McClosky, charged with a construction job on Wake, refuses to cooperate with Major Caton (Brian Donlevy), the island's Marine commandant. But after the attack on Pearl Harbor, McClosky changes his tune, becomes a team player, and, at the conclusion, ends up sharing a foxhole with Major Caton, blasting away at the Japanese with machine guns right up to the end.

During World War II, Tyrone Power portrayed more than one character who learns a lesson, does some growing up, and learns the importance of teamwork. Among these characters was Lieutenant Ward Stewart in *Crash Dive*. Stewart begins the film as a PT boat commander forced by the needs of the service into submarine duty. At first resentful over having to give up the PT boats, Power eventually is won over to the value of the submarine in the war in the Atlantic, and learns the value of "taking one for the team."

John Wayne, as "Wedge" Donovan in *The Fighting Seabees*, copies Cagney's and Carrol's sacrifice convention. At first Donovan is completely bullheaded about protecting his construction workers in hazardous, war-zone locations. He claims that these tough guys need no training, just some rifles. But, true to the plot formula in pictures such as these, when the Japanese attack a construction site, Donovan's well-meaning workers are slaughtered. He becomes a team player, helping to organize the first Seabee Battalion, a trained Navy construction group capable of both building and fighting.

Next, Donovan and his men are transported overseas to do a job. But once again, his temper and impatience get the best of him and he disobeys orders, taking his men on an expedition to eradicate some pesky snipers, leaving important facilities unguarded. Later, in what becomes the typical end-of-movie suicide mission, Donovan is killed puncturing an oil tank, pouring hot, flaming oil down on a battalion of Japanese.

NO INDIVIDUALISM

This to-the-death plot convention is not the only format Hollywood used to stress the importance of teamwork. In *They Were Expendable*, Wayne's character, Lieutenant J. G. Rusty Ryan, is out for personal gain and finds he has little chance for advancement in the PT boat service. Ryan figures that the quickest way to gain a reputation is to transfer to destroyer duty. His boss, "Brick" Brickley (Robert Montgomery), who is trying to prove the value of motor torpedo boats to "deaf-eared" US Navy brass, needs Rusty's skillful assistance. Brick observes Rusty writing a request for transfer and tells him that he doesn't appear to "want to play with the team," and is a "one-man band." But when they hear about the Japanese attack on Pearl Harbor, Rusty tears up the transfer letter and subsumes his ambitions under "the needs of the Navy" for the duration of the war. Later, Brick himself is faced with a similar situation. His PT boat force is not assigned combat missions, and instead runs only what he calls a "messenger service." Admiral Blackwell (Charles Trowbridge), commiserating, tells Brick that he understands, but the team comes first: "Listen, son. You and I are professionals. If somebody says 'bunt,' you lay down a bunt and let somebody else hit the home runs—our job is to lay down that sacrifice." Similarly, in *Air Force* and *Bombardier*, there are a dozen references to playing as part of the team, "knock 'em out of the box," "keep pitching," and lines like this from pilot "Irish" Quincannon (John Ridgely) to malcontent crewman Winocki (John Garfield): "You've played football, Winocki. You know how one man can foul up the works."

In *Bombardier*, when Major Chick Davis (Pat O'Brien) gives a Knute Rockne-style pep talk to his pilots before they take off on an important mission, they huddle, put their hands together in the middle, and he says:

Davis: You've all played football, haven't you?

Pilots: [in unison] Yes, sir!

Davis: Well, this is the kickoff!

MORAL INFERIORITY

"We will win because the enemy is morally inferior to us" is the fourth Illusion of Victory propaganda statement. Hollywood used this in three ways: as a suggestion that some of the enemy had sexually deviant tendencies; a simplistic rendition of the enemy as cowards; and a more thoughtful version of the previous concept—the enemy is morally bankrupt, therefore he does not possess the courage of his convictions necessary to forge on to victory.

SEXUAL DEVIATION: THE ENEMY'S WEAKNESS

In the 1940s, media references to homosexuality were never positive or even neutral. The underlying, unstated assumption in both the United States and in Hollywood in this era was that gay people were inferior soldiers. No reference is to be found of a homosexual American fighting man in any of these films, but there is plenty of suggestion that Hollywood characterized some Nazis as gay. For example, the Nazi Gestapo commandant in *Joan of Paris*, Herr Funk (Laird Cregar), is played as a dandy who peels his grapes and minces around his office, planning petty intrigues. At one point he interviews Paul (Paul Henreid), the dashingly handsome pilot whom the commandant and his men have pursued. Paul carries false identification, but this doesn't seem to fool the commandant. Nevertheless Funk does not immediately arrest Paul, justifying his decision to others by saying that he will have Paul followed so he can capture both the pilot and his crew. But it is reasonable to suggest that Funk may have had things other than duty on his mind. At one point the commandant admires Paul's hands, and when Paul exits the room, the Nazi changes a notation in Paul's dossier, indicating that his eyes were blue-green, not blue-grey.

Hollywood doesn't stop at suggestions of homosexuality. A burly Gestapo agent who is following one of Paul's crewmen gives every indication that he is a pedophile. The Nazi follows the crewman into a church, but becomes so fascinated with a little girl he finds there that he forgets to follow the crewman and the flyer escapes. Instead, the ghoulish Gestapo man plays with the little girl, and delights in allowing her to fondle his pistol.

At one time or another in Hitchcock's *Saboteur* (1942), nearly every antagonist character is suspect of either some form of sexual perversion or of being homosexual. There is a strong hint of an incestuous relationship between the boss villain and his daughter. Our hero meets Mr. Tobin (Otto Kruger), to all appearances a rich California rancher, but in reality he is the chief of an enemy sabotage ring. He introduces his daughter (Nancy Loring) and her baby to the hero, Barry Kane (Bob Cummings). The daughter's husband is never mentioned, and when Tobin does the introductions, he says to Kane, "And this is my daughter, Mrs. [he pauses, searching for a convincing lie] Brown." Then, while playing with the baby in the pool, Tobin makes a slip, asking the child to "come to daddy."

Later in the film, Kane falls in with saboteurs who assume that he is a member of their organization. Together, they travel by car across country. Saboteur No. 2, with the ironic name of "Freeman" (Alan Baxter), seems effeminate. In conversation, he reveals that he misses the long, golden curls he had when he was a child, and so he made sure his boy has them. The two thugs who are in the front seat of the car are listening to the radio, which is playing the swing music version of the main theme from the first movement of Tchaikovsky's Piano Concerto No. 1. The two thugs are singing the words written in the 1940s for this melody, renamed "Tonight We Love." As the men sing these words, they glance affectionately at each other. In the back seat, Kane appears disgusted by the two men's apparent plans for a romantic tryst tonight.

By suggestion in *Five Graves to Cairo*, even Field Marshal Rommel (Erich von Stroheim) appears to be cast as a closet homosexual. Although in real life, Rommel was not gay, this film portrays the famous field marshal as having an unnatural aversion to women: he is standoffish to Mouche (Anne Baxter), the sexy French maid, from the outset, and forbids his staff officers to have sexual liaisons with women. At one point, Mouche brings Rommel his coffee in the morning, and he strikes out at her with a riding crop, saying: "I don't like women in the morning—go away!"

YELLOW IN THE RISING SUN

Enemy cowardice is displayed in these pictures in many ways. Among them, in the climax of *Blood on the Sun*, newspaper editor Nick Condon (James Cagney) must escape his Japanese pursuers and seek asylum inside the gates of the American embassy in Tokyo. Condon has knowledge of secret information that if published in the United States will show that Japan has plans for world conquest. If Condon doesn't make it to the embassy and is caught by the Japanese, they will kill him. But all they manage to do is slightly wound him, and Condon makes it safely into the embassy. Secret Police Chief Yamada (Marvin Miller), tasked with preventing Condon from getting to the embassy, suddenly realizes in fear that he has created an international incident for which he will be honor-bound to pay with his life. Fearful of having to commit suicide, Yamada hopes to diffuse the entire event by mollifying Condon, reminding him that Christians in America have the saying "love your enemies." Condon hijacks the Bible with his reply, "Sure. Forgive your enemies—but first get even!"

In an air battle between the bomber squadron led by Chick Davis (Pat O'Brien) and intercepting Japanese Zeros over Nagoya in *Bombardier*, one Zero decides to "play chicken" with Davis's bomber, flying on a head-on collision course. The Japanese pilot expects Davis to veer off at the last instant. However, true to American movie heroics, the American holds his course, and we cut to the cockpit of the Japanese plane to see the surprised and panicked look on the Japanese flyer's face. He rolls over the stick and veers away. As if in punishment for his cowardice, his plane is destroyed when O'Brien's waist gunner gives the fighter a three-second burst as he goes by. This amazing marksmanship will be discussed later in this section.

Similarly, in an aerial encounter with the Japanese in *Flying Tigers*, the AVG boys dive out of the sun down at a flight of Zeros, machine guns blazing. As we cut to various Japanese pilots in their cockpits, we see that they are in a wide-eyed, cowardly panic.

The same sort of helpless panic is shown in the climax of *The Fighting Seabees*: Donovan (John Wayne) has just blown a hole in an oil tank, causing burning oil to flow down a hillside at a company of attacking Japanese infantry. Instead of attempting to circumvent the fire or at least retreating in order, the Japanese throw away their weapons and run away in utter disarray, screaming in panic. Similarly, in *Gung Ho*, a dozen Marines mount a bayonet charge against an equal number of Japanese. Instead of bravely standing and fighting, the enemy turns and runs.

ENEMY'S MORAL WEAKNESSES

Between the many German infantry assaults in *Sahara*, the defending Allied soldiers spend a great amount of time philosophizing about the enemy. Explaining how nine men could hold off five hundred Germans, Captain "Doc" Halliday (Richard Aherne) explains to Sergeant Joe Gunn (Humphrey Bogart), "Do you know why? Because we're stronger than they are—I don't mean in numbers, but in something else. Those men out there have never known the dignity of freedom."

Earlier in this picture, Director Zoltan Korda visually presents this moral low ground: two Germans have been captured, both severely dehydrated. Sergeant Gunn, desiring information about the location and strength of the Germans' unit, offers them water for information. The brute-browed sergeant arrogantly refuses, but the young private gives in, telling all he knows in exchange for water. Gunn decides to let both go free, sending them back to their unit with the news that there is water in the well they are defending. Gunn and his men plan to hold off the battalion as long as they can to prevent/delay the Germans from linking up with the troops fighting in the battle of El Alamein. What the Germans don't know is that the water hole has dried up. On the way back to their unit, the German sergeant murders the private (which only the audience sees). In the film's climax, after failing for two days to take the well, the entire German battalion throws away their guns in trade for the water, and (amazingly) surrenders to the two surviving Allied soldiers.

In *Tarzan Triumphs*, the German sergeant and two of his men chase Zandra, who, as previously noted, had escaped from German-occupied Palandria. Zandra crosses a river full of piranha by swinging over it on a handy vine. When the two German soldiers wade into the river to follow, they are attacked by the "cannibal fish." The horrified sergeant (Sig Ruman), only in the water up to the top of his boots, makes no attempt to rescue these men. He saves himself, standing safely on the shore, petrified, watching his men being eaten alive.

And in *This Land Is Mine*, Professor Sorel (Philip Merivale), headmaster of the school in a German-occupied French town, makes a statement that sums up the moral inferiority of the "master race":

> We seem weak because we have no guns, and our heroes are called criminals and shot against walls. They look strong with tanks and guns. Their criminals are called heroes. They teach vanity, self-love, everything that appeals to the unformed minds of children . . . but there is one weapon they can't take away from us, and that's our dignity.

On a lower plane of attack than Sorel's, the fifth Illusion of Victory category statement is "We will win because we are much more intelligent than the enemy." In many of these films, an American officer or noncommissioned officer tells his men that the enemy's chief weakness resides in his reaction to surprise maneuvers. In *Gung Ho*, Colonel Carlson (Randolph Scott) tells his men that the Japanese "have a weakness—it lies in their inability to adapt themselves to unusual situations."

A number of instances later in the film illustrate this point, including a sequence in which an all-important Japanese radio transmitter building had to be taken. Unsuccessful with a frontal attack, the Marines are pinned down. Two enterprising Marines circumvent Japanese defenders in a flanking maneuver and discover a huge steamroller, which they start up and use for mobile cover to assault the radio building. When the Japanese see what the Marines are doing, they panic and make wild gestures to each other rather than improvise and try to stop the steamroller. The makeshift "tank" rams the building, destroying the radio apparatus. In the confusion, the rest of the Marines mount a charge, killing the remaining Japanese forces.

In *Air Force*, the Japanese fleet in the Coral Sea is subjected to a surprise attack from Allied planes. When we cut to a shot on the bridge of the Japanese flagship, we are shown enemy admirals, wearing no helmets or "Mae Wests," apparently ready for a formal reception rather than a battle. The officers seem panicked, as if they can't cope with this surprise. They look and point in all directions, wide-eyed with fear and confusion.

THEY NEVER LEARN

In aviation movies, the Japanese are portrayed as unable to learn from the mistakes of the past. For some inscrutable reason, when shooting at American planes, the Japanese never seem to be able to learn to "lead" (shoot ahead into the oncoming path of) US planes. As a result, if the Japanese ever hit American planes, their bullet holes are generally found far behind the sensitive areas of the engine and pilot's compartment, back toward the tail of the aircraft. This inability to adjust for simple sideways motion was shown twice in *Flying Tigers*.

In both *China Girl* and *God Is My Co-Pilot*, the Japanese cannot seem to master the trick where the Flying Tigers attack them out of the sun. One would think that the significance of the sun in Japanese culture would give them a hint, but in these films, as General Chennault (Raymond Massey) says, the Tigers "just sit up there in the sun where [the Japanese] can't see us—until it's too late." Later, eighteen Japanese Zeros are on their way to bomb the Flying Tigers' airfield. Using a boxing metaphor, Chennault surmises that the enemy will attack the same way they always do. He explains it with a boxing metaphor: "The old one-two: lead with six from the east and cross with twelve from the west." Chennault dispatches his AVG fighter planes to counter this tactic. Sure enough, the Japanese attack exactly as expected and are wiped out. An officer quips, "They'll never learn."

Also, in *China Girl*, when an American pilot is told that three Japanese squadrons are attacking, he is surprised, since this is the enemy's first raid after dark. Sarcastically, he says, "Well, what do you know? They're learning to fly at night."

Presenting the careless, unprofessional acts of the enemy that cause their own deaths served two purposes in these films: it was good for Allied morale and an object lesson in military tactics for American troops. Among these was a really thoughtless German maneuver in *Crash Dive*: American commandos have just blown up a huge oil depot and are trying to escape back to their submarine. Down at the shoreline, the Americans' backs are to the ocean, and they are in a firefight with German soldiers. The flames from the burning oil tanks light up the sky behind the rocks that provide the Germans with cover. As long as the Germans continue firing from the safety of their elevated position and their cover, the Americans are pinned down and trapped.

Instead, the Germans rise up from these safe positions and stand erect, firing, backlit by the flames from their burning tanks, giving the Americans perfectly silhouetted and unobstructed targets. Of course, the Germans are mowed down, allowing the Americans to escape.

In *Objective Burma*, American paratroops dig in at the top of a hill and fend off night attacks as well as sneaky Japanese infiltrators. One Japanese infiltrator has been taught some English, but no subtlety. As the soldier crawls in the bushes near where a GI is dug in, he makes noise. The American calls out:

GI: Who goes there?

Japanese soldier: Where are ya, Joe? Where are ya, Joe? [The American throws a hand grenade in the general direction of the enemy's voice, and kills him.]

GI: [sarcastically] The name ain't Joe.

In the attack on the Makin Island radio station in *Gung Ho*, the enemy infantry's communications with their air cover have been cut off. When the Japanese flight commander arrives at the scene, he sums up the situation badly: he sees Japanese soldiers around the hospital but dives to attack them, because before the Americans left the hospital area, they painted a large American flag on the hospital roof. This commander doesn't take the time to think through his actions: Why would these American raiders take the time and effort to pinpoint their location for the Japanese from the air? And why were these American devils waving at the enemy planes? Why weren't they taking cover when the planes dove on them and bombed and strafed them? Instead, the flight commander and his men are depicted as mindless savages, so caught up on their bloodthirsty errand that just seeing the American flag below produced a blind, conditioned response that put them beyond the pale of reason.

On two occasions in *Back to Bataan*, Japanese sentries must have been selected for guard duty either because they were blind and deaf, or because they were just plain stupid. At the Philippine prison camp at Cabanatuan, an entire attack force gathers right below a guard tower and quietly discusses their attack. The guard above doesn't take any notice. Later in the picture, an even more oblivious guard is on sentry duty at a rice paddy. During the night, within a few feet of the guard, an attack force sneaks up. They hide their machine guns in the weeds surrounding the paddy and submerge themselves in the shallow water, breathing through hollow reeds. Amazingly, the Japanese guard does not notice any of this, and is killed by the guerrillas the next morning.

"HEIL, DUMMY!"

In a few films, enemy stupidity is even played for laughs. For example, in *All Through the Night*, best described as "Guys and Dolls meet the Nazis," "Gloves" Donahue (Humphrey Bogart) and "Sunshine" (William Demarest) use Brooklyn double-talk to con their way into a meeting of not-too-bright enemy agents. Later, when Donahue's friends arrive, a huge fistfight erupts between the Nazis and the "good guy" gangsters. Since neither side is wearing identifying uniforms, "Waiter" (Phil Silvers) separates friend from foe by yelling "Heil" to strangers. If an imbecile Nazi "Heils" back, (as all of them do, dropping their guard in the process), Waiter conks him with a two-by-four.

In *Berlin Correspondent*, a team of German censors stands over American journalist Roberts (Dana Andrews) who announces news in Germany over shortwave radio back to the United States. The censors can't figure out how the American manages to code information the Germans don't want released into these seemingly innocuous reports. Actually, the code is shown to be pretty simple. The next day, the newspaper syndicate for which Roberts works publishes stories embarrassing to the Germans. Not only that, but the Germans have no idea how Roberts obtains his information in the first place. Their most experienced detectives and spies, assigned to follow Roberts, are depicted as incompetent, not capable of even following Roberts without either losing him in revolving doors or being detected. On one occasion, Roberts has once again lost his detective "tail." Then he makes contact with the German Resistance agent who feeds him his information. To tease the poor German detective, Roberts returns to where he gave the detective the slip and helps the bumbling fool pick up the trail again. On another occasion, Roberts and a lady leave a restaurant and walk past what appears to be a beggar. Roberts recognizes the German detective in one more of his silly Inspector Clouseau-like disguises and greets him.

Nick Condon (James Cagney) also manages to fool his Japanese secret police "tail" in *Blood on the Sun*. As if he borrowed his routine from the script of *Berlin Correspondent*, Condon embarrasses the Japanese agent more than once, losing him, and then telling him where he and his lady are going "so you don't get in trouble." Later, Condon sneaks up on the agent from behind and asks, "Got a match, Mac?"

In *Tarzan Triumphs*, a Nazi assault team parachutes into the jungle. The plane that drops them is manned by an incompetent crew: due to their failure to double-check the last parachutist's static line, a lieutenant's chute hangs up on the airplane's tail. Only his reserve chute saves him. Then, when the flyers make a low, banking turn to look for the officer, they run into a huge flock of birds. The birds' impact startles the inept and panicked cockpit crew so badly that they crash.

The sixth Illusion of Victory category statement is "We will win because the enemy's soldiers are inferior to us in military strategies and tactics." This is a refinement of the prior statement, which claims that the enemy is very stupid indeed. The first tactical error that comes to mind is found in the previous paragraph. Although the German paratrooper force is of company strength, they bring along only one radio, which is lost when the lieutenant with the fouled chute is separated from the others. The lack of this one radio eventually causes the failure of the entire German expedition.

In films featuring the Japanese, a fatal flaw in their thinking appears to be the assumptions that they make. They seem to listen to their own propaganda about their impervious defenses and believe it. For example, in *Destination Tokyo*, the defiant American submarine *Copperfin* sneaks undetected into Tokyo Bay and rests on the bottom. The sub's crew is listening to the nightly broadcast from Japanese radio propaganda personality Tokyo Rose and enjoying the irony: "So impenetrable is the iron ring of defense of Japan that no ship dares to come within five hundred miles of her shores." Although the submerged *Copperfin* would have been a sitting duck for the many destroyers in Tokyo Bay, these ships pass over the sub time and time again without conducting sonar sweeps or any other such precautionary measures—at least that's the reality that Hollywood's screenwriters would have audiences believe.

In *The Purple Heart*, in a situation closer to actual events, Japan's intelligence personnel can't figure out how or from where Jimmy Doolittle's raiders were able to launch their attack on the Japanese mainland. First, because of a B-25's maximum range, they thought it unlikely that Doolittle's bombers were land-based. The Japanese refuse to consider the idea that an aircraft carrier, the *USS Hornet*, launched the planes, because firstly, the Japanese are absolutely convinced that a B-25 cannot be made to take off from the deck of a carrier. Because they were also fooled by Doolittle's tactics of attacking their targets from all four points of the compass, the Japanese were also sure that more than his actual sixteen bombers were involved in the attack. As many planes as they believe were involved in the attack would not fit on the deck of an aircraft carrier and still leave space for them to take off (which they were sure a B-25 couldn't do, anyway). Plus, as Tokyo Rose and other Japanese propagandists insisted, the Imperial Navy "regards this zone [where the *Hornet* launched the bombers] as impregnable."

President Roosevelt was so delighted by the Japanese's inability to think outside the box that he turned the well-kept secret of the Doolittle raid base into a joke. In a radio address to the nation about the Doolittle raid, FDR announced that the bombers attacked Japan from their base in "the [mythical] land of Shangri-La." In *Bombardier*, Buck's bomber group was supposedly flying a Doolittle-style mission. There is actually a shot showing a secretive land base from which they took off. When shot down over Nagoya (one of Doolittle's targets) and captured, Buck stalls for time by pretending to divulge the location he and the other ships came from. First, he points on a map of the Pacific to Midway Island, in real life the site of America's then-recent resounding naval victory over the Japanese. He says, "That's Midway—[grinning] I'm sure you've heard of that." Then he points to a blank spot on the ocean near Japan, and identifies this "base" to the Japanese commander as "the land of the wonderful Wizard of Oz."

THE PERILS OF IMPATIENCE

In the cat-and-mouse game between a Nazi sub stalking an American liberty ship in *Action in the North Atlantic*, the German captain is shown to make two critical tactical errors. First, although the liberty ship knows that the sub is following them, the sub captain does not attack her. He tells his first officer that he will just follow her to a place where she will rendezvous with her convoy, so the sub can sink more than one target. Of course, standing orders to vessels in a convoy in case of attack and separation are designed to foil such a plan. The ship has no planned rendezvous with the convoy, nor would they attempt a relinking if doing so meant leading an enemy sub back to other ships. The second error happens when American Captain Jarvis attempts to lose the sub in the night and fog by turning out all lights and sitting silently. The sub does the same for a short while, but its captain becomes impatient. If he had simply waited out the night, at first light he would have found the ship just a mile or so away. Instead, the captain decides to steam away, radioing his base to conduct an air search the next morning.

In *Crash Dive*, a Nazi Q-boat (a gunboat disguised as a friendly freighter) has ambushed an American sub, and is attacking the submerged vessel with depth charges. After taking quite a beating, the US sub "plays dead" by releasing a small oil slick and phony debris. Spotting this in the water, the elated Nazi captain says, *"Wunderbar,"* and assumes that the sub has been destroyed. The Q-boat comes to a stop and sits, dead in the water. With the enemy's guard down, the sub surfaces and easily torpedoes the stationary German ship.

AN OLD TRICK OR TWO

On *Wake Island*, Marine base commander Major Caton (Brian Donlevy) is a veteran of service in China. As the Japanese fleet approaches, it shells the island. But, using "an old Chinese trick," the Marines do not return fire. The Japanese, entirely too brazen, assume that their shelling has knocked out all the island's big guns. But rather than send out a landing party or a sortie of small ships to reconnoiter, they dispatch one plane to make a flyover. The Marines play dead and don't shoot at the plane. When the pilot reports back, the Japanese bring their troop ships and escort vessels up within range of the apparently dormant island guns, turn their ships broadside to the island, and begin to off-load their infantry. Of course, that's when the Marines open up, destroying many troop ships and other vessels.

In *Gung Ho*, the submarines that delivered the Marine raiders to Makin Island must pick them all up and escape before the Japanese fleet arrives. In the shots depicting the last few moments of loading the Marines on board the subs, director Ray Enright cuts away many times to a horizon filled with more and more Japanese vessels, as an enemy task force approaches. We know that this armada contains aircraft, since some of these planes have earlier made an air strike on the island. Nevertheless, during this critical time period, the Japanese do not launch aircraft to attack the subs, or even send out reconnaissance planes for an up-to-the-minute situation report on the Americans' escape. Also in *Gung Ho*, it was mentioned earlier that the Marines intentionally retreated back across the island for no apparent reason, drawing Japanese infantry into an ambush near the hospital in which their own planes bombed and strafed them. Yet it never occurred to the Japanese commander on the ground that this retreat might have some tactical significance, that giving up all this ground without reason might be a trap.

"HERE I AM: SHOOT ME!"

Back to Bataan features the same thoughtless tactics on the part of the Japanese found in *Objective Burma* and *Eagle Squadron*. In these films, there is a tendency for enemy soldiers, when alerted to a surprise attack on their home ground, to grab their rifles and run out a door, any door, right into American machine-gun fire. One-by-one, they file out to receive their bullets, as if no enemy tactician ever considered the possibility of looking outside first, firing from within the relative safety of their barracks walls, leaving by the back door or windows, throwing a few grenades out ahead of them, and so forth.

As well, in *Back to Bataan*, after the rescue of the Allied prisoners of war from the concentration camp at Cabanatuan, the Americans and Filipinos escape into the night through the jungle, followed a few minutes later by two platoons of Japanese troops. As if to notify everyone in the area that they were coming down the jungle path, they run, yelling and shouting "Banzai!" The only way they could have made the ambush the Filipinos arranged for them any more successful would have been to carry torches and march along the path in a straight line with a brass band playing.

In the climactic night attack by a company of Japanese against a half-dozen weary American paratroopers dug in on the top of a hill in *Objective Burma*, the enemy's officers chose only a one-sided frontal attack: the hill has four vulnerable sides, and the Americans are outnumbered almost ten to one, yet no flanking maneuvers of any kind were undertaken. Anticipating this ignorant and unimaginative Japanese tactic, the Americans had laid booby traps and land mines only in front of them and pointed their machine guns in just that direction.

In similar fashion in *Bataan*, the Japanese waste at least fifty men on a narrow frontal assault on the Americans' position. Although a simple flanking maneuver by a squad or even a few men appeared possible, the Japanese never attempted it. Instead, again and again they send banzai charges straight into the smoking machine guns of the Americans.

At the end of John Farrow's *China*, an entire Japanese battalion is wiped out because of their general's shortsightedness and his fondness for American cigarettes. First of all, his tactical error: he chooses a route of travel which takes his motorized, armored unit through a deep mountain gorge, the most perfect place for an ambush, or, even easier, as planned by Chinese guerilla fighters, a dynamite-instigated avalanche. However, someone was needed to stall the Japanese for a few minutes, so all the dynamite charges could be set. David Jones (Alan Ladd) volunteers. He approaches the lead vehicle, in which the Japanese commander was riding, and asks the general if he wants an American cigarette. While they stop and talk and smoke, the foolhardy general halts his entire column in this dangerous location. Finally finished with Ladd, the general decides to shoot him. By then the Chinese have had time to set and detonate their dynamite charges, and half of the mountain crashes down on the general and his troops.

In *Corvette K-225*, a Nazi U-boat commander misses the Canadian warship with a torpedo. Instead of firing a second "fish" from the relative safety of periscope depth, or retreating to torpedo another ship in the convoy, or even submerging to escape, the sub goes to "battle surface," and attempts to slug it out with the corvette with only the sub's single deck gun. The U-boat ends up in Davy Jones's locker.

THE ENEMY THAT COULDN'T SHOOT STRAIGHT

The seventh Illusion of Victory category statement is "We will win because the enemy is a poor marksman, compared to our boys, who are crack shots." Hollywood writers, borrowing a generic convention from the Western film, apparently wished to stress that although it is difficult to shoot straight, our boys do it considerably better than any Axis soldier. Therefore, the enemy is quite often pictured shooting at Americans and missing, followed by our soldiers shooting back at them and—of course—hitting the marks. Examples from naval, air, and ground engagements follow.

Aerial Incompetence

Reality check: It is a given that many of the real bombers of World War II were not the "flying fortresses" that their public relations-inspired nicknames indicated. Controversial statements have been made that if US bombers had been stripped of all the weight of men, machinery, and ammunition put on board to defend them from fighter/interceptors, that most American bombers could have simply climbed away from attackers to an altitude beyond enemy pursuit planes' ability to follow, and many, many fewer bombers would have been downed.

However, there are two problems with this thinking: first, the higher the altitude, the more difficult it is for a bomber to hit its target, so eventually a bomber would have to reduce altitude to make an accurate bomb run and take its chances with pursuit planes and anti-aircraft fire. Second, since sending basically "unarmed" planes aloft over enemy territory (beyond the range of American fighter escort planes) would make for unthinkable public relations, American bombers were weighted down with machine guns (plus crewmen to man them) forward, aft, top, waist, and belly. In addition, standard operating procedures for bombing missions whenever possible included fighter escorts. Seldom did the gunners on board these bombers actually shoot down the faster, more maneuverable enemy fighters. Most often, it was this US fighter cover that had its way with the enemy interceptors, allowing the bombers to make it through to the target. This was especially true later in the air war over Germany, when longer-range US fighter planes were able to protect bombers all the way to their objectives and back.

But then there was Hollywood's version of reality. In *Bombardier*, there is no fighter cover at all for Chick Davis's (Pat O'Brien's) squadron. Instead, they must have had the luckiest deadeye gunners in the Air Corps. In a pitched battle in the sky just east of Nagoya, Japan, which was their bombing target, a flight of Japanese fighters does battle with Davis's bombers, resulting in the destruction of all but two of the fighters, who unbelievably flee rather than fight it out. The number of those sitting-duck bombers destroyed? Zero.

Air Force is replete with poor enemy marksmanship and flying ability compared to American gunners. One member of the B-17 bomber *Mary Ann*'s crew asks a pilot who engaged in dogfights with the Japanese how good the enemy was: "They're pretty good when they've got the edge, ten or twelve to one, but every time you get one alone, he lights out like a scared sage hen."

Later in *Air Force*, a wounded Marine major tells of the heroism, marksmanship, and flying ability of his pilots at Wake Island: "Those four Grummans [Marine fighter planes] took on sixty Nips this afternoon. They shot down plenty of them, too." In fact, the audience is later informed that only two Grummans were shot down and one plane badly damaged in this skirmish. Later, doing some bombing of their own, the *Mary Ann* engages in aerial battle with Japanese fighter planes, and despite how difficult it is for a B-17 bomber in World War II to actually hit speedy Mitsubishi pursuit planes, her crew shoots down Zero after Zero. However, in a Hawksian tip of the cap to reality, the bomber at least sustains some damage and puts in at Clark Field in the Philippines for repairs. While they are there, seven Japanese planes bomb the field, but apparently can't hit anything of value, even as large a target as a B-17.

Later, when the *Mary Ann* is repaired and airborne, her crew stumbles onto the location of the Japanese fleet. What follows, although not identified as such, is likely the Battle of the Coral Sea. Incredible accuracy on the part of Allied fighter planes and bombers results in an enormous amount of enemy tonnage sunk, with nearly no Allied bombs missing their mark. The few Japanese fighter planes attacking the bombers are easily destroyed, including one fighter that, after being damaged, crashes onto a Japanese ship.

In *Wake Island*, a Japanese cruiser is about to arrive at a position fifteen miles away from the island, out of range of the American guns, from which it plans to shell the island into submission. But Lieutenant Cameron (McDonald Carey), in the Americans' one remaining Grumman fighter, loads up four bombs and dive-bombs the cruiser through a hail of typically inaccurate Japanese anti-aircraft fire, putting all his "eggs" down the smokestacks of the vessel, which explodes and sinks.

During the Luftwaffe air attack on the American liberty ship in *Action in the North Atlantic*, the enemy's dive bombers, facing a few paltry anti-aircraft guns on board the ship, drop six bombs and miss their target all six times. The seventh bomb comes the closest: a near miss. In response, brilliantly accurate American gunners shoot down both attacking planes.

Japanese air-to-ground accuracy was shown to be as poor as the Germans'. In *China*, a Japanese plane attempts to strafe a truck containing the film's protagonists, but misses it almost entirely. However, a sharpshooting Chinese guerilla fighter shoots down the Zero with a few short bursts from a Thompson machine gun. Later, one Chinese soldier says, "It is not unusual: twice before I have seen him [the Chinese marksman who shoots down the plane] do the same thing." Even America's allies are better shots than the Japanese.

American and Allied forces were no less successful in out-gunning the enemy on the ocean, as evidenced in *Action in the North Atlantic*. After a German wolf pack of subs attacks the convoy, the Allied destroyer escort attacks the subs, destroying three of them with depth charges in the filmic time of two minutes. In reality, it takes hours of work or extreme luck to get just one sub with depth charges: to sink three within minutes is to portray these destroyer crews as being the antisubmarine equivalent of Annie Oakley. Compare this to a much more realistic British non-propaganda postwar film, *The Cruel Sea*. In this picture, Captain Ericson (Jack Hawkins) and his crew spend the entire war and two convoy escort corvettes looking for subs to sink, and manage to get just one.

But during the war, these films portrayed the Allies as astoundingly eagle-eyed. In *Crash Dive*, Lieutenant Ward Stewart (Tyrone Power) and his PT boat need to drop only four depth charges to sink a German sub. Later in the picture, attesting to the Americans' superior aim, from only two thousand yards away, a German Q-boat's seven large deck guns can't manage to hit a sub that's dead in the water, facing the Q-boat broadsides, waiting for their men in a rubber boat to paddle safely back aboard. However, the American sub's single deck gun manages two hits on the Q-boat.

John Ford's *They Were Expendable* perhaps sets the all-time record for enemy inaccuracy. In this film, a few American PT boats can manage to get close enough to torpedo and sink an amazing amount of Japanese cruisers, destroyers, barges, and even a small aircraft carrier, but the Japanese, who see them coming and fire everything they've got, are shown to consistently miss. Ford photographs the PTs roaring to the attack with Japanese shells hitting the water all around them, but never once scoring even a partial hit. Only when one PT boat is sabotaged and floating dead in the water merely one hundred yards from land can the Japanese manage a direct hit. And at that, it took the enemy many rounds to zero in on the defenseless boat. Incidentally, besides sinking all that tonnage, the PT's crewmen also deftly shoot down a half-dozen attacking Japanese fighter planes. In some cases, these victories are shown to occur because Japanese flyers are inaccurate strafers and bombers, sometimes because the Japanese aircraft always attack from the same predictable compass direction, but always because the Americans are much better shots.

German naval anti-aircraft fire was no more accurate than their Japanese allies, even with a larger target, as demonstrated in *A Guy Named Joe*. Despite the hail of anti-aircraft fire from a German carrier and all of its escorts, a single bomber, piloted by Pete Sandidge (Spencer Tracy), makes a dive-bomb drop on the flattop, and they cannot stop him. His hits are so accurate that in only one pass, he damages the carrier so badly that it sinks. General Billy Mitchell would have been proud, but in reality, during World War II, Germany never managed to deploy an aircraft carrier.

In a scene in *Air Force*, Japanese infantry have landed and are fighting their way toward the airstrip and the *Mary Ann*, which is trying to quickly take off. The Japanese are firing furiously but hitting practically none of the US Marine defenders, who pick them off like ducks in a shooting gallery. Earlier, defending the *Mary Ann* while it's refueling, hefting 60-pound 50-caliber Browning machine guns by cradling them in their arms, two crewmen from the *Mary Ann* manage to shoot down three attacking Japanese fighters flying at over three hundred miles per hour.

The first battle in *Sahara* is between Sergeant Gunn's (Humphrey Bogart) tank and a German Messerschmitt fighter, which could fly faster than the Japanese Zero. The grinning German makes four strafing passes at the tank, but does it no harm; only a lucky ricochet hits one of Gunn's men. But with a single artillery shot from their tank's cannon, the Americans manage to shoot down the German plane.

In *The Fighting Seabees*, perhaps the most incredible shot of the war takes place. A mortar is a very difficult instrument to aim. Like most artillery, a mortar is generally zeroed in on the target by being fired at a high angle into the air, the landing area observed, errors in distance and/or direction noted, then fired again, the error noted, and finally operators might begin to zero in on something, provided their target doesn't move. But in this film, with only one try, a Seabee mortar man scores a direct hit on a Japanese tank, 150 yards away, moving right to left at 20 miles per hour. He did so by simply looking left, setting the mortar down on the ground, and firing a single shot.

In *Across the Pacific*, Rick Leland (Bogart) must stop a light bomber from taking off from a jungle airfield. If he doesn't, this plane will bomb the Panama Canal. Leland singlehandedly subdues a guard stationed at a heavy machine gun and uses the weapon to destroy the bomber as it is taking off. Meanwhile, none of the other Japanese guarding the airstrip who are wildly shooting at Leland manage to hit him. Irritated with these pesky Japanese firing at him, Leland turns his machine gun their way and—of course—easily kills all of them.

HOW MANY SHOTS DOES IT TAKE...

In *Sahara*, Sudanese Sergeant Major Tambul (Rex Ingram) ventures into "no man's land" between the German and the Allied lines. He must silence or kill an escaping Nazi prisoner before the man can tell his comrades that Sergeant Gunn (Bogart) and his men are bluffing—that they are defending a dry water well. Tambul succeeds in killing the Nazi, but on his way back to friendly lines, the Germans spot him and begin shooting at him. Eleven German shots ring out before the huge sergeant is hit the first time, but the big man gamely staggers on. Finally, it takes a German machine gun raking back and forth across Tambul's body to bring him down.

Similarly, in *Bataan*, one malaria-crazed American soldier runs amok and leaves the safety of his lines to charge the enemy. It takes eight or nine Japanese shooting at him to hit the man once, and then there are many more misses before they finish him off. Later, as previously mentioned in discussing deceit in hand-to-hand fighting, a Japanese soldier who played dead stands, aims his rifle at Seaman Purckett (Robert Walker) from a distance of only three feet, and, incredibly, misses.

As previously mentioned, in *Blood on the Sun*, Nick Condon (James Cagney) is ambushed by Japanese agents outside the American embassy in Tokyo. They must not fail to kill the American journalist or he will break a story revealing a secret Japanese plan for world domination. Japanese "sharpshooters" less than one hundred yards away with scoped rifles miss him three times. Finally, at point-blank range, a Japanese agent with a handgun is only able to wound Condon.

RESOURCEFULNESS

The eighth of our Illusion of Victory propaganda statements is "We will win because the Allies are resourceful and original thinkers, while the enemy blindly obeys and cannot think as individuals." During the war, American filmmakers often portrayed Axis soldiers as automatons, mindless robots, incapable of independent thinking. Americans, of course, are portrayed as the opposite: the very Yankee individuality and creativity that helped found the United States and set the country's independent philosophy makes them superior to the enemy and will aid America in defeating them, both strategically and tactically.

Often simple dialogue reminds American audiences of this supposed enemy disadvantage. In *Berlin Correspondent*, an English prisoner talks back to a burly Nazi concentration camp guard: "No! I'll never learn your way—blind obedience, without reason, without thought, without soul!"

Snide comments about the enemy's lack of critical thinking ability abound. During the silent stand-off between the liberty ship and the German sub in *Action in the North Atlantic*, two sailors discuss their Nazi submarine opponents. The first sailor says, "I wonder what them guys on the sub are thinkin' about?" Sailor no. 2 responds, "Aw, they're Nazis. They don't think."

Crossing the seas, in *Blood on the Sun*, Condon discusses with Iris (Sylvia Sidney) the place of women in Japanese society. She says: "They're not considered human beings—they're not even allowed to think—it's against the law."

In *Guadalcanal Diary*, again reinforcing Japanese mendacity (cued again and again in these films by their deception in the Pearl Harbor attack), two officers share what they have learned about the Japanese since they arrived on the island. The first says, "We know [the Japanese] are not supermen, just tricky." The second responds, "Aw, we out-shoot 'em and we usually out-guess 'em, because our men have learned to act as individuals."

This very resourcefulness is one of the main reasons shown for the survival of the Americans in hand-to-hand combat against overwhelming odds in *Bataan*. The Americans would pull imaginative tricks, such as throwing dust in the enemy's face (borrowed from B-Westerns), and even surprising the enemy by using some of his own tricks on him, such as judo. On one occasion, Corporal Todd (Lloyd Nolan) has just used a rifle-mounted bayonet to kill a Japanese soldier in hand-to-hand combat. Then he uses the bayonet to prop up the dead body to serve as a decoy, drawing enemy fire. Then Todd sees from which direction the enemy's potshots at the decoy are coming. Todd cleverly flanks their position and lobs a grenade on top of them. Other examples of American inventiveness have already been mentioned, such as Colonel Carlson painting an American flag on the roof of the Japanese hospital in *Gung Ho* to draw the enemy into an area that soon would be ground zero for a Japanese air strike.

"THOUSANDS WILL RISE UP TO TAKE OUR PLACE . . ."

"We will win because our system of government does not depend on any individual" is the ninth Illusion of Victory statement. This line of argument flies counter to the importance to the Germans of strongmen like Hitler or to the Japanese leaders like Emperor Hirohito and General Tojo. This message appears often in American war films of the period, most often in film plots about enemy occupation, such as *Manila Calling* (1942), *Hangmen Also Die!* (1943), and *The Moon Is Down*. Typifying the way this works is a speech by Victor Laszlo (Paul Henreid) to Nazi Major Strasser (Conrad Veidt) in *Casablanca*. It is the same as countless brave retorts made by Allied patriots in the face of the enemy who, because of the enemy's devotion to a single leader, cannot comprehend the strength of diversity found in a democracy. This flaw in Axis strategic thinking usually leads the enemy to think that the capture or execution of a leader or group of leaders will cause the end of a resistance or guerilla movement. Laszlo, referring to the possibility that the Nazis could identify and kill the leaders of anti-Nazi Resistance throughout Europe, disabuses Major Strasser of that idea: "What if you killed all these men? What if you murdered all of us? From every corner of Europe, hundreds, no, thousands would rise up to take their place. Even Nazis can't kill that fast."

In *Captains of the Clouds*, the protagonists listen to a Churchill speech, in which the British prime minister bravely suggests that even if England were to fall to the Germans, he expects that the rest of the British Empire will continue the fight:

> We shall not flag or fail: we shall go on to the end. We shall fight in France, we shall fight on the seas and the oceans. We shall fight with growing confidence and growing strength in the air. We shall defend our island, whatever the cost may be. We shall fight on the beaches, we shall fight on the landing grounds, we shall fight in the fields, and in the streets, we shall fight in the hills. We shall never surrender. And even if, which I do not for a moment believe, this island, or any part of it, were subjugated and starving, then our empire beyond the seas, armed and guarded by the British fleet, would carry on the struggle, until in God's good time, the new world, with all its power and might, steps forth to the rescue and the liberation of the old.

In *The Edge of Darkness*, the Nazis are sure that they can end the mood of insurrection in the captured town of Tronus if they begin selective executions. In reprisal for the killing of a German soldier who raped a Norwegian woman, ten citizens of the town are to be executed in the town square. These people were selected by the Nazis because they were suspected to be resistance leaders. As these ten are digging their own graves and the German firing squad is moved into position, the entire town, armed with guns supplied by the British, attacks in force. Even a pacifist minister sets aside his Bible and wields a machine gun against the enemy.

In *This Land is Mine*, we see the passing of the torch of resistance from one person to his replacement, and then to his replacement. Professor Sorel begins the fight as the secret editor of an underground anti-Nazi newsletter. His activities are discovered and he is later executed. But before Sorel is taken into custody, he charges Albert (Charles Laughton) to carry on the fight. Albert, a namby-pamby schoolteacher afraid of his own shadow, is enraged by the execution of Sorel, his mentor and father figure, and gathers up all his courage. In a courtroom scene, he delivers a stirring anti-Nazi, pro-resistance speech. Shortly thereafter, expecting the arrival of the enemy at any moment to arrest him, Albert reads to his pupils the French *Declaration of the Rights of Men*, which the Nazis have forbidden. Before he finishes, the Nazis burst in and take him away to be shot. But Albert has barely been removed from the room when Louise (Maureen O'Hara), another schoolteacher, takes up reading the French Declaration to his students at the point where Albert has left off.

And in the conclusion of *Corvette K-225*, the battered warship proudly limps into port along with the liberty ships it has safely escorted. Cricket (Fuzzy Knight) asks "Pop" (Barry Fitzgerald) if he thinks the K-225 will be refitted in time to escort these liberty ships back to Canada. Pop answers, "If it's not them, there'll be plenty of others."

AMERICA THE MELTING POT

The tenth Illusion of Victory category statement is "We will win because America is a melting pot containing the diversity of talents necessary to triumph." The American armed forces are shown to be organizations full of diverse people from very different kinds of backgrounds. An example is how the Polish former construction worker in *Gung Ho* comes up with the idea of using a steamroller as a tank, the Jewish intellectual air crewman in *The Purple Heart* can so elegantly spout international law at the Japanese, and why a backwoods hick in *Guadalcanal Diary* can bring Sergeant York-style turkey-shoot tactics to bear on hapless Japanese marines. As Jeanine Basinger points out in *The World War II Combat Film: Anatomy of a Genre*, all of this heterogeneity is suggested by the diverse composition of the standard World

War II cosmopolitan outfit. One of the standard exposition devices of the genre is for audiences to encounter a squad of men sitting around, waiting for the action to start, that includes (for example) a schoolteacher from New England, a Southern farm boy, a Brooklyn cab driver, a Mexican-American from California, and a fresh-faced kid from some small town in the Midwest (51–58).

There were a few exceptions. Hollywood went to great pains to include Americans from nearly all ethnicities, but with the exception of *Bataan* and *Crash Dive*, excluded African Americans. Two films demonstrate the more classic World War II combat film diversity.

The first is *Air Force,* featuring the Mary Ann's pilot, "Irish" Quincannon; Petersen, a Swede from Minnesota; Weinberg, a Brooklyn Jew who turns out to be a native-born German; Butch, the Marine "from Joisey"; Chester and Sergeant White, of plain Midwest white Anglo-Saxon Protestant (WASP) background; and Joe Winocki, a hard-headed Polish American.

The second example is *Gung Ho*, featuring a WASP commander, an Italian-American officer from the wrong side of the tracks who came up through the ranks; a Midwest Norwegian; a Filipino recruit; a man from Poland; another from Greece; another from that exotic country of Brooklyn; plus boys from America's deep South, the Ozarks, California, and so forth.

But perhaps, in marked contrast to the uniform, homogeneous image given of the enemy, the ultimate diversity is not seen in their last names, or in the countries in which their fathers were born, but in themselves, as reflected in this scene at the end of *Destination Tokyo*. Just home from a difficult and dangerous mission, the sub steams under the Golden Gate Bridge. The sailors we have grown to know and care for during the course of the movie are on deck, as one-by-one they tell each other what they intend to do when the sub docks and their liberty begins:

Sailor No. 1: I'm hopping the first train for the farm, and when I get there, I'm bustin' open a barrel of cider just for me.

Sailor No. 2: I'm gonna go to a platter shop and I'm gonna get drunk on Dinah Shore records.

Sailor No. 3: Every night for a week I've been dreaming about green vegetables—four heads of lettuce all in a row.

Sailor No. 4 [the "wolf"]: I'm dreamin' about somethin' else [dames!]

Sailor No. 5 [the submarine's cook]: There'll be somebody hangin' over a hot stove for me for a change.

Sailor No. 6: Me, I'm gonna take my girl out in a canoe, and I'm gonna propose to her—and have seven kids!

Sailor No. 7 [the sub's pharmacist's mate]: If you wait 'till I'm a doctor, I'll deliver 'em for ya for free.

AN INTERNATIONAL FLAVOR

The eleventh Illusion of Victory category statement is the logical extension of the tenth: "We will win through the united strength of our allies." An example comes from *Action in the North Atlantic*. Captain Jarvis (Raymond Massey) has just sailed his ship into Halifax Harbor, site of the forming of a Merchant Marine convoy to "deliver the goods" to our allies fighting in Europe. Looking at the different flags of this international effort, Massey says to First Mate Rossi (Humphrey Bogart): "We'll live to see the day when we'll sail right into Hamburg and Bremen with these ships."

In *Sahara*, Bogart, as Army Sergeant Joe Gunn, is teamed with an international allied cast. His small outfit consists of Americans, British, French, a South African, a Sudanese, an Australian, one Irish, and an Italian who, although a prisoner of war (POW), sides with the Allies against the Germans. *Captains of the Clouds* has the same diverse flavor, as Royal Canadian Air Force recruits come from, in addition to Canada, America, Australia, Argentina, England, and Ireland.

Warner Brothers' *Objective Burma* was banned in England because the irate and insulted British said that it gave the historically inaccurate impression that the Burma campaign as all-American. The film did stress one mostly American raid, but it also found time to give credit to the Chinese, British, Australians, and Nepalese who were primarily responsible for fighting the war in that sector of Asia.

As we have come to expect from Hollywood films, American involvement usually was portrayed as the deciding factor in the success of a combat operation. As previously mentioned in discussing war allegories, American intervention in the European conflict (*Saboteur*, etc.) usually tipped the scales of the war. In *Casablanca*, the allusion to American involvement tipping the scales in favor of victory is evident in the scene in Rick's café in which the Germans begin to sing their World War I patriotic song, "*Die Wacht am Rhein*." This causes most of the patrons, many of whom were patriotic French or French sympathizers, to be uncomfortable, but as usual, this international aggregation appears powerless to stop the Germans from doing what they want. Czech freedom fighter Victor Laszlo (Paul Henreid), however, is the catalyst: he strides over to Rick's orchestra and orders them to play "*La Marseillaise*." The bandleader hesitates until Rick, the owner and an American, nods his approval. Stimulated by the American, the band strikes up the French national anthem, and the now reinforced Allies lustily and, in some cases, tearfully sing it, drowning out the song of the frustrated Germans.

As previously mentioned, the German is ultimately defeated in *Lifeboat* only when the survivors, Americans and English, simply "have had enough," and combine together to kill him.

A number of films display America's allies as fierce and skillful fighters, a sure indicator of eventual victory. In *Berlin Correspondent*, a Nazi colonel sends the men who fail him to serve on the Russian front. He tells his mistress/assistant that he is so disgusted with them, he wishes he could have them shot. She reminds him that sending the men to fight against the Russians is tantamount to executing them. In *Back to Bataan*, a similar fate seems to await any Japanese patrol that ventures out looking for the extremely dangerous Filipino guerillas. One frustrated Japanese colonel complains that when he sends out a company, they see nothing; when he sends out a squad, no one returns.

These are the kind of tough, able allies America praised in its films. As well, pictures such as *Thirty Seconds Over Tokyo*, *The Purple Heart*, *Eagle Squadron*, *Mrs. Miniver*, *China Girl*, *Flying Tigers*, and many more stressed how the Chinese, British, and all of America's civilian allies were "our kind of people."

THE MILLION-PLANE FLYOVER

Another aspect of the Illusion of Victory that by war's end became a cliché is the twelfth statement: "We will win because of our superior numbers." Regardless of the fact that the United States began the war under-armed, under-manned, and under-supplied, and that the Axis combined could probably put more men into the field than the United States, it was not too long into 1942 before films began to conclude with the obligatory "million-plane flyover," columns of marching men, or some other indication of America's supposed overwhelming numerical superiority.

At the conclusion of *Eagle Squadron*, the sky is filled with Spitfires and bombers, accompanied by rousing, patriotic music, while the names of German cities to be bombed such as Hamburg and Bremen flash on the screen, each getting bigger and bigger until the final one, "BERLIN," fills the screen. *Flying Tigers* and *Bombardier* each ended with huge, multi-plane flyovers, courtesy of their studios' animation departments, accompanied by the "Battle Hymn of the Republic" and the *Bombardier's* theme song, respectively. The same flyover scenario is played out in *God Is My Co-Pilot*, *Across the Pacific*, and *Captains of the Clouds*.

Working the fly-by into the story is sometimes done in a more creative way than pasting it on the end of the movie. In *Eagle Squadron*, the end scene takes place a few days after the climactic raid in which Brewer's (Robert Stack) gallantry was conspicuous, and for which he is now being decorated during a parade on the flight line. In the middle of the ceremony, the "scramble" siren sounds, calling pilots to man their planes. The flyover is supposed to portray the many planes that took off in this scramble. In *God Is My Co-Pilot*, a similar call to action provides motivation for the big flyover. But perhaps *Mrs. Miniver* manages to work it into the story in a clever fashion. Village vicar Henry Wilcoxon has just delivered a stirring oration from the pulpit of his bombed-out church. As the music rises, so does the camera view tilt up, right through a strategically positioned bomb hole in the church's roof, to reveal a cloud-filled sky full of Spitfires flying off to meet the Hun in a "V for Victory" formation. Once again, a Satanism appeal (bombing a church and killing civilians) is used in concert with an Illusion of Victory appeal to make a doubly effective propaganda statement.

"We will win because the enemy underestimates our will" is the thirteenth Illusion of Victory propaganda statement. With the ability to look at the war from the vantage point of seventy years later, it is clear that both the Germans and the Japanese underestimated the impact of Allied resolve and the ferocity of America's collective counterattack. The Germans, buoyed by easy victories in Europe, were more concerned about the aid America was sending England than the Americans themselves. Japan expected that the United States, whom they deemed cowardly, lazy, and unwilling to sacrifice their comfortable lifestyles, would sue for peace right after Pearl Harbor. Of course, the Japanese did not anticipate their mistake in not notifying the United States and declaring war well in advance of their attack. As a result, Pearl Harbor was not, as Japan had planned, simply the first battle of the war: it was, instead, a "Day of Infamy," a sneak attack that demanded fierce American revenge. As is seen in the films of the period, the American and Allied fighting spirit was portrayed as being constantly underestimated by the enemy.

ALLIED TENACITY

Much longer-winded than Nathan Hale, Captain Ross (Dana Andrews) in *The Purple Heart* gives this oration before he and his men are led out of the courtroom to be executed:

> True we Americans never knew much about you Japanese—and now I realize [that] you know even less about us. You can kill us, all of us or part of us. [His voice rising, with clenched fists] But if you think that's going to put the fear of God into the US of A and stop them from sending other flyers to bomb you, you're wrong, dead wrong! They'll come by night and they'll come by day, thousands of them. [Nearly shouting] They'll blacken your skies and burn your cities to the ground and make you get down on your knees and beg for mercy! This is your war: you started it, and now you're going to get it, and it won't be finished until your dirty little empire is wiped off the face of the earth!

The arrogant Nazi attitude of superiority and of Norwegian timidity was the ruination of the commandant of the garrison at Tronus in *Edge of Darkness.* Discussing the townspeople with a Gestapo agent, the lieutenant says he is not worried that he has only 150 men to guard a town of 800. His arrogantly incorrect assessment of the Norwegians concludes that it doesn't matter if his 150 men are up against 800, 8,000, or 80,000: "We have guns, and they are afraid to die."

But in his hubris, the lieutenant erroneously assumes that this imbalance, armed vs. unarmed, would persist; that the townspeople would not secretly receive guns from England, and, even if armed, Norwegians would still not have the courage to fight. Both of these assumptions are mistaken. When the revolt begins, the amazed lieutenant is incapable of coping with the situation, continues to underestimate the vehemence of the attack, and even botches the defense of his own headquarters. Later, when all is lost, a few minutes before he commits suicide, he can only shout in desperation, "These rabble cannot win! They must not win!"

Nazi overconfidence in strength of arms is also reflected in comments by the German colonel in charge of the expeditionary force in *Tarzan Triumphs.* Observing a leopard fight a boar in the jungle, he comments to his men that the strong always win. Later, having temporarily captured Tarzan, the overconfident Nazi repeats this observation to the jungle man. But later, Tarzan escapes and leads an uprising of the people of Palandria, liberating them, wiping out the Nazi contingent.

In *Eagle Squadron*, Ajax, the arrogant flight commander of the Luftwaffe squadron which fought the American flyers over occupied France earlier in the day, overflies the British aerodrome, dropping a parachute containing a mascot cat that survived the crash of one of the three planes the Germans had shot down. The parachute also contains a message, which pilot Officer Leckie (Eddie Albert) reads to the men:

Leckie: Hello, Eagle Squadron. If you are daring for more fights, every day we will be here. However, remember, only cat has nine lives, and when *Amerikanas* fight Luftwaffe, that is not enough. [Note the pidgin English.] So we say for Coe and Bell and Meeker: they were, when we found them, altogether dead. Brave men, but foolish. Heil Hitler! Signed, Ajax.

Another Pilot: Well, can ya beat that?

Yet Another Pilot: Boy, will we knock their ears down tomorrow! [All
the other pilots loudly agree.]

As mentioned earlier, in pictures such as these, enemy boasts such
as this one just beg to be contradicted. This film is no exception. Later
in the film, Brewer (Robert Stack) is a part of a commando raid into
German-occupied France. There, he steals a Messerschmitt mounted
with a super-secret weapon and shoots down three pursuing German
planes on the way back to England. One of the German flyers Brewer
shoots down is the overconfident Ajax.

Typical of Axis hubris at the highest military levels are the quote by
Japanese Admiral Yamamoto in *Blood on the Sun* (Yamamoto promises
that he will be in the White House when Japan dictates its terms of
peace) and the comments of Field Marshal Rommel (Erich von Stroheim) in *Five Graves to Cairo*. Rommel promises, "We shall take that
big fat cigar out of Churchill's mouth and make him say 'heil!' five
times."

In *Cry Havoc*, surrounded by the Japanese Army, a scared and frustrated nurse tells the others that she doesn't know any more why they
continue to carry on the fight, since "we can't win." Pat (Ann Sothern)
surprises the others by emphatically responding that "we can't lose!"
Pat explains that she had learned that the Japanese battle plan in the
Pacific assumed that after Pearl Harbor they would speedily overrun
the Philippines. But the enemy hadn't counted on the stiff, unbending
American and Filipino resistance. "We just didn't like the idea of [the
Japanese] walking through us that easy . . . and we've kept 'em here
over two months and made 'em use over two hundred thousand men
right here on Bataan. . . . We'll hold 'em as long as we can, and the boys
in the other places'll hold 'em, too, till we push 'em right back where
they came from. They're coming [here], and we don't have a chance,
but we're winning the war, that's what we're doing. That's why this little
peninsula's so important. It's just winning the war, that's all."

In response to a speech in *China* in which a Japanese general makes
his country's imperialistic aims clear, Jones (Alan Ladd) responds:
"General, in all the countries that you and your gang have put the finger
on [note the gangster vocabulary in Jones's references], there are millions and millions of guys just like me pretty much living their lives in
the same pattern. And the pattern of our lives is freedom. And it's in

our blood, giving us the kind of courage that you and your gang never dreamed of. And in the end, it's that pattern of freedom that'll make guys like you wish you'd never been born!"

In *This Land Is Mine*, the German commander of the occupation force and the collaborator French mayor and are riding in a car through the streets of the town after confiscating the Resistance printing press and arresting the men who operate it. The mayor thinks that if "you break up the printing presses, you break up rebellion." To answer this poor underestimation of the will of the people, a Resistance fighter, hiding in a rooftop garret, lobs a hand grenade at the car.

THE SINKING FLAG

The fourteenth Illusion of Victory category statement is "All signs point to our winning." This is a general category to describe the icons of Illusion of Victory statements, a more graphic representation of the Allies' inevitable triumph.

Perhaps the most dramatic of these icons is the end shot of the Battle of the Coral Sea sequence in *Air Force*, in which massive damage was inflicted on the Japanese fleet, and many of their ships were sunk. Director Howard Hawks intercut documentary footage into this battle sequence, and the last documentary shot he used was the best: all that was visible of a sinking Japanese ship was its flag at the top of the mast. As the audience watches in great satisfaction, the symbol of the rising sun sinks into the sea.

Not to be outdone, in *Edge of Darkness*, director Lewis Milestone adds the Norwegian version of Hawks's emotional defeat symbol. The end of the film is the beginning of a new phase of the war for the Norwegians of Tronus. The entire town has given up their former lives, and the townspeople have become citizen-soldiers. They have won the first battle, but the rest of the war for them, a guerrilla war, has begun. Although a new German garrison has taken over the now-empty town, things are not as before. When the villagers left the town for the safety of the forest, they tore down the German flag. So when a soldier tries to fly a new German flag, the audience is shown a shot of it being pulled up the flagpole. Then we hear a gunshot and see the flag falling again. Then we cut to a shot of a Norwegian woman with a smoking rifle, as she and her comrades fade back into the forest. On this occasion as well as the Coral Sea example, the notes of the music score accompanying these visuals descend chromatically downward with blaring trumpets, amplifying the enemy flags falling.

In a lighter vein, in the brawl between Bogart's gangsters and the Nazis in *All Through the Night*, Barney (Frank McHugh) joins Waiter (Phil Silvers) in conking foolish Nazis on the head with two-by-fours. As they do so, Barney symbolically chalks a huge "V" for "victory" on their backs, and piles them in a corner.

In *Casablanca*, when Vichy prefect Major Renault (Claude Rains) sees what Rick (Humphrey Bogart) has sacrificed to allow Victor Laszlo to escape, he has a change of heart. Renault says that Rick is not only a sentimentalist, "but you've become a patriot." Renault, who has poured himself a drink of Vichy water, realizes the symbolism of what he has in his hand and disgustedly tosses the Vichy water into the trashcan. To add insult to injury, he kicks the can.

NON-SOLIDARITY

This last "we will win" icon leads us into the fifteenth and final Illusion of Victory category statement: "Many Axis citizens themselves do not believe in their own cause." In the middle of *Casablanca*, Major Strasser (Conrad Veidt), while interrogating Laszlo (Paul Henreid), says that he would be willing to let the Czech freedom fighter go free in return for revealing the names of the heads of the undergrounds in Paris, Oslo, and Athens. Laszlo interjects and adds "and Berlin." Major Renault (Claude Rains) is wavering in his loyalty long before the final scene of the movie. He reveals this for the first time when he tells Major Strasser that his loyalties are in the wind, and that the current wind just happens to be blowing from Vichy. Later, to remind Strasser that Germany does not have a winning record, Renault reminds Strasser that he was with the American Army when they "stumbled into Berlin" at the conclusion of World War I. Rick's (Humphrey Bogart) selfless act at the conclusion of the film revives Renault's ultimate sense of right and wrong, and it seems time for him to change sides. After kicking the trash can, he tells Rick that he will pay him the bet he lost (that Laszlo would not get out of Casablanca alive) by financing their passage to Brazzaville, where he and Rick could together join a Free French garrison.

And in *Berlin Correspondent*, Karen Hauen (Virginia Gilmore) is at first a Nazi sympathizer engaged to a Gestapo colonel, even though her father opposes the Nazis. But then she sees her father arrested, beaten, and sent to a "mental hospital" for extermination, and this picture of "justice in the new Germany" makes her change sides. At the end of the picture, Bill Roberts (Dana Andrews) and Karen hijack a German plane to make their escape to Switzerland and safety. However, the German pilot manages to disarm Andrews. Then he smiles, hands the gun back to the amazed American, and says

Pilot: You must have dropped this.

Andrews: You mean you want to get out of Germany?

Pilot: Confidentially, it will be a pleasure.

As with the other Illusion of Victory statements, what the audience experiences is a gutsy, emotional appeal, making the case that ultimately the weight of the enemy's own weaknesses and, conversely, Allied strengths, will insure Allied victory.

5

GOD IS ON OUR SIDE!

The Apocalyptic/Biblical Appeals

A mighty fortress is our God, a bulwark never failing. A helper, He, amid the flood of mortal ills prevailing.

For still our ancient foe doth seek to work us woe. His craft and power are great, and, armed with cruel hate, on earth is not his equal.

Did we in our own strength confide, our striving would be losing. Were not the right man on our side, the man of God's own choosing.

Dost ask who that may be? Christ Jesus, it is He. Lord Sabaoth His Name, from age to age the same, and He must win the battle.

And though this world with Devils filled, should threaten to undo us, we will not fear for God both willed His truth to triumph through us.

There are two reasons this chapter begins with the lyrics to this sixteenth-century hymn by Martin Luther, "A Mighty Fortress Is Our God." The first is that they embody the essence of Christian belief in the power of God to intercede for His people against the forces of the devil. This is important to understand as we analyze the propaganda statements in this category. Secondly, these verses were chosen because Director Lewis Milestone chose this hymn as a recurring theme in the musical score of the propaganda film about the revolt of a town full of Norwegians against Nazi occupation, *Edge of Darkness*. In this picture, the archetypal doctrine proclaimed by the lyrics of this classic hymn

Figure 5.1.   Emboldened by the belief that God is on their side, the people of a Norwegian fishing village take up arms in revolt against the Nazis in *Edge of Darkness* (1943).

becomes the underlying theme of the picture: these Norwegians, the people of God, will defeat the forces of the devil—the Nazis—through their own efforts, but empowered by the Almighty.

This major appeal category contains two very similar types of analogous relationships between the characters and events of the Bible and those occurring in the war. Apocalyptic and Biblical appeals are propaganda that create and illustrate a relationship between God and the propagandist's country that implies or overtly expresses heavenly approval and support.

APOCALYPTICISM

According to war rhetoric scholar Ronald Reid, in war propaganda, apocalypticism is the reinterpretation of modern-day occurrences into Biblical metaphor: two belligerent countries cease to be themselves and take on the identities of the forces of good and evil in the final conflict as foretold in the final book of the Bible (229).

Harold Lasswell's research on World War I propaganda described a media phenomenon he called Satanism, in which a sharp good vs. evil distinction is drawn between us and our enemy. We are virtuous and they are evil; America employs democracy as the ideal form of government while the enemy, as in World War II propaganda, is fascist and totalitarian; America is peace-loving and non-aggressive, while, in contrast, our enemies are bellicose and imperialistic (77). There are two differences between Lasswell's concept of Satanism and Reid's description of Apocalypticism in war propaganda. The first is that when Lasswell called these appeals Satanism, he was referencing what rhetorical critics have dubbed "God and devil terms." That is, making sharp rhetorical distinctions between "us" and "them."

Apocalypticism more specifically refers to happenings predicted in the Revelation of John and in the Book of Daniel in the Bible. Apocalypticism takes the elements of this predicted conflict between good and evil and casts the belligerents in stark contrast in this battle. Contrasts include light vs. darkness, false gods vs. the Lamb, the sheep vs. the goats, and the forces of God vs. the armies of the Antichrist.

Reid explains Apocalypticism this way: as found in the books of Revelations and Daniel, human history has been interpreted as

> a long struggle between the forces of God and Satan, Christ and the Antichrist. Early Christians (as well as some today) were living in the prophetic "dark days," but Christ will soon return. The Antichrist would be destroyed in an apocalyptic struggle, and Christ's early kingdom would last for a millennium, after which another struggle would take place, and the world would end. (232)

In war rhetoric, the speaker's government is portrayed as representing the people of God; the enemy is, by default or by explicit definition, the footman of the Antichrist. Lasswell's Satanism appeals just amplify the differences between us and them.

US propagandists maintained that since Americans are the agents of the Creator, God must be on our side. Therefore, Americans are the children of light and the eventual beneficiaries of the millennium. For example, in the Spanish-American War, hawkish war correspondent Richard Harding Davis quoted an American general as saying, "This is God Almighty's war: we are only his agents" (Friedel, 54). Logical deduction tells us whom the enemy represents in such a scenario.

In a radio address on May 27, 1941, President Roosevelt said:

> Today the whole world is divided between human slavery and human freedom—between pagan brutality and the Christian ideal. . . . We reassert our abiding faith in the vitality of our constitutional republic

as a perpetual home of freedom, of tolerance, and of devotion to the word of God. (192)

BIBLICAL APPEALS

Reid wrote that Biblical typologies are appeals that draw similarities between Biblical personalities and present-day people. However, in examining World War II propaganda films, I extend Reid's typology definition to similarities between contemporary situations or actions and stories found in the Bible.

To differentiate between Apocalypticism and Biblical typologies, Reid says that typologies involve the similarity between present-day events and Biblical accounts of what has already occurred, while Apocalypticism concerns itself with prophesies that have not yet come to pass. "However," Reid said, "both involved the same exegetical method, which presumed the historicity of Scriptures and interpreted them as foretelling the future" (232).

THE ANTICHRIST

First we will examine individual Apocalyptic appeals and then Biblical typology appeals. The first propaganda statement is "The enemy is the Antichrist." The Antichrist is the antagonist in the apocalyptic conflict in which the devil and his followers battle the combined forces of God. This results in the triumph of God over the Antichrist. Typical of this in these films is the characterization of the enemy as devil-like, or seemingly devil-possessed, certainly the agent of the Antichrist. In *Casablanca*, for example, Rick's rival saloon keeper, Ferrari (Sydney Greenstreet), tells Laszlo (Paul Henreid) that it would take a miracle to get him out of Casablanca, "and the Germans have outlawed miracles." Later, the young woman from Bulgaria (Anita Brandel) explains to Rick the reason that she and her husband have fled their native land: "Things are very bad there, Monsieur. The devil [read Nazis] has the people by the throat. We do not want our children to grow up in such a country." As well, Ugarte (Peter Lorre), who murdered German couriers carrying the letters of transit, labels these deceased Nazis as "poor devils."

Besides the overwhelming presence of Luther's hymn throughout *The Edge of Darkness*, the "conversion" of the town minister from pacifist to freedom fighter is an important moment, especially for many 1940s religious Americans still wrestling with the need to fight for their country. How do you square fighting and killing with the commandment, "Thou shalt not kill"? At a secret town meeting disguised as a church service, the townspeople have a chance to speak their minds about whether they should take up arms against the Germans. The minister stands firm behind the commandment and maintains that fighting the Nazis—or anyone—is sinful. But later in the film, as he observes the leaders of the community digging their own graves in the town square prior to their execution, he makes a decision: the minister realizes that although the work of the devil is afoot, he has remained neutral. Perhaps his character recalls another quote from scripture, in which Christ warns his disciples: "So, because you are lukewarm, and neither hot nor cold, I will spit you out of my mouth." This realization changes the minister from a man of peace to an avenging angel, and from his perch in the belfry, he machine-guns the German firing squad. This act begins the bloody battle in which many Tronus townspeople and the entire German garrison are killed.

In *Mrs. Miniver*, Mr. Ballard (Henry Travers) is speaking to Mrs. Miniver (Greer Garson) about the beauty of the Bible and predicts the eventual failure of the Antichrist. He says:

Ballard: And no one that's thrown [the Bible] over for a set of "Gobbles 'n Gorin'" [Nazi leaders Goebbels and Goring] is gonna win this war. That's my comfort, ma'am.

In *God is My Co-Pilot*, adding a theologian's belief that the Almighty and the Chinese and Americans fighting the Japanese in China are on the same side, the priest, "Big Mike" (Alan Hale), tells Flying Tiger Colonel Scott (Dennis Morgan) that they—clergyman and fighter pilot—both fight the forces of evil, each in his own way.

A more subtle reference to the enemy's connection with the devil required screenwriter Dudley Nichols to know a little German: in *This Land Is Mine*, Walter Slezak portrays Nazi Major Von Keller, whose last name, in German, translates "out of the underground," or hell. And if Von Kellar is the devil, his assistant, Lieutenant Schwartz, is his dark-side minion, since Schwartz in German means "black."

FALSE GODS

Part of the prophecy in Revelations predicts that there would be false gods and false prophets in the times to come. This is the second propaganda appeal in this section: "The enemy raises up false gods against the Lord."

The clearest reference to this is in *Bombardier* during the discussion between Chaplain Craig (John Miljan) and reluctant bomb-dropper Paul Harris (Russell Wade), whose pacifist mother has been sending him letters urging him not to kill.

Paul expresses the concern that his bombs will hit innocent civilians instead of his intended targets. Uplifting music plays underneath the chaplain's recitation:

> Paul, there's a little prayer for that. God, give me not the spirit of fear, but of power and of love for the oppressed, a sound mind and a clear eye. [His voice rises in intensity.] God, make me a good bombardier that I may destroy the poison in his cup, and quench the violence of fire, and overcome the false gods who make war with the Lamb. For He is the Lord of lords, and the King of kings, and they who are with Him are called and chosen, and faithful.

Harris, relieved of his guilt, converts to the padre's point of view, and later in the film, as he drops his bombs, he prays, "God, make me a good bombardier."

In *Sahara*, as discussed previously, the Italian and the Nazi POW argue. The Italian, Giuseppi (J. Carroll Naish), has been treated well by his Allied captors and considers them friends. The Italian makes the case to rabid Nazi Major Von Falkan (John Wengraf) that Hitler is the Antichrist; he tells the German that Mussolini can only dress his men to look like murderers:

> Giuseppi: He cannot, like Hitler, make them feel like that. He cannot, like Hitler, scrape from their conscience the knowledge [that] right is right and wrong is wrong, or dig holes in their heads to plant his own ten commandments: steal from the neighbor, cheat thy neighbor, kill thy neighbor!

> Von Falkan: You Italian swine! You dare to insult the Fuehrer?

Giuseppi: That would take an artist. I am but a simple mechanic. But are my eyes blind that I must fall to my knees to worship a maniac who has made of my country a concentration camp, who has made of my people slaves?

Infuriated, Von Falkan beats Giuseppi to death.

In *Back to Bataan*, to portray the Japanese as worshippers of a false god, director Edward Dmytryk adds a bit of business to two scenes. No matter where Japanese soldiers are in this film, in an office or in an official ceremony, if they utter the name of the emperor, they stop and turn to bow to the Northeast, the direction of Tokyo.

Director Frank Lloyd puts extra emphasis on this Japanese practice of emperor worship in *Blood on the Sun*. Condon (James Cagney) must hide the copy of Japan's secret plans in a place in his room where no one will think to look for it. Since the Japanese are not even allowed to gaze at the face of the emperor, Condon hides it behind a photo of Hirohito on the wall. When the goons of the Secret Police come to search his room, they, of course, will not look at the picture, much less search behind it. They only discontinue their search long enough to reverently bow to the image of their sun god. They even go so far as to put Condon's dressing screen in front of it, so the picture is veiled from their eyes as they resume their search of the rest of the room. So, besides showing us this pagan practice, Lloyd also makes the point that the worship of a false god can cause the Japanese to fail at their tasks, suggesting perhaps that these devotions might even lead them to fail in their prosecution of the war.

Certainly a Japanese infantry tactic comes to mind in this context. In films that include Japanese Army assaults on Allied positions, the enemy is not pictured as being terribly imaginative. Rather, as we have seen, they seem to favor what are called "banzai" charges, suicidal frontal assaults. To Japanese tacticians, this appeared to be an attractive alternative, since it does not take much skill or intelligence for thousands of eager-to-die soldiers to assault a stronghold in human waves. Since to die for the emperor means eternal salvation, the Japanese soldier was quite willing to submit to even as senseless a death as this. However, when this method of attack is not successful, either through poor military strategy or slavish devotion to a single course of action, the Japanese in these films do not experiment with other methods of assault more effective and less fatal to their soldiers. The *Kamikaze* ("divine wind") suicide pilots who dove their explosives-loaded aircraft into Allied ships were shown as equally eager to die for their emperor-god.

LIGHT VS. DARKNESS

Michael Osborn writes that light and darkness are archetypal symbols for survival vs. death, sight vs. blindness, and "the warmth and engendering power of the sun" (necessary for successful agriculture) vs. "the cold, suggesting stagnation and thoughts of the grave. . . . When light and dark images are used in a speech, they indicate and perpetuate the simplistic, two-valued, black-and-white attitudes which rhetoricians and their audiences seem so often to prefer" (117).

Appropriately, the third Apocalypticism category propaganda statement is "We are the forces of light, who do battle against the forces of darkness." This light vs. darkness polarity is clearly similar to the Satanism appeals. And as has been noted before, there is a synergy of effect that occurs often between two or more of these propaganda appeals that work together. In fact, this statement uses the opposing dynamics of Satanism to affect a more specific statement; in this case, a theological allusion.

The light vs. darkness analogy is found throughout Revelations and is used to identify the children of God (light) and the children of Satan (darkness). But this is nothing new to Hollywood, which, with the exception of Hopalong Cassidy and a few others, communicated to its audience which cowboy characters were either good or bad by how light or dark their hats were. This is another reason for noting earlier that *Berlin Correspondent* contained many icons from the "B" Western, including clumsy, obvious switches between the heroine's light and dark wardrobe colors. In this film, Karen Hauen (Virginia Gilmore) wears all white, up until the time that she agrees to spy on American reporter Bill Roberts (Dana Andrews) for her fiancé, a Gestapo colonel. He, of course, always wears black. So while spying, Karen wears black outfits. Once she discovers the error of her ways and changes back to the good side, she wears white for the remainder of the picture. The Gestapo colonel's mistress/assistant also wears black through most of the picture, until she helps the protagonists escape. Then she becomes a "child of light," and wears white.

In *China Girl*, a Kunming schoolteacher reads a poem to his pupils in defiance of the Japanese air raid going on outside. This poem, he says, is "for all who stand against evil and darkness." He goes on to say that there is a larger thing, a light that they cannot kill, "though they bomb many things that we love here in Kunming. It is the knowledge of good in your hearts." A moment later, a bomb hits the roof of the school, and it falls in on the teacher, killing him.

In *Mrs. Miniver*, although he mixes his shades of gray, and the screenwriter jumbles verses (in order: verses 2, 3, 5, 6, 4), the vicar's reading from Psalm 91 nonetheless speaks to an apocalyptic theme about light and darkness: "Surely [God] shall deliver thee from the snare of the fowler and from the noisome pestilence. Thou shalt not be afraid for the terror by night, nor the arrow that flyeth by day, nor for the pestilence that walketh in darkness. . . . He shall cover thee with His feathers, and under His wing shalt thou trust. His truth shall be thy shield and buckler."

Biblical typology appeals, like Apocalyptic ones, create analogous relationships between persons and events in the Bible and those that are happening in the present. The difference between the two lies in the applicable tense: Apocalyptic appeals deal with those personalities, concepts, and events that are foretold in Daniel and Revelations, and thus have not yet happened. Biblical appeals find analogues with those events, personalities, and concepts written in the Bible that have already occurred.

GOD IS ON OUR SIDE

The first Biblical typology propaganda statement is simply that "God is on our side." As displayed at the beginning of this section, the hymn "A Mighty Fortress Is Our God" proclaims that for the Norwegians of *Edge of Darkness*, the "Right Man" is on our side, and He must win the battle. As well, victory appears predestined, since "God hath willed His truth to triumph through us." Similarly, the Vicar's sermon in *Mrs. Miniver* ends with, "This is the people's war. Fight it with all that is in us! And may God defend the right!" As the priest finishes his sermon and a wide shot camera tilts up to the aforementioned hole in the roof to see a Spitfire fly-by, the hymn "Onward Christian Soldiers" begins, and swells to crescendo.

They Were Expendable ends in a similar fashion, with the "Battle Hymn of the Republic" sung by a choir while a paraphrased version of General Douglas MacArthur's "I Shall Return" ("We Shall Return") is superimposed over the sky at sunset. The conclusion of *Cry Havoc* ends similarly: as the nurse volunteers file out of their bunker, now prisoners of the Japanese, the "Battle Hymn" begins.

Luther's hymn also states, "The Spirit and the gifts are ours, through Him who with us sideth." In *Gung Ho*, in the midst of a skirmish in which the Marines seem to be losing, Luther's lyric is paraphrased. Private Harbison (Alan Curtis), a former minister, and his squad are pinned down by the Japanese. An officer tells him that they are in an awful spot, but Harbison optimistically assures him that "the Lord fights on the side of the right." Sure enough, a few minutes later, Marines stage a daring breakthrough, rescuing the squad.

In *Five Graves to Cairo*, there is an ironic Biblical typology. In a message sent to Hitler, Field Marshal Rommel (Erich von Stroheim) assures the Fuehrer that he will be able to push on to Egypt and take Cairo on schedule: "They say the Red Sea once opened by special arrangement with Moses. A similar mishap will not occur this time."

As we have seen often in the films of World War II, whenever an enemy makes such a boast, he will live to eat those words. So it was with Rommel, whose supply dumps are pinpointed by a British spy and destroyed by Allied forces. This ironic parting of Rommel from his supplies marks the beginning of the end for the Afrika Corps.

WITH DIVINE ASSISTANCE

In *Action in the North Atlantic*, Captain Jarvis (Raymond Massey), his lifeboat rammed and sliced in half by the German U-boat, vows to take revenge. Lieutenant Rossi (Bogart) reminds Jarvis that the Nazi submariners can no longer hear him. Massey resolutely responds that "God can." Later in the picture, on a new liberty ship pursued by yet another U-boat, Jarvis and Rossi decide strategy. The captain is confident in their heavenly ally: "Our first job is to shake off that sub. Our next job is to get this ship to Murmansk and deliver the goods. With God's help, that's what we'll do." Not only does the ship make it to Murmansk, but they manage to destroy another German sub along the way.

The second Biblical typology propaganda statement is "Americans put their faith and trust in God." Like Captain Jarvis's "with God's help" statement above, there are many occasions in the films of World War II in which the men display their faith in the Almighty. For example, in *Objective Burma*, paratroopers are informed that they are about to leave on a dangerous mission. As per normal procedure, it is announced that services for all faiths will be conducted before takeoff. These services are well attended. In the planes in route to the big jump, many men are seen praying, and one man fingers his rosary beads. Later, when the men hear that half of their unit has been wiped out in a Japanese ambush, a man drops down on one knee to pray for them.

Similarly, *Guadalcanal Diary* begins on board a troop ship on a Sunday morning, where all the enlisted men are participating in a good old Protestant service led by a Catholic chaplain. To emphasize how far American ecumenism extended in wartime, by far the best-singing Marine in this makeshift congregation appears to be Sammy. When another Marine compliments Sammy on his nice singing voice, he says, "I should be good. My father is a cantor in the synagogue."

And in *Lifeboat*, the survivors kill the Nazi Willi (Walter Slezak) who, because he hoarded water and food, was the only one with enough energy to row the boat. Rittenhouse (Henry Hull) remarks that they've "killed our motor." Joe (Canada Lee), looking up to heaven, disagrees: "No. We still got a motor."

A number of famous people, including war correspondent Ernie Pyle, are quoted as saying that there are no atheists in foxholes. The main subplot in *God Is My Co-Pilot* and one of the many sub-plots of *Destination Tokyo* concern men coming to grips with faith in God. In *Co-Pilot*, Colonel Scott (Dennis Morgan) had always been a self-reliant man, never counting on anyone else, not even God. His friend the missionary priest (Alan Hale) insists that God aids all the Flying Tigers when they go up to fight the enemy, but Scott still won't believe. Finally, Scott is grounded for medical reasons and can't lead an important mission, described by General Chennault (Raymond Massey) as "a milestone on the road to Tokyo and to final victory."

Heartbroken, Scott decides to try praying for a miracle. The miracle happens and General Chennault relents on his grounding order, allowing Scott to fly one last mission. As the film ends and Scott flies up to meet his squadron, we hear the final words of a poem the priest recited to Scott earlier in the picture: "and they believed."

In *Destination Tokyo*, "Pills" (William Prince), the submarine *Copperfin's* pharmacist's mate, is at best an agnostic bordering on atheism. He tells fellow crewmen, "I only believe what I see." But later, like Colonel Scott, Pills has a revelation. Their sub is hiding on the bottom of Tokyo Bay, and young crewman Tommy Adams (Robert Hutton) develops appendicitis. Pills, with only a little pre-med college training, must operate on Tommy or he will die. Faced with something beyond his control, the medic is terrified. As his young patient on the operating table goes under the anesthetic, Tommy recites the "Lord's Prayer," but becomes unconscious before he can finish. In a moment of faith, Pills appends a heartfelt "Amen" to the young man's prayer. Of course, Pills successfully performs the operation. Later in the picture, as the *Copperfin* is under depth charge attack, the crew is very edgy. One frightened crewman, thinking out loud, asks Pills if he thinks prayers do any good. Pills answers, "I know they do."

In *Gung Ho*, Private Harbison is shot and Rube (Rod Cameron) shoots the Japanese soldiers who ambushed him. The ex-minister utters these last words: "Thy will be done on earth as it is in . . ." and he dies before he can say "Heaven."

"AND THE SEA WILL GIVE UP HER DEAD . . ."

The third Biblical typology statement is most often found in the burial scenes that are written into many World War II combat films. The propaganda statement is "Christian soldiers will go to heaven." In *Destination Tokyo* and *Action in the North Atlantic*, there are burial scenes at sea in which the officer in charge reads comforting words for the crew and all who view these films. In *Destination Tokyo*, consigning crewman Mike's body to the depths, Captain Cassidy (Cary Grant) prays that God "grant him eternal rest, through Jesus Christ, our Lord." Similarly, in *Action in the North Atlantic*, before the liberty ship's dead are buried at sea, Lieutenant Rossi reads from John 11:25: "I am the resurrection and the life; he who believes in me will have life everlasting." And from the service for burial at sea, he reads: "And the sea will give up her dead, in the sure and certain hope of the resurrection."

In the at-sea service for their deceased helmsman, the crew of Corvette K-225 stand at attention as an officer reads these words: "We, therefore, commit his body to the deep, looking for the general resurrection in the last day, and the life of the world to come, through our Lord Jesus Christ, at whose second coming in glory the sea shall give up her dead, and the corruptible bodies of those who sleep in Him shall be changed, and made like unto His glorious body, according to the mighty workings whereby he is able to subdue all things into Himself, I now commend thee to the deep. Amen."

During the brief burial service for their fallen captain, *Bataan's* Private Epps (Kenneth Spencer) offers one of the beatitudes from the Gospel of Matthew: "Blessed are the pure at heart, for they shall see God" (5:8).

This promise of salvation includes noncombatant victims, as well, as we see in *China*. Carolyn Grant (Loretta Young) comforts a dying young girl who has been raped and brutalized. She reads from Psalm 23: "The Lord is my shepherd, I shall not want. He maketh me to lie down in green pastures; He leadeth me beside the still waters; He restoreth my soul. He leadeth me in paths of righteousness for His name's sake. Even though I walk through the valley of the shadow of death, I fear no evil; for thou art with me; thy rod and thy staff, they comfort me . . . my cup overfloweth . . . and I will dwell in the house of the Lord forever."

These comforting words are used again by Joe in *Lifeboat*, as they consign the lifeless body of a drowned baby to the deep. It is a shame that in two of the three war films studied that feature African-American men, Caucasian producers and directors saw fit to add to the servile racial stereotype of the 1940s the implication that only black people have the ability or inclination to quote the Bible and have an overriding faith in its contents. However, in terms of propaganda, these instances serve to introduce opportunities for the inclusion of Biblical appeals.

Occasionally, filmmakers combined a slur on the enemy's religion, or lack of it, with Americans' statements of faith. In *Guadalcanal Diary*, US Marines intercept a Japanese dispatch from a commander to his men. A Marine reads it out loud. In part, it says that "we are convinced of help [for you] from the imperial heaven. . . ." This makes the Marines laugh out loud, and a Southern boy drawls: "only God's children go to heaven."

Again in *Lifeboat*, this exclusive notion about salvation is allegorized in the interest of reinterpreting the Bible for the war effort. Early on, Rittenhouse (Henry Hull) argues that the Nazi, Willi (Walter Slezak), should be allowed on board the boat. Kovic (John Hodiak) argues that the German will always be a "rattlesnake," and saving him will cause the other survivors harm. But Rittenhouse argues, "On the other hand, if we treat him with kindness and consideration, we might be able to convert him to our way of thinking. It's the Christian way."

But, as we have already observed, the Nazi works his malevolence against them, seeing the survivors' forgiving attitude toward him as weakness and an opportunity. Eventually, they have to kill him. The audience's conclusion? Nazis are unredeemable, and one cannot respond to them in a Christian manner. So the propaganda message for the American public is that the only thing left for Nazis is extermination.

As well, in *The Purple Heart*, after Captain Ross's bomber crash-lands in China, the flyers learn that the Doolittle raid was a success. Speaking to two Chinese who help them escape, Ross (Dana Andrews) says that the raid "should put the fear of God into them." But one Chinese man says: "Japanese do not fear God, only bombs."

HEAVEN OR HELL

The fourth Biblical typology propaganda statement is a logical application of Christian doctrine. If one fears and obeys God, one goes to heaven. But if one disobeys God's law, and this seems applicable to the Axis powers, "the enemy will go to Hell." Howard Hawks's *Air Force* pictures a visual metaphor regarding the enemy's likely eternal resting place. But before the punishment, the crimes: when the crew of the *Mary Ann* observes the destruction of Pearl Harbor, crewman and aerial gunner Winocki (John Garfield) simply curses, "Damn them, damn them."

Later, we witness this damnation in action, figuratively speaking at least. A Japanese fighter pilot machine-guns young crewman Chester

(Ray Montgomery) while he helplessly descends to earth, clinging to the shrouds of his parachute. Winocki and Crew Chief Robbie White (Harry Carey, Sr.), toting 50 caliber machineguns from the Mary Ann, shoot down the dastardly Japanese, who crashes in flames into a grove of trees. Hawks clearly shows us in silhouette the lifeless body of the Japanese pilot in the Hell of his flaming cockpit. Then Hawks cuts to Winocki, as he pats the side of his machinegun and looks on with revengeful satisfaction. Finally, at the end of the picture, (supposedly much later in the war) the men are preparing a bombing raid on Japan. Their commander reinforces their goal to usher Japanese into the netherworld by simply saying, "Good luck to you, and give 'em Hell!"

The theme song in *They Were Expendable* also alludes to sending the enemy to perdition: "We're the men who are sending them down below, sentries of the Navy." However, this must be viewed as a double meaning: "down below" referring to either the depths of the sea, or, perhaps, in a less literal sense, the depths of Hell.

There are no shades of gray in the tirade of the Italian against the Fuehrer in *Sahara*. However, the conclusion of Giuseppi's (J. Carroll Naish's) oration is fitting for the topic at hand: "Must I kiss the hand that beats me, lick the boot that kicks me? No! I'd rather spend my whole life in this dirty hole than escape to fight for things I do not believe against people I do not hate—and for your Hitler, it was for people like him that God . . . my God . . . created Hell!"

JUDASES AND QUISLINGS

The fifth Biblical typology statement harkens to the betrayal of Christ: "Only a Judas betrays his country." Films that expound on this statement portray characters who betray their country as opportunists who become collaborators and quislings for personal gain.

Finding parallels between the fallen apostle who betrays Christ for thirty pieces of silver, both *Saboteur* and *Bombardier* display American-born Nazi spies who attempt to disrupt American defense work and steal top secret equipment for money. In the former film, Kane (Robert Cummings) confronts master saboteur Tobin (Otto Kruger) with the evil of his crimes, and the audience receives a full measure of the spy's arrogance.

Kane: A man who kills other Americans for money, a man like you, can't last in a country like this.

Tobin: [sarcastically] A pretty speech: youthful, passionate, idealistic.

In *Bombardier*, when an enemy fifth columnist meets Cadet Connors (Robert Ryan) to attempt to get his hands on the top-secret Norden bombsight, he says: "I'm glad you decided not to be a chump, Joe. If you're half as smart as I think you are, you're going to be one of the richest boys in the country." Then Connors gives the signal, and Major Chick Davis (Pat O'Brien) and the Military Police move in on the spy and arrest him.

The man who betrayed the airmen of *The Purple Heart* was the Japanese occupation governor of a Chinese province and a collaborator (H. T. Tsiang). He also follows the Judas pattern of this propaganda statement, betraying the flyers to ingratiate himself with his Japanese overlords. He also makes false testimony in court against them. But ironic justice catches up with this man, as his own Americanized son (Benson Fong) kills him.

In *The Edge of Darkness* and *This Land is Mine*, a cannery owner, a French mayor, and a railroad superintendent all collaborate with the Nazis for money and stature. Two of the three end up paying with their lives, and the fate of the third is uncertain. In *The Edge of Darkness*, another collaborator is a weak individual who tells the Germans where he thinks the Norwegians buried the guns they received from the British. Fortunately, his sister informs resistance leaders about the betrayal, and the Nazis don't find the guns. Later, however, he atones for his betrayal, sacrificing his life to warn the Norwegians that they are walking into an ambush.

"NO GREATER LOVE . . ."

The sixth Biblical typology category statement is "No greater love hath a man than to give up his life for a friend." Many times in these films we have observed people sacrificing their lives to save their comrades or to achieve an important military objective that will save others, or to atone for their misdeeds. What follow are a few representative occasions.

We have examined cases in which men who have done wrong (James Cagney's character in *Captains of the Clouds*, John Carroll in *Flying Tigers*, Alan Ladd in *China*) later atone for their sins by taking on suicide missions which save the lives of their friends. *Bombardier* also comes to mind when sacrifice is discussed. During a very hazardous course of flight training, Cadet Carter (Walter Reed) rides a crashing plane to the ground, belly-landing it safely because his buddy Hughes (Eddie Albert) is too afraid to parachute-jump to safety. Harris (Russell Wade) volunteers to be swung by the heels upside down out of the bomb-bay door at 5,000 feet to grab and release a flare line caught on the plane's rear wheel. Hughes, redeeming himself for his early cowardice, eventually and ironically dies saving a man from falling through the bomb-bay hatch, but in doing so, falls to his death. When Connors's (Robert Ryan's) plane is crashing in flames over Nagoya, he goes down with the ship so that he can finish destroying the Norden bombsight, preventing it from falling into enemy hands. Once Buck (Randolph Scott) gets free from the custody of the Japanese, he could have attempted to escape. Instead, he chooses to drive a flaming truck around the target area, catching camouflage netting on fire, lighting up the bombing objective and shouting up to the skies for the bombardiers to drop their deadly cargos on him—which they do.

In *Blood on the Sun*, Condon (James Cagney) chooses what appears to be certain death, holding off a band of Japanese secret police so that Iris (Sylvia Sidney) can escape to America with evidence to prove the existence of the Tanaka Plan for world domination.

Much to the credit of producer Milton Sperling, *Crash Dive* featured not only an instance of sacrifice, but one in which African-American submarine cook Oliver Jones (Ben Carter) is allowed a combat role, volunteering for a very hazardous mission, and is shown fighting bravely alongside his white counterparts. This was an unusual bit of casting for Sperling, running counter to the contemporary stereotype, which held that the black man was too cowardly or superstitious to fight bravely alongside the white man. In addition, as a welcome change in combat films, the minority representative survives. These men are chosen from all the sub's volunteers because they were unmarried, a clear sign that they might not return. Their task, as described earlier, was to destroy a German sub-tending base. In their escape, three men, including Jones, fight a delaying action against the Germans so that the other commandos in their group can escape. Later, two withdraw, leaving the old Chief (James Gleason) to hold the Germans back while the last commandos swim to safety. As noted earlier, there is often a reason for a character like the Chief to stay when it means certain death, or at best, capture. Chief's reason for staying was a dark moment in his past: during World War I, he committed what he considered a cowardly act, choosing to avoid a mission in which his shipmates were killed. So this time, the Chief chose to sacrifice his life to save others and atone for his sins.

Kenneth Burke wrote that not all scapegoats need be objects of scorn. Some are "too good for this world," and therefore of highest value, or, as the Bible says, "the most perfect sacrifice." Burke calls this simply "the Christ theme" (1973, 40). In many cases in these films, the Biblical value on the highest degree of love is conferred upon many a decent, innocent American soldier, who "lays down his life for a friend."

Bataan features superimposed titles at both the beginning and the end that praise the sacrifices made by the defenders of that island. At the beginning, it says: "To those immortal dead, who heroically stayed the wave of barbaric conquest [note the name-calling], this picture is reverently dedicated."

And at the end, once again interpreting defeat as victory, the title reads: "So fought the heroes of Bataan. Their sacrifice made possible our victories in the Coral and Bismarck Seas, on Midway, on New Guinea, and Guadalcanal. Their spirit will lead us back to Bataan."

In addition to fighting men, noncombatants are often shown risking or sacrificing their lives. In the war/fantasy film, *A Guy Named Joe*, Dorinda (Irene Dunne) is a highly skilled and experienced pilot in the Air Corps' Women's Ferry Service. When she learns that her lover, Ted (Van Johnson), has volunteered to fly what could be a suicide mission, Dorinda, a better pilot, steals the plane and flies the mission in his place, succeeding in not getting herself killed.

As in *Bataan*, *Sahara*, and others, there is often a moment of decision, a sort of Gethsemane in the film when it is possible for characters to decide to let "this cup pass from me." In *Cry Havoc*, the women, civilian nurse volunteers, must decide to stay or flee to safety. If they stay on the besieged island of Bataan, they can care for its wounded defenders, but if they do, they will likely not be able to escape before the Japanese overrun Allied positions. When one nurse asks, "For what?" another answers that that is up to her to decide. Someone else asks:

> Nurse No. 1: How important is it for us to hold out here? What's the good of holding onto a piece of ground like this?
>
> Nurse No. 2: We're talking like we're doing all the fighting. Where the Army is is where they need us. A man died in my arms tonight. And now I wouldn't leave here if I knew that it was my last day on earth.

Of course, they all vote to stay on, and, in the climax, all still alive are captured by the Japanese, and led off to an uncertain fate.

In both *Joan of Paris* and *Five Graves to Cairo*, civilians Joan (Michelle Morgan) and Mouche (Anne Baxter) manage to occupy the Nazis' time and attention for a few minutes to allow Royal Air Force flyers and a British spy to escape from enemy-held territory to continue the fight. Later the Nazis execute both women.

In *Purple Heart*, the airmen are told by the Japanese that they must reveal where their air raid originated (from the aircraft carrier *Hornet*), or they will all be executed. In a private meeting, the men decide that if one of them votes to talk, they all would. No one does; in a secret ballot, they all choose to sacrifice their lives rather than disobey orders. Speaking for all the flyers, Lieutenant Greenbaum (Sam Levene) tells the court that the flyers are delighted that their refusal to reveal where they are based means that Japan must guard against further raids from all directions: Russia, China, and the sea.

In the polemical *Sahara*, Sergeant Joe Gunn (Humphrey Bogart) borrows his style, if not his vocabulary, from Winston Churchill in answering the question from one of his men as to why they must, in all probability, sacrifice their lives in obscurity in the desert just to keep the Germans from taking a dry, useless water well:

> Why did your people go about their business in London when the Germans were throwing everything in the book at 'em? Why did your little boats take the men off the beach at Dunkirk? Why did the Russians make a stand at Moscow? Why did the Chinese move whole cities thousands of miles inland when the Japs attacked them? Why Bataan? Why Corregidor? Maybe they were all nuts. But there's one

thing they did do. They delayed the enemy, and they kept on delaying them until we got strong enough to hit him harder than he was hittin' us. I'm no general, but it seems to me that that's one way to win.

Thus we see that both the Apocalyptic and Biblical typology appeals concretely and symbolically link Christian values, Biblical themes, and Christian expectations of salvation to the Allied war effort.

6

DEFENDING OUR HOMES

The Territorial Appeal

Many aspects of the appeals we have examined so far at least imply a threat to America, American homes, families, and the American way of life. Man is a territorial creature who will instinctively defend his property and territory against outsiders (Ardrey). As I have discussed, the five appeal categories are noteworthy not only because of their prominence in the history of war rhetoric, but because of how well they work with each other.

Guilt itself implies that imperialism, or, at the very least, a bully's threatening belligerence, is the enemy's practice. Up to now, he has not

Figure 6.1. Marines show how fiercely Americans defend their territory against an overwhelming Japanese task force in *Wake Island* (1942).

been satisfied in lording it over his own people. It requires no proof to state that the goal of imperialism is to co-opt the territory of another, oftentimes resulting in the replacement of their present system of government. It is also a matter of historical fact that in this planet's history, many limited incursions into the territory of another have resulted in the escalation of the conflict from a minor dispute to total war. Satanism carries with it the implication that if the enemy were to win, his alien values, his savagery, and his way of life might be unleashed upon us. This implants in audiences a distaste, even a hatred, for the enemy. As well, it leaves the seed of fear of the enemy and of what his victory would mean to the people of the United States.

Apocalyptic/Biblical typology appeals make it clear that the enemy is a pagan, an atheist, or the worshipper of some false god who intends on establishing Satan's reign in America and the world. But these territorial inferences are not the primary goals of the Guilt, Satanism, and Apocalyptic/Biblical appeals; rather they are residual propagandistic benefits that result from their use. In short, there is ample justification for a major propaganda appeal category that promotes man's territorial imperative as the primary appeal, not a secondary by-product. Robert Ardrey wrote: "If we defend the title to our land or the sovereignty of our country, we do it for reasons no different, no less innate, no less ineradicable, than do lower animals. The dog barking at you from behind his master's fence acts for a motive indistinguishable from that of his master when the fence was built" (5).

Ardrey also offered evidence from nature and from human history that when any creature is forced to defend his territory, he fights harder, longer, and more viciously than he would if he was fighting on neutral territory or invading some other creature's territory. There is something innate—an instinct as old as the species—to defend one's nest, one's home, one's own preserve, and it applies as much to mockingbirds as to man (220).

Properly presented, an appeal to this instinct is a powerful tool in the hands of a skilled propagandist.

"A NEW ORDER"

An excellent example of the first Territorial category statement, "The enemy threatens our democratic institutions and our way of life," is found at the end of John Farrow's *China*. In David Jones's (Alan Ladd's) climactic argument with the Japanese general (Chester Gan), the enemy officer boasts:

> Contrary to public belief, the Japanese people have always held your country in great esteem. Yes, we have finally decided to take it away from you. In fact, we have already moved toward that aim [he looks at his watch], and the fate of Pearl Harbor will be the fate of all so-called free democracies who dare to oppose the imperial Japanese government. We and our allies, for the ultimate good of all nations concerned, have determined to establish a new world order.

In *All Through the Night*, Nazi agent Ebbing (Conrad Veidt) attempts to butter up "Gloves Donahue" (Humphrey Bogart), gangster to gangster, appealing to their supposed similarities to show that Nazis and hoods both want to overthrow America's way of life: "You and I are alike: you take what you want, and so do we. You have no respect for democracy; neither do we."

Later in the film, in a speech to his fellow hoodlums, urging them to help him fight the Nazis, Gloves provides territorial answers to the objection of one of the gang bosses, who argues that he doesn't care who runs the country as long as they leave him alone: "Listen, big shot—they'll tell you what time to get up in the morning, and what time to go to bed at night. They'll tell ya what you can eat, what kinda clothes to wear, what ya drink. They'll even tell ya what morning paper you can read."

A scene in *Action in the North Atlantic* reminds audiences that they may not be able to count on the simplest components of the American dream if the Nazis have their way. This explains why the liberty ship's carpenter went to sea:

> Carpenter: Before the war, I had my own business and my own house and got a little money put away.
>
> Mate: Whaddya doin' out here, then?

Carpenter: Well, I wanna keep my business and my house, and I figure that this is a smart way to do it.

Similarly, in *They Were Expendable*, "Dad" (Russell Simpson), the American owner of the Filipino shipyard where the PT boats are being repaired, is offered the chance to go along with Rusty (John Wayne) and his crew and escape the rampaging Japanese. But Dad, sitting on his front stoop and lifting a jug of homemade whisky for a drink, says that he spent forty years building his shipyard, and "if I leave it, they'll have to carry me out." So he will guard his shipyard and wait for the Japanese with his jug and shotgun. Director John Ford, reprising the mournful harmonica rendition of "Red River Valley" from *The Grapes of Wrath*, pulls back to a wide shot of the old man as he sits resolutely on his porch, unwilling to leave his home, and ready to doggedly defend his territory.

In *Saboteur*, Tobin (Otto Kruger), the enemy agent, explains to Kane (Bob Cummings) why a wealthy American rancher/industrialist with society connections wants to help overthrow the American government. Tobin explains that Kane, being an average American, can't understand that to a rich man like himself, power is the only thing that is outside his grasp, and our form of democratic government puts a limit on any one man's power. He prefers the kind of totalitarian system the Axis would impose on this country, which might allow him greater privilege as a member of the ruling elite. Also, once again attesting to the synergy of the appeals we have examined, toward the end of this conversation we catch a glimpse of some of Tobin's perverse desires hinted about in the Satanism chapter:

Kane: Why is it that you sneer every time you refer to this country? You've done pretty well here. I don't get it.

Tobin: No, you wouldn't. You're one of the ardent believers, the "good American." Oh, there are millions like you, people that plod along without asking questions. I hate to use the word "stupid," but it seems to be the only one that applies. The great masses—the moron millions. Well, there are a few of us who are unwilling to just troop along, a few of us who see that there's much more to be done than to live small, complacent lives; a few of us in America who desire a more profitable type of government. When you think about it, Mr. Kane, the competence of totalitarian nations is much higher than ours: they get things done.

Kane: (sarcastically) Yeah. They get things done. They bomb cities, sink ships, torture, and murder so you and your friends can eat off of gold plate. It's a great philosophy.

Tobin: I neither intend to be bombed or sunk, Mr. Kane. That's why I'm leaving [for Cuba] now. And if things don't go right for you, if, ah, we should win, then I'll come back. Perhaps I can get what I want then. Power. Yes, I want power as much as you want your job, or that girl. We all have different tastes, you see. Only I'm willing to back my tastes with the necessary force.

In *Cry Havoc*, the women are discussing the war and how it all came to happen. One of them, Pat (Ann Sothern), is confused about it. Andra (Heather Angel) and her sister, Sue (Dorothy Morris) answers her, laying out a Territorial scenario clear to everyone:

Andra: I'll tell you what's going on, Pat. A world revolution, a war to the death. . . .

Sue: This is a very simple war. Oh, it's big, and terrible, and it's frightening, but in other wars, lots of times you didn't exactly know why you were fighting. But that's not so in this war. This war we're all fighting for the same thing. We all know what it is . . . our lives. Because if we should lose this war, we'd all be dead. You, you and me, millions and millions of us. And those of us who were down under the ground would be the luckiest. Because those of us who weren't would be slaves. That's why it's a simple war.

SWEETHEARTS AND KIDS

The second Territorial category propaganda statement is "The enemy threatens our loved ones." In many combat films, there are scenes in which "back home" is discussed, flashed back to, and sometimes brought right to us in the middle of a war zone. For example, nurse Sandy (Donna Reed) visits the PT boat officers for a dinner at their

Philippine headquarters and reminds them all of their own sweethearts. In *Destination Tokyo*, Cary Grant tells the sweet story of how proud he was when he took his young son for his first haircut, and the boy announces to all the men in the barbershop, "This is my daddy!" These digressions implicitly remind the combatants and the audience that American soldiers are risking their lives to defend those they left behind back home. Films such as *Destination Tokyo* begin and end with the sub's crew saying goodbye to and greeting their loved ones after their mission, and films such as *Air Force* and *Wake Island* begin with farewells to the combatants' families. These aid immeasurably in bringing each man's ultimate territorial war objective, the protection of their homes and families, into sharp focus.

There are many pointed references to the consequences of an Axis victory. In *Thirty Seconds Over Tokyo*, when pilot Ted Lawson (Van Johnson) is asked why he thinks it's "okay to bomb Tokyo," he replies: "Because, I figure, it's drop a bomb on them, or pretty soon they'll be dropping a bomb on Ellen [his pregnant wife back home]."

In one scene, *Cry Havoc* digresses to remind us of both the sacrifices made by the gallant defenders of Bataan, and also why they made those sacrifices. The nurses have the sad duty of having to take inventory of the huge pile of personal belongings of dead soldiers. They take note that a twenty-two-year-old soldier had a wife and two children, and they admire the picture that the young man carried with him. One of the women also observes that the soldier had been carrying around a marble, which she imagines was the prized possession of one of the man's kids, and that it was probably given to him as a treasured keepsake when he left for war.

In both *Air Force* and *Flying Tigers*, men listen to FDR's "Day of Infamy" speech over the radio, and, through the use of close-ups, we are privy to their thoughts. In *Air Force*, while listening to the speech, pilot Quincannon's (John Ridgely's) eyes dart to a little toy airman he has hung up in the Mary Ann's cockpit. The toy was given to him by his little son before they left home. Similarly, Flying Tiger "Mack" (Jimmie Dodd) listens to FDR and with a concerned look on his face stares at a picture of his mother, father, and relatives back home.

In *Guadalcanal Diary*, there is a scene reminiscent of the cinematically famous ending scene in *All Quiet on the Western Front* (1931). A Marine falls, mortally wounded. He reaches out his hand for his helmet, which flew off when he fell. In it is a picture of his wife and children. Director Lewis Seiler cuts to a close up of the helmet, as the dying man's hand comes into frame, touches the photo, spasms, and falls limp as he dies.

Quentin Reynolds's stirring "forward" narration to *Eagle Squadron* contains more than an explanation that these Americans volunteered to help England before the United States was "stabbed in the back":

> These boys knew what we are learning now. They knew that the security of our country must depend upon our dominating and controlling the air—the tragedies of the past months [Pearl Harbor, etc.] have finally taught us as a nation what these boys knew then. In London they saw ghastly death and destruction fall from the skies; they saw the heart of Britain bleed—but never break. They came to know the civilians of London and found them just like their neighbors in California, and Texas, Oregon, Maine—these they found were our kind of people, with our ideals and our hatred of tyranny. And each time they walked through battered London they winced— one day this might happen in their home town.

This Land Is Mine presents the specter of Nazi regimentation, lack of freedom of choice, and militarism hanging over our families. Speaking to schoolteacher Albert about the importance of a good Nazi education, Major Von Kellar says, "The children of today are the soldiers and mothers of tomorrow." This kind of message was particularly distressful for parents who hoped that the sacrifices they were making would prevent their children from having to endure similar hardships.

Although territorial disputes in the animal kingdom are usually settled when the invader is repulsed, *Homo sapiens* are different. Pushing back the enemy beyond one's own boundaries is often followed by a vengeful counterattack on the territory of the invader. This punitive difference between us and "lower creatures" is the third Territorial statement: "We shall turn the tables on the enemy and threaten his territory."

TOTAL WAR

Carl von Clausewitz wrote that there are two kinds of war, limited war and total war (79). In a limited war, there may be a repulsion of the interloper followed by a reestablishment of the status quo, like the skirmish between an animal defending his territory and a temporary invader. But total war results in the overthrowing of the territory of one of the belligerents, followed by a new order of some sort.

Like World War I, World War II was a total war, followed by the establishment of different forms of governments and new national boundaries on the part of many nations allied on both sides of the conflict. When Pearl Harbor was bombed, President Roosevelt made it quite clear that the overthrow of the Japanese government would be the only result that would satisfy the United States. Frustrated with two successive wars instigated by Germany, America's European allies would also insist on the total defeat of Germany. So the "reverse Territoriality" that this statement implies is more than rhetoric: it is the desire and commitment of the major Allied governments to overthrow the governments of the Axis powers and replace them with systems less likely to reinstigate hostilities and again threaten our governments and our way of life.

In the speech given by the Air Minister (Stanley Ridges) at the conclusion of *Eagle Squadron*, the final goal of the war is clear: "And now that . . . our two great countries are actively allied, let us continue to work together, no matter where it may be, for the final overthrow of the enemy, and for the establishment of an enduring peace."

A number of films make reference to Tokyo and Berlin, seats of government of the enemy, as the ultimate military objectives of the conflict. As previously mentioned, *Eagle Squadron* lists "Berlin!" in large letters, as its ultimate goal. In *Gung Ho, Guadalcanal Diary, A Guy Named Joe*, and *God Is My Co-Pilot*, characters refer to their final objective as "going to Tokyo," "striking at the heart of the Japanese octopus," preparing for the first strike on Tokyo "since the Doolittle raid," and having reached "a milestone on the road to Tokyo."

Thus, Territoriality appeals at two levels. First, it taps into the "lower" instincts we share with the animal kingdom, and is not satisfied when only our sphere of influence, our domain itself, is no longer threatened. However, in today's world, many countries—including the

United States—have quite an inflated sense of territoriality, which can result in defending one's territory, quite literally, all over the globe. Also, at the "preventative" level, the human territorial being's intelligence allows him to think beyond the moment, to consider the future. Once attacked, *Homo sapiens* have the ability to consider and plan to prevent further incursions by the interloper. This often takes the form of seeing to it that the enemy no longer has the ability to conduct such destructive enterprises.

CONCLUSION

The End?

The end results of American propaganda during World War II were—by today's standards—never empirically measured. No one obtained hard statistical evidence of these films' influence on the American population: no reliable, quantifiable effects studies were ever performed to gauge attitude change and/or reinforcement. So all historians can do is examine the hints, the indications.

All researchers interested in the effects of these films might do at this late date is search available records about the amount of traffic at local recruiting stations after a particularly inspiring war film played nearby. They might look to the upsurge of bond sales, the downsurge of rationing complaints, and so on that followed the release of an exceptional propaganda film, and make purely speculative guesses about likely correlations.

Another approach might be determining the commercial success of these films. This could be accomplished by consulting trade publications such as *Variety*, in which the commercial and critical achievements of these films were regularly reported. However, there are many other mitigating variables that can affect a film's box office, including how large a chain of theaters the studio owned. Plus, in this analysis, I have observed that sometimes good movies contain excellent propaganda (e.g., *Mrs. Miniver* or *Air Force*) and sometimes much lesser "B"-

Figure 6.2. Floating around the Atlantic after their ship was torpedoed, a hetero-geneous group of American survivors and a German U-boat captain enact an alle-gorical version of World War II in Alfred Hitchcock's *Lifeboat* (1944).

type pictures also employ the five categories of propaganda appeals very well (e.g., *Gung Ho* or *Black Dragons*).

OBSERVATIONS

In the absence of hard data, I'll conclude this study with some reflec-tions and observations from the vantage point of the war's end until the present.

But first, a prologue: In the horror/science fiction picture *Them!* (1954), America's detonation of the first atomic bomb at White Sands caused a genetic mutation among a colony of ants, creating a race of giant, carnivorous insects. At the end of that film, the last of the ants destroyed by US Army flamethrowers, one actor exclaims that he is thankful that now the enemy is defeated, "it's all over." But another character questions that conclusion. He wonders about the possibility that America's subsequent atomic tests and explosions could have caused new horrors that are as yet undiscovered.

Similarly, this book ends on an ambiguous note, wondering if America has seen the last of the residual effects of the propaganda Hollywood propagated in World War II. Did the half-life of America's propaganda effects expire when the Japanese signed unconditional surrender papers on the *U.S.S. Missouri* in Tokyo Bay on September 2, 1945?

In 1941, a generation of "jitterbugs," the first offspring of the age of radio and talking pictures, had achieved their majority. What kind of a world greeted them? Just a world engulfed in the greatest conflict this planet has yet endured. Due to the Office of War Information, plus unprecedented cooperation by the then dominant media of motion pictures and radio (and yes, the kind of propaganda we've examined here was also found on radio), the mindset of this generation was radically redirected from thoughts of high school dances and a new Ford in their futures. Instead, these young people, men and women, were reshaped into one of the most unified, single-minded populations in the history of the human race and later given the title of *The Greatest Generation* in Tom Brokaw's fine book. This we can be reasonably sure of, because, as we have discovered, Hollywood was both an influence in, and a dutiful mirror of, American public opinion.

War was simple, the movies told them. Americans of many diverse backgrounds left their homes, came together to train hard, learned to be "team players," to sacrifice, and to use good old Yankee brain-power and ingenuity against an enemy that was racially, culturally, politically, and intellectually inferior, incapable of overcoming this aggregation of indomitable Americans. And, as an insurance policy, the God of our fathers had made it abundantly clear that when the chips are down, He would be on hand to insure our victory. On both the war fronts and the home front, Hollywood's motion pictures both instilled this mindset, and, true to propagandistic method, repeated its key messages over and over again in nearly four hundred feature films released between 1941 and 1945.

True to Hollywood's prophecy of victory, the United States and its allies won. The world, being America's personal oyster, became open as never before to America's will. The United States proudly assumed the role of the most powerful, most influential nation on the planet.

After experiencing all this, World War II's generation of Americans might very well come to the conclusion that in the future things might very well stay that way. It was quite reasonable for the Greatest Generation to jump to the conclusion that with the same national commitment, the same level of teamwork, and with the same spirit that enabled the United States to achieve victories in the first two world wars, America could not possibly fail in future conflicts. Why couldn't omnipotent America respond similarly the next time the "enemies of freedom" rise up to threaten this new *pax Americana*? It was as if Americans bought into the notion that we, too, were some sort of master race.

It's not hard to see how the residual effects of this mindset still influence our nation and its collective ego. "We're the cops of the world," protesting 1960s students sarcastically chanted. But they were not heard or heeded by presidents and congresses still firmly grasping to a belief in America's omnipotence and manifest destiny of world leadership. If a nation melds this self-important posture with an ethnocentric, racist attitude toward Asians, it is not hard to see why this country so easily became entrenched in an unwinnable land war in Vietnam. Our country's politicians and military leaders seemed to sincerely believe our own propaganda, that Asians were tiny, inferior creatures who fell neatly into only two categories: the godless communist robot masses, or helpless peasants desperate for the protection and civilizing influences of the United States. Didn't we do that in the war against the Japanese? Didn't we rescue the Filipinos and the Chinese? We saw that happen in film after film.

In postwar years, this stereotype has come to be the defining attribute of what has been called the "ugly American" syndrome. In the movies and in presidential speech after speech in the thirty years following World War II, this *America uber alles* (America above everything) mind-set was constantly reinforced.

Films such as *China Gate* (1957), *The Quiet American* (1958), and *The Ugly American* (1963) helped to create the image of the Chinese Communists as one of the two new "Great Satans" of the postwar era. The other was, of course, the Soviet Union. These two bad guys made worthy replacements for the Japanese and the Nazis. These early Vietnam War films and dozens more like them pictured Asians such as the Vietnamese as uncivilized children requiring American nurturing and care. US foreign policy was determined to provide these services, hoping by doing so to forestall the inevitable effects of President Eisenhower's simplistic "domino theory," which warned that if one Asian country's "democratic" government toppled to communism, they all would.

To an America not yet ready to forget Pearl Harbor, the image of a scheming, slant-eyed communist enemy manipulating and encouraging every Indo-Chinese incident of anti-Americanism was quite vivid and easily believable. When demonstrations of Southeast Asian nationalistic fervor were explained away as "communist-inspired," those name-calling characterizations were not challenged. Cued by the intellectually devastating social effects of McCarthyism propaganda back home and coupled with the ongoing real Soviet threat in Europe, Americans were more than willing to accept the urgency of an American imperative to protect Southeast Asia from "the cancer of godless communism."

THE CONFLICT ABOUT THE "CONFLICT"

Catapulting forward from V-J Day twenty years, America found itself "hip-deep in the big muddy" of Vietnam. And much to the amazement and shock of their parents, students on America's college campuses suddenly appeared, waving signs demanding "peace now!" The young people of the greatest generation, transformed during the ensuing two decades into the parents of the post-World War II "baby boom," found a peace in Vietnam movement impossible to fathom. Hadn't the movies of World War II often reminded them that they were sacrificing, fighting, and dying so that their children could live and grow up with the gift of liberty? As well, hadn't America's president, an authority figure endowed during World War II with the godlike wisdom of FDR, proclaimed to the country that the war in Vietnam was righteous and necessary?

But to conform with the successes of the past, war must be fought with a massive, all-consuming national effort, shouldn't it? That's what it took to win World War II. President Lyndon Johnson, as well as John Kennedy and Dwight Eisenhower before him, used all the correct rhetorical appeals found in this book when they told Americans that the enemy bears total responsibility for this conflict; that the new Satan is an inferior, Godless savage; that because of the "domino theory," these communists threaten our very democratic institutions, our democracy, our families; that God not only supports our efforts, but will undoubtedly intervene on our behalf; and that because we are Americans, that special, tough, mongrel superhuman breed destined to "make the world safe for democracy," we must persist against communists in the jungles of Vietnam, where we will surely triumph.

Undaunted, many thousands of children of the baby boom refused to accept the values John Wayne, Randolph Scott, Dana Andrews, Cary Grant, Humphrey Bogart, and the rest of World War II's mediated models preached to their parents. Instead, these values were criticized as "imperialist," and the armed services and national defense establishment so often praised in World War II became the evil "military-industrial complex." America, the most powerful nation in the world, the nation with the H-bomb, couldn't use it. Barry Goldwater lost an election for president because he merely hinted that if he were elected he might consider using low-yield nuclear weapons in Vietnam. Nuclear politics and world opinion had made such a tactic impossible.

Although the Greatest Generation wished and believed things to be the same, nothing was as cut and dried as it used to be. "Hell no, we won't go!" clashed discordantly with "Gung Ho!" The generation whose values and attitudes were hardened in the kiln of a life-or-death struggle with Hitler and Tojo could not, or would not, see the important differences until it was too late for the 1.45 million Asians and Americans killed in the Vietnam War.

That war is over and America lost. If the residual effects of World War II propaganda in some way assisted in that failure, what of it? It's behind us, and Americans have apparently learned the important lessons of that conflict. After all, when Congress balked at Ronald Reagan's folly in Nicaragua, they said that they feared an escalated American involvement would "lead to another Vietnam." But have Americans learned enough?

BEYOND VIETNAM

It's too simplistic to attribute the blame for America's foolish Vietnam involvement on any single influence, including beliefs and attitudes taught by movies and other wartime media influences. As Edward R. Murrow said of Joe McCarthy, "He didn't create this situation of fear, he merely exploited it," as did other US entities, organizations, industries, and personalities. But it would be equally too simplistic to discount them. It is true that the media of mass communication, then and now, often reflect and exploit, rather than guide, national attitudes and values.

But observing campaign managers for presidential hopefuls position their candidates' speeches for their key sound bites on the evening news, or how the hair (sans Donald Trump) and clothing styles of mediated models are so quickly emulated by a numbed, desensitized, and submissive viewership, one must give serious consideration to the myth-making, attitude-forming capabilities of American mass communication. One has only to reflect on how George H. W. Bush was able to successfully exploit these old attitudes during the 1988 presidential campaign, scaring the nation into believing that Michael Dukakis was "weak on defense" and unwilling to thrust America into the forefront of the battle to defend freedom around the globe. And in his second debate with the Massachusetts governor, Bush, in confessing his lack of faith in the United Nations to "do the job" of peacekeeping around the world and protecting it from the threat of communism, chided his opponent for putting great stock in that organization.

The management of consumer demand through commercial propaganda and molding and shaping attitudes and beliefs through political/social propaganda is not new. It was practiced well before World War II. But propaganda took a great leap forward between 1941 and 1945. Using the medium of the motion picture, Hollywood's propaganda during World War II both reflected and inflamed mainstream public opinion. Today, as the United States must live with the fallout from the atomic bombs they dropped, Hollywood must share some of the blame for the residual effects of the propaganda they unleashed upon the world.

And even though such post-Vietnam War films as *The Deer Hunter*, *Platoon*, *Full Metal Jacket*, *Hamburger Hill*, and others irritate still painful nerves, America as a nation may already be on its way to blotting out the memory of the tragedy of Vietnam, to a "repositioning" of America back to a more reactionary, World War II modality. If the United States didn't find victory in Vietnam then under President Reagan, America could flex its mighty muscles to overcome communists in tiny Grenada, and count coup against terrorist sympathizer Muammar Gaddafi in a one-night bombing raid on Libya.

And wouldn't the United States be able to quickly demonstrate its continuing dominance and ability to manipulate world affairs by straightening out those silly little conflicts in the Middle East? Just like in Asia, these are just more simple people who need American help—simple people who live in deserts floating on oil? America could just run on over there, knock off Saddam Hussein, secure enough cheap oil to keep the United States polluting the air for another century and transplant American-style democracy, McDonald's, and Colonel Sanders into the Middle East the way we did into Japan after World War II. No one would object to that, right?

How could any of that possibly go wrong?

In 1948, Harold Lasswell once theorized that one of the responsibilities of mass communication is the "surveillance of the environment" (37), so that by virtue of its role in society, the mass media serve as "watchdogs" for the people. In turn, one of the responsibilities of mass communications scholarship is to keep a watchful eye on the watchdogs. This book's approach to that responsibility has been to point out the kind of propaganda that has come before, and, in this chapter, provide a few anxious looks backward and forward as the same propaganda appeals are used to justify more war against more adversaries, including the new enemies we have created.

Americans need to understand themselves better, so they can tell the sizzle from the steak. The United States needs to recognize how vulnerable they are to the effects of the mass media that surrounds them. If we can gauge the ability of mediated images to persuade us, if we can avoid clinging too tightly to artificially created values and attitudes not relevant to new and changing conditions, then we can perhaps truly benefit from the lessons history can teach us.

Otherwise, as philosopher George Santayana has famously written, "Those who do not remember the past are condemned to repeat it" (284).

ANNOTATED FILMOGRAPHY

ACTION IN THE NORTH ATLANTIC (1943, WARNER BROS.)

Director: Lloyd Bacon
Screenplay: John Howard Lawson; Guy Gilpatric (story)
Cast: Humphrey Bogart, Raymond Massey, Alan Hale, Julie Bishop, Ruth Gordon

The adventures of a merchant marine crew in the North Atlantic, hauling arms and supplies to America's allies. A Nazi sub sinks their first ship, and they spend many days in a life raft. Later, on a new ship in a large convoy, they are threatened by a wolf pack of subs. But Bogart and Massey pilot their ship to safety, and then fight off a sub and planes that attack them, finally delivering the goods to our Russian allies.

Propaganda Appeals: Guilt, Satanism, Illusion of Victory, Biblical Typologies, Territoriality

ACROSS THE PACIFIC (1942, WARNER BROS.)

Director: John Houston
Screenplay: Richard Macaulay, based on the serial "Aloha Means Goodbye" by Robert Carson

Cast: Humphrey Bogart, Mary Astor, Sydney Greenstreet, Victor Sen Yung

A US agent posing as a corrupt army officer who has been dishonorably discharged appears to join forces with a Japanese agent. Assigned to crack a spy ring, instead on December 6, 1941, the American ends up spoiling a Japanese attempt to blow up the Panama Canal.

Propaganda Appeals: Guilt, Satanism, Illusion of Victory, Territoriality

AIR FORCE (1943, WARNER BROS.)

Director: Howard Hawks
Screenplay: Dudley Nichols
Cast: John Ridgely, Gig Young, Harry Carey, John Garfield, James Brown, Ray Montgomery

The story of the crew of the Air Corps bomber *Mary Ann* on a flight from California to Pearl Harbor on December 7, 1941. Finding Pearl under attack, they fuel up and move on to Wake Island and finally to the Philippines. They fight their way through many perils to get to Manila, from where they plan to launch a counterattack against the Japanese. Finally, they find the Japanese fleet, direct Allied air forces to attack it, and join with other flyers in sinking Japanese ships during the Battle of the Coral Sea.

Propaganda Appeals: Guilt, Satanism, Illusion of Victory, Biblical Typologies, Territoriality

ALL QUIET ON THE WESTERN FRONT (1930, RKO-PATHE)

Director: Lewis Milestone
Screenplay: George Abbott; Del Andrews, Maxwell Anderson (adaptation), based on the novel by Erich Maria Remarque
Cast: Lew Ayres, Louis Wolheim, John Wray, Arnold Lucy, Ben Alexander

An epic story of a group of German schoolboys recruited by their jingo-istic schoolmaster into the German Army to fight the Allies in World War I. As the boys witness death and the carnage of war, they realize its folly and become men. Enthusiasm gives way to disillusionment and finally to a resigned stoicism. This antiwar film ends when the featured character returns to the front only to join most of his schoolmates in the ranks of those who die on the battlefield.

Propaganda Appeals: Guilt, Satanism, Illusion of Victory, Territoriality

ALL THROUGH THE NIGHT (1941, WARNER BROS.)

Director: Vincent Sherman
Screenplay: Leonard Spigelgass, Edwin Gilbert; Leo Rosten, Leonard Spigelgass (story)
Cast: Humphrey Bogart, Conrad Veidt, Kaaren Verne, Frank McHugh, Peter Lorre, William Demarest

A film that could be subtitled, "Guys and Dolls Meet The Nazis," Bo-gart's character plays an undeniably crooked but true-blue American gambling boss who enlists his fellow New York gangsters, burly team-sters, and newspaper circulation goons to discover, attack, and defeat a band of Nazi saboteurs bent on the destruction of a battleship about to leave the Brooklyn Navy Yard on its maiden voyage.

Propaganda Appeals: Guilt, Satanism, Illusion of Victory, Territoriality

APPOINTMENT IN BERLIN (1943, COLUMBIA)

Director: Alfred E. Green
Screenplay: Michael Hogan, Horace McCoy; B. P. Fineman (story)
Cast: George Sanders, Marguerite Chapman, Onslow Stevens, Gale Sondergaard

A Royal Air Force (RAF) officer manages to infiltrate Nazi propaganda headquarters in Berlin. He gets the job of broadcasting Nazi propaganda, but his scripts contain coded intelligence messages to London.

Propaganda Appeals: Satanism, Illusion of Victory, Territoriality

BACK TO BATAAN (1945, RKO)

Director: Edward Dmytryk
Screenplay: Ben Barzman, Richard H. Landau; Aeneas MacKenzie, William Gordon (story)
Cast: John Wayne, Anthony Quinn, Beulah Bondi, Fely Franquelli, "Ducky" Louie, Richard Loo, Philip Ahn

The story of the American and Filipino guerilla fighters who extracted huge losses from the Japanese invaders from the fall of Corregador until and after MacArthur's return. The film stresses the loyalty of the Filipinos to America and the Yanks' dedication to Filipino liberation. After many brave and heroic engagements with the enemy, Wayne's character leads Filipinos in a desperate struggle to hold a key supply road so that the Japanese could not send reinforcements to their troops trying to repel MacArthur's "return" landing on Leyte.

Propaganda Appeals: Guilt, Satanism, Illusion of Victory, Territoriality

BATAAN (1943, MGM)

Director: Tay Garnett
Screenplay: Robert H. Andrews
Cast: Robert Taylor, George Murphy, Thomas Mitchell, Lloyd Nolan, Robert Walker, Desi Arnaz

A group of volunteers destroys a key bridge on Bataan and then gamely holds onto the bridgehead, preventing the enemy from rebuilding and crossing it. Although wave after wave of Japanese attackers finally overcomes the last of these thirteen men, their sacrifice gives the Americans time, which in turn, allows the defenders of the Philippines to hold out much longer against the Japanese, resulting in the enemy's strategic defeat in Southeast Asia.

Propaganda Appeals: Guilt, Satanism, Illusion of Victory, Apocalypticism and Biblical Typologies, Territoriality

THE BATTLESHIP POTEMKIN (1925, MOSFILM)

Director: Sergei Eisenstein
Screenplay: Nina Agadzhanova
Cast: Alexsandr Antonov, Vladimir Barsky, Gigori Aleksandrov, Ivan Bobrov, Mikhail Gormorov

Eisenstein's account of the mutiny of the crew of the famous battleship, which leads to his famous Odessa Steps sequence, in which Cossacks, employed by the Czarist government, slaughter helpless civilians of Odessa who gather to demonstrate their support for the mutineers.

Propaganda Appeals: Satanism, Illusion of Victory

BERLIN CORRESPONDENT (1942, 20TH CENTURY FOX)

Director: Eugene Forde
Screenplay: Steve Fisher, Jack Andrews
Cast: Dana Andrews, Virginia Gilmore, Mona Maris, Martin Kosleck, Sig Ruman

In the days just prior to December 7, an American journalist manages to transmit the truth about what is going on in Germany back to America, right under the noses of a group of particularly stupid Nazi censors. When the journalist, played by Andrews, aids in the escape to Switzerland of an anti-Nazi German, he is arrested and thrown into a concentration camp. In the inevitable escape, he outsmarts his captors and escapes Germany for safety in Switzerland.

Propaganda Appeals: Satanism, Illusion of Victory, Territoriality

BLACK DRAGONS (1942, MONOGRAM)

Director: William Nigh
Screenplay: Harvey Gates
Cast: Bela Lugosi, Joan Barclay, George Pembroke, Clayton Moore,
Robert Frazer, Edward Peil

In this "poverty row"–produced film, Lugosi plays a talented but mad
German plastic surgeon who transforms members of the infamous Japanese Black Dragon Society into the likenesses of American defense
contractors and industrialists. The original men have been kidnapped
and murdered. The Black Dragons then attempt to sabotage American
defense industries. Double-crossed and thrown into prison by the Japanese, the surgeon escapes, follows the dragons to America, and murders
each of them. Finally, American police and G-men catch up with Lugosi.

Propaganda Appeals: Guilt, Satanism, Territoriality

BLOOD ON THE SUN (1945, UNITED ARTISTS)

Director: Frank Lloyd
Screenplay: Lester Cole, Nathaniel Curtis; Garrett Fort (story)
Cast: James Cagney, Sylvia Sidney, Porter Hall, Wallace Ford, Rose-
mary DeCamp, Robert Armstrong

A highly fictionalized account of how the fabled secret Tanaka Memorial Plan for Japanese world conquest was uncovered in 1928 and spirited
out of Japan to America by an American journalist and a Chinese double agent. Cagney and Sidney achieve this by overcoming and outsmart-
ing an array of incompetent Japanese secret police. This results in Baron Tanaka's suicide and the passing of power in Japan to General Tojo
and Admiral Yamamoto.

Propaganda Appeals: Guilt, Satanism, Biblical Typologies, Territoriality

BOMBARDIER (1941, RKO)

Director: Richard Wallace
Screenplay: John Twist; Martin Rackin, John Twist (story)
Cast: Pat O'Brien, Randolph Scott, Robert Ryan, Eddie Albert, Walter Reed, Barton MacLane, Anne Shirley

For two-thirds of the film, *Bombardier* is a typical training film of Army Air Corps personnel for high-altitude precision bombing. Then, in the last third, it changes to a combat film. Scott's character flies a lone bomber over the target to light it up with incendiary bombs, but is shot down short of the target. He escapes from his Japanese captors and manages to set the camouflage netting over the target area, a Mitsubishi assembly plant, on fire. This lights up the objective for the rest of the bomb group, which destroys it.

Propaganda Appeals: Guilt, Satanism, Illusion of Victory, Apocalypticism and Biblical Typologies, Territoriality

CAPTAINS OF THE CLOUDS (1942, WARNER BROS.)

Director: Michael Curtiz
Screenplay: Arthur T. Horman, Richard MacAulay, Norman R. Raine; Arthur T. Horman, Roland Gillett (story)
Cast: James Cagney, Dennis Morgan, Brenda Marshall, Alan Hale, Reginald Gardiner, George Tobias

Cagney plays a rebellious "seat of the pants" Canadian bush pilot who wishes to join the Royal Canadian Air Force (RCAF) to fight the Nazis. However, Cagney's unwillingness to submit to service discipline and fly by RCAF regulations leads to the death of his friend, Hale, followed by his disgrace and cashiering. Assuming Hale's identity, Cagney volunteers for duty ferrying bombers to England. When a flight of unarmed bombers is attacked by a Messerschmitt, some are picked off. Cagney, his crewman killed, uses his bush-pilot savvy to chase down the faster and more maneuverable German fighter and ram him. Thus by his death, he atones for his sins and saves the rest of the bomber flight.

Propaganda Appeals: Satanism, Illusion of Victory, Biblical Typologies, Territoriality

CASABLANCA (1943, WARNER BROS.)

Director: Michael Curtiz
Screenplay: Julius and Philip Epstein, Howard Koch, based on the play *Everybody Comes to Rick's* by Murray Burnett and Joan Alison
Cast: Humphrey Bogart, Ingrid Bergman, Claude Rains, Conrad Veidt, Paul Henreid, Sydney Greenstreet

The familiar love story of Rick, who "sticks his neck out for nobody," and Ilsa, his long-lost love. For our purposes, *Casablanca* is an allegory of American isolationism followed by eventual joining of the war against the Nazis. Bogart, like America, was sympathetic, but because of his past, uncommitted to "Europe's War," but in the end, he gives up safety, security, and the beautiful Bergman to assure that Henreid's character, a Czech Resistance leader, can get to America to continue to lead the fight against the Nazis.

Propaganda Appeals: Guilt, Satanism, Illusion of Victory, Apocalypticism and Biblical Typologies, Territoriality

CHINA (1943, PARAMOUNT)

Director: John Farrow
Screenplay: Frank Butler, based on the play by Archibald Forbes
Cast: Alan Ladd, William Bendix, Loretta Young, Philip Ahn, Richard Loo

Like *Casablanca*, *China* is another anti-isolationist allegory. In this film, we see a parallel to America's selfish reluctance to involve itself in the war until it becomes directly affected. Ladd's character is an unscrupulous oil dealer willing to sell his product to either the Chinese or the Japanese, whoever will pay him. Then he meets Loretta Young's character and her small band of Chinese schoolgirls, and helps them escape from the enemy. Seeing the savagery with which the Japanese treat the Chinese they have conquered, he decides to enter the fight on the side of America's ally. Ladd joins Chinese guerilla fighters and sacrifices his life to help destroy a Japanese troop column.

Propaganda Appeals: Guilt, Satanism, Illusion of Victory, Biblical Typologies, Territoriality

CHINA GIRL (1942, 20TH CENTURY FOX)

Director: Henry Hathaway
Screenplay: Ben Hecht; Darryl F. Zanuck (story)
Cast: George Montgomery, Jean Tierney, Victor McLaglen, Lyn Bari, Alan Baxter, Sig Ruman

In yet another allegory of American non-involvement followed by commitment to the war, Montgomery's character portrays a news photographer out only for a buck, nearly oblivious to the suffering of the Chinese at the hands of the Japanese. Finally his "China Girl" and her father teach him by their example about sacrifice and honor. When they are killed by the Japanese, Montgomery takes up the machine gun, and like Alan Ladd in *China* and Humphrey Bogart in *Casablanca*, joins the fight.

Propaganda Appeals: Guilt, Satanism, Illusion of Victory, Biblical Typologies, Territoriality

COMMANDOS STRIKE AT DAWN (1942, COLUMBIA)

Director: John Farrow
Screenplay: Irwin Shaw; C.S. Forester (story)

Cast: Paul Muni, Anna Lee, Lillian Gish, Cedric Hardwicke, Ray Collins, Robert Coote

Muni's character, a peaceful man living in a Norwegian fishing town, witnesses the brutal Nazi occupation and decides to go to war. He forms a resistance group and kills the chief German commander, so he must escape to England. But he returns, guiding a group of British commandos on a mission to destroy the secret airstrip the Germans are building near his town.

Propaganda Appeals: Guilt, Satanism, Illusion of Victory, Territoriality

CORVETTE K-225 (1943, UNIVERSAL)

Director: Richard Rosson (and Producer Howard Hawks [uncredited])
Screenplay: John Rhodes Sturdy
Cast: Randolph Scott, James Brown, Ella Raines, Barry Fitzgerald, Andy Devine, Noah Beery Jr.

Scott's Canadian navy captain is anxious to assume command of a new corvette and return to sea. His last ship was torpedoed by a Nazi sub, which then brutally machine-gunned the survivors in their lifeboats. McLain gets his new ship, and the K-225 accompanies a convoy across the Atlantic, protecting them from German submarine wolf packs. The corvette sinks one sub and then conducts a climactic surface battle with (of course) the very U-boat that machine-gunned McLain's former crew. The sub is destroyed, and the battered corvette proudly completes its escort mission, conveying a group of Allied liberty ships to an English port.

Propaganda Appeals: Guilt, Satanism, Illusion of Victory, Territoriality

CRASH DIVE (1943, 20TH CENTURY FOX)

Director: Archie Mayo
Screenplay: Jo Swerling; W. R. Burnett (story)

Cast: Tyrone Power, Anne Baxter, Dana Andrews, James Gleason, Harry Morgan, Ben Carter

Power's character, an American PT boat commander, is reassigned to serve aboard a submarine. This officer then meets and woos his own captain's girlfriend, not knowing who his rival is. Of course, this creates conflict between the two officers. But in typical wartime fashion, all this is set aside as Power's character leads a successful commando raid on a secret North Atlantic sub tending station. In the height of this action, the two officers reconcile. This film also features a rare occurrence in films made during World War II in which an African American is, at least partially, in combat.

Propaganda Appeals: Guilt, Satanism, Illusion of Victory, Territoriality

THE CRUEL SEA (1953, EALING STUDIOS)

Director: Charles Frend
Screenplay: Eric Ambler; Nicholas Monsarrat (story)
Cast: Jack Hawkins, Donald Sinden, John Stratton, Denholm Elliott, John Warner, Stanley Baker

This film portrays life aboard a Royal Navy corvette, the *HMS Compass Rose*, assigned to convoy escort duty in the North Atlantic. Compared to the fictionalized, almost unbelievable events in *Action in the North Atlantic*, the propagandistic Hollywood version of life on convoy duty, *The Cruel Sea* is gritty and real. After three years of foul sea and near misses, the *Compass Rose* finally sinks a submarine, but in the battle is herself sunk. Later, the *Compass Rose*'s survivors, including Hawkins's character, who is promoted and commanding a frigate, the *HMS Saltash Castle*, manage to sink another sub. Ironically, after V-E Day, the *Saltash Castle* is assigned to escort to port German submarines that have surrendered.

Propaganda Appeals: A postwar film, not expressly intended for propaganda

CRY HAVOC (1943, MGM)

Director; Richard Thorpe
Screenplay: Paul Osborn, based on the play by Allan Kenward
Cast: Margaret Sullivan, Ann Sothern, Joan Blondell, Marsha Hunt, Heather Angel, Frances Gifford

Nine civilian women volunteer to join nurses on Bataan who are tending to the soldiers conducting the heroic stand on that island against the Japanese. From the burlesque queen to the art student to the Southern society debutante, all were unprepared for war, death, and sacrifice. But all "grow up," serve valiantly, fight, and a few of them die. In the climax, these women stay behind when General MacArthur's main forces retreat to Corregidor. They are captured by the Japanese in an apparent defeat. But the picture takes great pains to point out that these women's sacrifices helped delay the enemy, causing his strategic defeat in that theater of operations.

Propaganda Appeals: Guilt, Satanism, Illusion of Victory, Biblical Typologies, Territoriality

COUNTER-ESPIONAGE (1942, COLUMBIA)

Director: Edward Dmytryk
Screenplay: Audrey Wisberg, based on a novel by Louis Joseph Vance
Cast: Warren William, Eric Blore, Hillary Brooke, Thurston Hall, Fred Kelsey, Forrest Tucker

A notorious jewel thief works for British intelligence during the blitz. Pursued by Scotland Yard both because he's a thief and also because he's suspected of spying for the Germans, William's character manages to evade everyone who's after him and uncover a spy ring.

Propaganda Appeals: Guilt, Satanism, Illusion of Victory, Territoriality

DESTINATION TOKYO (1944, WARNER BROS.)

Director: Delmer Daves
Screenplay: Delmer Daves, Albert Maltz; Steve Fisher (story)
Cast: Cary Grant, John Garfield, John Ridgely, Alan Hale, Dane Clark,
William Prince, Robert Hutton

The somewhat polemical and highly fictionalized account of the men of
the submarine *USS Copperfin*, which supposedly sneaks into Tokyo Bay
so that a shore party can obtain weather and atmospheric data to aid the
Doolittle raid flyers. Once Grant and his crew finish their mission and
retrieve their shore party, the sub sneaks out of Tokyo Bay, and, just for
good measure, sends a Japanese aircraft carrier and a destroyer to the
bottom. Then they triumphantly return home to San Francisco to their
wives and/or sweethearts.

Propaganda Appeals: Guilt, Satanism, Illusion of Victory, Biblical Typologies, Territoriality

EDGE OF DARKNESS (1943, WARNER BROS.)

Director: Lewis Milestone
Screenplay: Robert Rossen, based on the novel by William Woods
Cast: Errol Flynn, Ann Sheridan, Walter Houston, Ruth Gordon, Judith
Anderson, Helmut Dantine

This is the story of the rebellion staged by the population of an entire
Norwegian village against the Nazi occupation. It portrays the people of
the town as they first question whether they are committed enough to
sacrifice everything, even their lives, for their freedom. They decide to
accept a British offer to secretly deliver them arms and ammunition,
avoid the consequences of a betrayal by a quisling, and defeat the Germans, but at great loss of life. German reinforcements arrive and the
remaining townspeople take to the hills to continue the fight.

Propaganda Appeals: Guilt, Satanism, Illusion of Victory, Apocalypticism and Biblical Typologies, Territoriality

EAGLE SQUADRON (1942, UNIVERSAL/WALTER WANGER)

Director: Arthur Lubin
Screenplay: Norman Reilly Raine; C. S. Forester (story)
Cast: Robert Stack, Leif Erickson, Diana Barrymore, Jon Hall, Eddie Albert, Nigel Bruce, John Loder

"This is the story," as the narrator says, "of our countrymen who didn't wait to be stabbed in the back," the American pilots who joined the RAF to fight the Germans before America's official entrance into the war. Wanger has written that this film was made specifically to foster closer Anglo-American cooperation. Robert Stack, the hero, undergoes a conversion in the film from happy-go-lucky flyboy to dedicated patriot and freedom fighter. He changes his attitude as a result of witnessing the conduct of Barrymore's character and her countrymen during the Battle of Britain.

Propaganda Appeals: Guilt, Satanism, Illusion of Victory, Territoriality

ENEMY AGENTS MEET ELLERY QUEEN (1942, COLUMBIA PICTURES)

Director: James P. Hogan
Screenplay: Eric Taylor; Manfred Lee, Frederic Dannay (story)
Cast: William Gargan, Margaret Lindsay, Charley Grapewin, Gale Sondergaard, Gilbert Roland, Sig Ruman

Ellery Queen, a fictional mystery writer, usually appears in literature as a novelist who assists the police in solving puzzling crimes. This time he assists his police inspector father in solving the murder of a smuggler murdered by fifth columnists for industrial diamonds the victim smuggled into the United States in a mummy case.

Propaganda Appeals: Guilt, Satanism, Illusion of Victory, Territoriality

ESCAPE (1940, MGM)

Director: Mervyn LeRoy
Screenplay: Arch Oboler, Marguerite Roberts, based on the novel by
Grace Zaring Stone (as Ethel Vance)
Cast: Robert Taylor, Norma Shearer, Conrad Veidt, Alla Nazimova,
Felix Bressart, Albert Bassermann

Taylor's character, an American, discovers his mother has been imprisoned in a Nazi concentration camp. He goes to Germany, and with the
help of a German countess and a doctor, hatches a plan to rescue
Taylor's mother and escape to the United States.

Propaganda Appeals: Guilt, Satanism, Illusion of Victory

THE ETERNAL JEW (1940, DFG)

Director: Fritz Hippler
Screenplay: Eberhard Taubert
Cast: This film is a documentary. Appearing in the film via archive
footage are hundreds of Jewish people, and many famous people, including Albert Einstein, Charles Chaplin, and Adolf Hitler.

One of the most evil of the Nazi hate films, The Eternal Jew characterizes all Jewish people (especially those from Poland) as dirty, evil
people bent on taking over the world. Comparing Jews to rats and
vermin, the film clearly suggests that like rats, Jews must be exterminated. In the ending, Hitler announces that the Jewish race will be annihilated.

Propaganda Appeals: Satanism, Territoriality

THE FIGHTING SEABEES (1944, REPUBLIC)

Director: Edward Ludwig
Screenplay: Borden Chase, Aeneas MacKenzie; Borden Chase (story)

Cast: John Wayne, Dennis O'Keefe, Susan Hayward, William Frawley, Leonid Kinsky, J. M. Kerrigan

This film dramatically documents the founding of the Navy's construction battalion, the Seabees, putting Wayne's character into the middle of the story. It dramatizes the Navy's early failures in war zone construction and the loss of life among the civilian workers. Wayne plays a construction contractor who, at first reluctantly, and later heroically, helps O'Keefe's character organize the Seabees and lead them in battle.

Propaganda Appeals: Guilt, Satanism, Illusion of Victory, Territoriality

FIVE GRAVES TO CAIRO (1943, PARAMOUNT)

Director: Billy Wilder
Screenplay: Charles Brackett, Billy Wilder, based on the play by Lajos Biro
Cast: Franchot Tone, Anne Baxter, Akim Tamiroff, Erich von Stroheim, Peter van Eyck, Fortunio Bonanova

An English tank corps corporal, the lone survivor of his unit, stumbles into an Egyptian village hotel a few minutes ahead of Field Marshal Rommel's victorious Afrika Corps. The Brit, played by Tone, poses as a hotel employee, and at first attempts to assassinate the Field Marshal. Later, he steals the map locations of Rommel's secret buried supply dumps and delivers the information to British headquarters, thereby halting the German advance against Cairo.

Propaganda Appeals: Guilt, Satanism, Illusion of Victory, Biblical Typologies, Territoriality

FLYING FORTRESS (1942, WARNER BROS.)

Director: Walter Forde
Screenplay: Edward Dryhurst, Brock Williams, Gordon Wellesley

Cast: Richard Greene, Carla Lehmann, Betty Stockfeld, Donald Stewart, Sidney King

A pilot and a playboy who also is a pilot first join the RAF Ferry Command to fly B-17 bombers from the United States to England. Later they join the Royal Canadian Air Force so that they can not just ferry Flying Fortresses but bomb Germany as well. On the climactic bombing mission over Germany, the film's trio of screenwriters dip heavily into fantasy: they have the bomber hit by German anti-aircraft fire and one engine is on fire. One of the heroes climbs out on the wing and extinguishes the fire. Of course, to advertise the sturdiness of the Fortress, they make sure that the B-17 makes it back home safely.

Propaganda Appeals: Guilt, Satanism, Illusion of Victory, Territoriality

FLYING TIGERS (1942, REPUBLIC)

Director: David Miller
Screenplay: Kenneth Gamet, Barry Trivers; Kenneth Gamet (story)
Cast: John Wayne, John Carroll, Anna Lee, Paul Kelly, Gordon Jones, Edmund MacDonald, Richard Loo

Wayne's character, the commander of this squadron, recruits brash loner Woody Jason (Carroll) to join the Flying Tigers, American volunteers who fly P-40 Warhawks against overwhelming numbers of Japanese planes. But Woody refuses to play by the rules and is the cause of a fellow pilot's death. When Wayne volunteers to fly a cargo plane loaded with nitroglycerine in what amounts to a suicide mission, Woody, who has learned his lesson, stows away on board and helps Wayne bomb the target. The plane is hit and Wayne and Woody are supposed to bail out, but only Wayne jumps. Woody, badly wounded, does not, and guides the ship down to hit just one more target, a Japanese supply train.

Propaganda Appeals: Guilt, Satanism, Illusion of Victory, Biblical Typologies, Territoriality

FOREIGN CORRESPONDENT (1940, WALTER WANGER PRODUCTIONS)

Director: Alfred Hitchcock
Screenplay: Charles Bennett, Joan Harrison; James Hilton, Robert Benchley (dialogue)
Cast: Joel McCrea, Laraine Day, Herbert Marshall, George Sanders, Albert Bassermann, Robert Benchley

McCrea's character, an American reporter, is sent by the editor of a New York newspaper to England to be the paper's newest foreign correspondent. He becomes involved in a web of intrigue as he uncovers a plot to sabotage talks aimed at avoiding a war in Europe. But they are unsuccessful and England and France declare war on Germany. In the climax, the principal German spy dies, and the reporter radios a story to New York warning of German treachery and Nazi plans to involve the entire world in war.

Propaganda Appeals: Guilt, Satanism, Illusion of Victory, Territoriality

GOD IS MY CO-PILOT (1945, WARNER BROS.)

Director: Robert Florey
Screenplay: Peter Milne, Abem Finkel, based on the book by Robert Lee Scott Jr.
Cast: Dennis Morgan, Dane Clark, Alan Hale, Raymond Massey, John Ridgeley, Andrea King, Richard Loo

Another Flying Tigers picture with much better aerial combat sequences than the Wayne film (spiced with radio banter between Richard Loo ["Tokyo Joe"] and the Americans; "Joe," a Japanese ace, learned to fly in Southern California). Based on the memoirs of Colonel Robert L. Scott of his days with General Claire Chenneault's American Volunteer Group force in China, the film explains how the Tigers were able to out fly and out fight the Japanese despite the enemy's far superior numbers and materiel. Scott also relates his own struggle over faith in God. In the end, Scott defeats "Tokyo Joe," is shot down himself and survives, only to be grounded with malaria. Finally, Scott prays to be allowed to go on one last mission, and his prayer is answered.

Propaganda Appeals: Guilt, Satanism, Illusion of Victory, Biblical Typologies, Territoriality

GUADALCANAL DIARY (1943, 20TH CENTURY FOX)

Director: Lewis Seiler
Screenplay: Lamar Trotti, Jerome Cady, based on the novel by Richard Tregaskis
Cast: Preston Foster, Lloyd Nolan, William Bendix, Richard Conte, Anthony Quinn, Richard Jaeckel

This film follows a typical company of US Marines from the troop ship to their assault landing on Guadalcanal to their eventual relief by the Army months later. In between, we are introduced to the men, follow their exploits, watch them turn from brash boys into battle-hardened veterans, and see some of them die. A truly pivotal World War II combat film, it combines equal amounts of vicious anti-Japanese propaganda with generous, down-to-earth development of the quintessential American GI.

Propaganda Appeals: Guilt, a huge dose of Satanism, Illusion of Victory, Territoriality

GUNG HO! (1943, UNIVERSAL/WALTER WANGER PRODUCTIONS)

Director: Ray Enright
Screenplay: Lucien Hubbard, Joseph Hoffman; W. S. LeFrancois (story)
Cast: Randolph Scott, Alan Curtis, Noah Beery Jr., J. Carrol Naish, Sam Levene, Robert Mitchum, Rod Cameron

A highly idealized reenactment of the Marine Raiders' famous Makin Island raid, from the formation of the battalion, through their training, to the wildly successful raid on the objective. Amazingly, 600 raiders attack 1,800 Japanese on the island, kill every enemy soldier, and lose only thirty of their own men in the process. Having achieved their goal, they escape in submarines just minutes before the Japanese fleet arrives.

Propaganda Appeals: Guilt, Satanism, Illusion of Victory, Biblical Typologies, Territoriality

A GUY NAMED JOE (1943, MGM)

Director: Victor Fleming
Screenplay: Dalton Trumbo, Frederick Hazlitt Brennan; Chandler Sprague, David Boehm (story)
Cast: Spencer Tracy, Irene Dunne, Van Johnson, Ward Bond, James Gleason, Lionel Barrymore, Barry Nelson

Part fantasy, part love story, part war film, this picture has the hero, Tracy's character, killed off in the second reel. Especially helpful to those back home who have lost loved ones in the war, the film shows Tracy, a pilot, coming back to earth as a sort of "guardian angel" to look after other pilots. Tracy leads one of them, Johnson's character, through training and into combat. In the climax, Tracy reconciles his old sweetheart to life without him and frees her to accept Johnson's proposal of marriage. This is also the only World War II picture to feature a woman flying a combat mission.

Propaganda Appeals: Illusion of Victory, Biblical Typologies

HANGMEN ALSO DIE! (1943, ARNOLD PRESSBURGER FILMS)

Director: Fritz Lang
Screenplay: John Wexley; Bertolt Brecht, Fritz Lang (story)

Cast: Brian Donlevy, Walter Brennan, Anna Lee, Gene Lockhart, Dennie O'Keefe, Margaret Wycherly

During the Nazi occupation of Czechoslovakia, the brutal Reich Protector of Prague, Reinhard Heydrich, is assassinated. His killer is a doctor and a Czech patriot who tries to hide out, but the cover is blown on his safe house. He then hides with a woman whose father (Brennan's character), a professor discredited by the Nazis, has been banned from teaching. With the help of a Czech collaborator, the Nazis begin a series of reprisal killings aimed at making Heydrich's assassin surrender. If he does not, more innocent people will be killed. The professor is among those arrested for the next batch of executions. But the Czech resistance instead manages to frame the collaborator for the assassination.

Propaganda Appeals: Guilt, Satanism, Illusion of Victory, Territoriality

THE HITLER GANG (1944, PARAMOUNT)

Director: John Farrow
Screenplay: Frances Goodrich, Albert Hackett, Kurt Neumann
Cast: Bobby Watson, Roman Bohnen, Martin Kosleck, Victor Varconi, Louis Van Rooten, Alex Pope

Using the plot style of a Hollywood gangster film (a gangster rises up through the ranks of criminals to lead his own criminal empire), this pseudo-documentary purports to show the rise of Adolph Hitler and his "gang" of followers into a powerful force in their country, and finally for Hitler to become chancellor of Germany.

Propaganda Appeals: Satanism, Territoriality

HOTEL BERLIN (1945, WARNER BROS.)

Director: Peter Godfrey
Screenplay: Jo Pagano, Avah Bessie, based on the novel by Vicki Baum

Cast: Faye Emerson, Helmut Dantine, Raymond Massey, Andrea King, Peter Lorre, Alan Hale, George Coulouris

Like *Grand Hotel*, this film tells the interwoven stories of a number of different characters staying in a hotel. It's 1945, the Third Reich is crumbling, and the end is a few months away. Among them are a German Resistance fighter, recently escaped from a Nazi concentration camp, a snoopy hotel maid who's on the make, a German general caught up in one of the plots to assassinate Hitler, the leader of a group that plans to escape to South America and later return to Germany to take power, an SS official, and a famous actress. Nearly all are trying to escape to a neutral country and away from the devastation in Berlin that will precede and follow Germany's *Gotterdammerung*. The resistance fighter makes his escape, the maid betrays anyone she can, the general kills himself, and so on.

Propaganda Appeals: Guilt, Satanism, Illusion of Victory, Territoriality

IMMORTAL SERGEANT (1943, 20TH CENTURY FOX)

Director: John M. Stahl
Screenplay: Lamar Trotti, John Brophy
Cast: Henry Fonda, Maureen O'Hara, Thomas Mitchell, Allyn Joslyn, Reginald Gardiner, Melville Cooper

A timid young Canadian corporal is a member of a British patrol in the North African desert, led by a veteran sergeant whom the young man admires greatly. During the patrol, the downing of an Italian plane turns into a tragedy when the aircraft crashes onto one of the patrol's vehicles, and many are killed. Later, the sergeant is also mortally wounded. Now the corporal is in charge of the three men left alive and must remember the lessons he has been taught. Channeling his beloved sergeant, the now confident corporal leads the three remaining soldiers on a successful attack on a patrol of Germans at an oasis. Leading this attack leads this changed man to a battlefield promotion. Now an officer, he even summons the gumption to propose to his girl.

Propaganda Appeals: Satanism, Illusion of Victory, Territoriality

JOAN OF PARIS (1943, RKO STUDIOS)

Director: Robert Stevenson
Screenplay: Charles Bennett, Ellis St. Joseph; Jacques Thery, Georges Kessel
Cast: Paul Henreid, Michelle Morgan, Paul Henreid, Thomas Mitchell, Laird Cregar, May Robson, Alan Ladd

In this story, Henreid's character, a Free French flying ace with a Nazi price on his head, along with four other RAF flyers (one severely wounded) is shot down near Paris. All are pursued by the Gestapo. Morgan's character takes Henreid in, falls in love with him, and, through the aid of the Resistance, arranges for all the flyers but one, who dies of his wounds, to escape to England. But in doing so, Joan must play a dangerous game of deception with Cregar's character, the Gestapo chief in Paris. In the end, the flyers escape and Joan faces a firing squad.

Propaganda Appeals: Guilt, Satanism, Illusion of Victory, Territoriality

LIFEBOAT (1944, 20TH CENTURY FOX)

Director: Alfred Hitchcock
Screenplay: Jo Swerling; John Steinbeck (story)
Cast: Tallulah Bankhead, John Hodiak, William Bendix, Walter Slezak, Henry Hull, Mary Anderson, Heather Angel, Hume Cronyn, Canada Lee

A World War II allegory. A standoff between a submarine and an armed freighter/passenger ship results in the sinking of both vessels. The civilian survivors of the battle take into their lifeboat the sole survivor of the U-boat. The German at first fools them into thinking that he is a harmless crewman who speaks only German. Later, the man is revealed to be the sub's captain, who speaks English. The Nazi deceives the survivors into believing that he will navigate their boat to Bermuda, but instead aims for a planned rendezvous with his submarine tender. After hoarding food and water and murdering one of the survivors, he is killed by the rest. Later, much wiser, and more wary of the Nazi menace, the survivors are rescued.

Propaganda Appeals: Guilt, Satanism, Illusion of Victory, Apocalypticism and Biblical Typologies, Territoriality

MANILA CALLING (1942, 20TH CENTURY FOX)

Director: Herbert I. Leeds
Screenplay: John Francis Larkin
Cast: Lloyd Nolan, Cornel Wilde, James Gleason, Carole Landis, Martin Kosleck, Ralph Byrd, Elisha Cook

In a plot very similar to *Bataan*, *Manila Calling* tells the story of American radio engineers who get caught up in the Japanese invasion of the Philippines. Fleeing the Japanese, these engineers encounter a band of Filipino scouts, and together they attack a plantation that has one huge radio transmitter. The group decides to use this radio to send propaganda messages of hope and encouragement to the people of the Philippines. They know they can't hold out indefinitely surrounded by Japanese troops, but they do it anyway. They hold out as long as they can, transmitting their messages as Japanese bombing attacks reduce their number to a few, and finally, as in *Bataan*, to the last man.

Propaganda Appeals: Guilt, Satanism, Illusion of Victory, Biblical Typologies, Territoriality

MRS. MINIVER (1942, MGM)

Director: William Wyler
Screenplay: Arthur Wimperis, George Froeschel, James Hilton, Claudine West, based on the book by Jan Struther

Cast: Greer Garson, Walter Pidgeon, Theresa Wright, Dame May Whitty, Henry Travers, Henry Wilcoxon, Reginald Owen

The saga of an upper-middle-class British family, beginning just prior to England's entry into the war: it chronicles the Minivers's personal contributions to the war and what it cost them. Their son gets married and leaves Oxford to join the RAF. Clement, his father, uses his motor launch to help rescue soldiers at Dunkirk, while his son fights Messerschmitts overhead. As a member of the home guard, Clem also hunts for a fugitive German pilot who crashed near their village. But the Nazi, wounded, makes it to the Miniver house. Mrs. Miniver manages to disarm him when he faints. The film ends with a terrifying bomb raid in which Vin's young wife is killed. The following Sunday the church's vicar preaches to the people and to us that it is "the people's war," as this film so eloquently states.

Propaganda Appeals: Guilt, Satanism, Illusion of Victory, Biblical Typologies, Territoriality

MISSION TO MOSCOW (1943, WARNER BROS.)

Director: Michael Curtiz
Screenplay: Howard Koch, based on the book by Joseph E. Davies
Cast: Walter Huston, Ann Harding, Oskar Homolka, George Tobias, Gene Lockhart, Eleanor Parker, Richard Travis, Helmut Dantine

A highly propagandistic pseudo-documentary based on US Ambassador Joseph E. Davies's memoir about his experiences as the US envoy to the Soviet Union. Davies begins as a critic of the Soviet Union, Josef Stalin and communism, but softens on much of his objections after his experiences. Even Stalin's show trials in the 1930s in which the dictator persecuted his opponents were characterized as purges of Japanese and German spies.

Propaganda Appeals: Satanism, Territoriality

THE MOON IS DOWN (1943, TWENTIETH CENTURY FOX)

Director: Irving Pichel
Screenplay: Nunnally Johnson, based on the novel by John Steinbeck
Cast: Sir Cedric Hardwicke, Henry Travers, Lee J. Cobb, Dorris Bowdon, Margaret Wycherly, Peter van Eyck

Beyond shock, the first reaction of a Norwegian coal mining town when the Germans invade is a surprise. At first, the German commandant, a gentleman, asks the town mayor to work with him for peaceful coexistence. Although the people are angry, for a while things are calm. But as little acts of sabotage against the mine's operations escalate, and finally when Norwegians kill German soldiers, the commandant has no choice but to order reprisals. Some townspeople have obtained explosives from the British, so when finally the mayor and other town leaders are hanged in reprisal, simultaneously the town resistance blows up the mine.

Propaganda Appeals: Guilt, Satanism, Illusion of Victory, Biblical Typologies, Territoriality

THE MORTAL STORM (1940, MGM)

Director: Frank Borzage
Screenplay: Claudine West, Hans Rameau, George Froeschel, based on the novel by Phyllis Bottome
Cast: James Stewart, Margaret Sullavan, Robert Young, Frank Morgan, Robert Stack

Although the studio went to great pains not to mention Germany by name or mention the persecution of the Jews (they were called "non Aryans"), this film resulted in all movies produced by MGM being banned in Germany. It tells the story of two young people in love who lived through it. Sullavan's character's father is arrested for his ideas, and when she visits him in prison, he advises her to flee to another country. He dies soon after. Stewart and Sullavan attempt to escape the country, but are hunted down. Sullavan's character is killed.

Propaganda Appeals: Guilt, Satanism

OBJECTIVE, BURMA! (1945, WARNER BROS.)

Director: Raoul Walsh
Screenplay: Ranald MacDougall, Lester Cole; Alvah Bessie (story)
Cast: Errol Flynn, James Brown, William Prince, Henry Hull, George Tobias, Warner Anderson, John Alvin
Oscars: Nominations for Best Original Story, Best Film Editing, Best Music Score

This is the controversial account of a paratrooper raid into Burma right before the Allies' big push to retake it from the Japanese. The reason for the furor about it (and its banning in England) is because it gave the impression that the British had little to do with the Burma campaign. In the film, Flynn's raiders destroy a vital enemy camp and communications center, and then, after losing many men, stage a heroic last stand against the Japanese, holding out until the main attack force arrives.

Propaganda Appeals: Guilt, Satanism, Illusion of Victory, Territoriality

PRIDE OF THE MARINES (1945, WARNER BROS.)

Director: Delmer Daves
Screenplay: Albert Maltz, Marvin Borowsky, based on a book by Roger Butterfield
Cast: John Garfield, Eleanor Parker, Dane Clark, John Ridgely, Rosemary DeCamp, Ann Doran, Ann Todd

Based on a true story, the film chronicles the life before war of a macho Philadelphia steel worker, Al Schmid, and how he finally falls for his future wife. Next, in the Marines, Schmid finds himself in the battle for Guadalcanal manning an M 1917 Browning machine gun. In a fierce battle, one of his friends dies, another, Lee Diamond, is wounded, and Schmid himself is blinded by a Japanese grenade. But despite being wounded, Schmid and Diamond manage to kill two hundred attacking enemy soldiers. The rest of the story centers on Schmid's rehabilitation. Never happy on relying on others and embarrassed about receiving the Navy Cross as a blind man, the Marine must learn to cope with his affliction. With the help of rehabilitation specialists and his soon-to-be wife, he adapts to his new situation. John Garfield, a method actor, plays Schmid. To research his role, Garfield met and actually lived with the Schmids for several weeks.

Propaganda Appeals: Guilt, Satanism, Illusion of Victory

THE PURPLE HEART (1944, 20TH CENTURY FOX)

Director: Lewis Milestone
Screenplay: Jerome Cady; Darryl F. Zanuck (story)
Cast: Dana Andrews, Richard Conte, Farley Granger, Richard Loo, Don Barry, Sam Levine, John Craven

In response to reports of Japanese mistreatment of Allied prisoners, this film is a fictionalized account of the kangaroo court trial, conviction on false charges and subsequent execution of three B-25 crewmen from the Doolittle Raid. In reality, another crewman POW died of mistreatment at the hands of the enemy and one additional air crewman out of the eighty Doolittle raiders died during the crash landing of his B-25 in China. In this film, a crew of eight are given a kangaroo court show trial, found guilty, and, at the end of the picture, marched off to be executed. In the film, these flyers, under orders not to reveal how they were able to penetrate Japan's "Iron Wall" of defense to successfully bomb Tokyo, undergo torture and choose to accept execution rather than reveal their base to the Japanese. Their refusal to admit that they actually flew their bombers off the flight deck of the *USS Hornet*—and not from some base in China, Russia, or "Shangri-la," as FDR had joked—causes an important Japanese general to commit suicide.

Propaganda Appeals: Guilt, Satanism, Illusion of Victory, Biblical Typologies, Territoriality

SABOTEUR (1942, UNIVERSAL)

Director, Alfred Hitchcock
Screenplay: Peter Viertel, Joan Harrison, Dorothy Parker
Cast: Robert Cummings, Priscilla Lane, Norman Lloyd, Otto Kruger, Alan Baxter, Norman Lloyd

A home front spy thriller, Cummings' character, a defense worker, is accused of setting a sabotage fire at his aircraft plant in which a worker was killed. Wanted by both the police and the spies, he chases the saboteur, played by Lloyd, across the country. Along the way he encounters an initially reluctant Lane, who, in typical 39 *Steps* Hitchcock fashion, eventually warms to Cummings and becomes his ally. The two try in vain to prevent the saboteurs from destroying a newly built warship at the Brooklyn Navy Yard. The famous climax occurs when Cummings pursues Lloyd to the top of the Statue of Liberty, where Lloyd falls to his death.

Propaganda Appeals: Guilt, Satanism, Illusion of Victory, Biblical Typologies, Territoriality

SAHARA (1943, COLUMBIA)

Director: Zoltan Korda
Screenplay: John Howard Lawson, Zoltan Korda; James O'Hanlon (adaptation); Philip MacDonald (story)
Cast: Humphrey Bogart, Dan Duryea, Bruce Bennett, J. Carroll Naish, Rex Ingram, Richard Aherne, Louis Mercier, Guy Kingsford

A "lost patrol" picture, *Sahara* is also an allegory depicting the physical, intellectual, and moral superiority of the Allies over the Germans. Less than a dozen assorted soldiers from many of the allied countries dig in and hold an oasis in the desert, denying a thirsty German battalion the use of a well. This finally causes the Nazis to surrender, although these Allied soldiers were greatly outnumbered. This sacrifice—since nearly all these men were killed—was purported to help the British defeat the Germans at El Alamein by denying them the use of this battalion.

Propaganda Appeals: Guilt, Satanism, Illusion of Victory, Apocalypticism and Biblical Typologies, Territoriality

SO PROUDLY WE HAIL! (1943, PARAMOUNT)

Director: Mark Sandrich
Screenplay: Allan Scott
Cast: Claudette Colbert, Paulette Goddard, Veronica Lake, George Reeves, Barbara Britton, Sonny Tufts

Partially based on books by men and women who actually served in the Philippines after the Japanese invasion, this tale chronicles the story of a group of nurses, called the "Angels of Bataan," who stayed to the very end to care for wounded American and Filipino soldiers holding out against the Japanese on this island. Centering on a tragic love story between Reeves and Colbert's characters, the plot shows in flashback the sacrifices offered by these women to support General MacArthur's fighting men.

Propaganda Appeals: Guilt, Satanism, Illusion of Victory, Biblical Typologies, Territoriality

TARZAN TRIUMPHS (1943, RKO)

Director: William Thiele
Screenplay: Roy Chanslor, Carroll Young; Carroll Young (story)
Cast: Johnny Weismuller, Johnny Sheffield, Frances Gifford, Stanley Ridges, Sig Ruman, Philip Van Zandt

In an attempt to involve their series of ape man films in the war effort, RKO delivers yet another anti-isolationist allegory, albeit a silly one. In this fantasy, for a somewhat unclear reason, the Nazis invade an African city-state and enslave its natives. Their neighbor, Tarzan, refuses to help his neighbors, asserting, "Nazis leave Tarzan alone, Tarzan leave Nazis alone." But when the Germans kidnap his son, Tarzan goes ape, attacks and frees the natives, precipitating an uprising. Now allied, together they destroy the enemy.

Propaganda Appeals: Guilt, Satanism, Illusion of Victory, Territoriality

THEY WERE EXPENDABLE (1945, MGM)

Director: John Ford
Screenplay: Frank "Spig" Wead, based on the book by William L. White
Cast: John Wayne, Robert Montgomery, Donna Reed, Ward Bond, Jack Holt

The exploits of a squadron of PT boats in the Philippines, from Pearl Harbor until the fall of Corregador. The squadron proves the worth of the motor torpedo boat, sinking everything they are sent out to attack, from troop barges to heavy cruisers and even a small Japanese aircraft carrier. But one by one, lack of parts and enemy action reduces the PT force until the last boat is gone. Finally, four of the squadron's officers are ordered out to Australia "to do a job, to get ready to come back." They go home to train others in the successful PT boat tactics they developed.

Propaganda Appeals: Guilt, Satanism, Illusion of Victory, Biblical Typologies, Territoriality

THIRTY SECONDS OVER TOKYO (1944, MGM)

Director: Mervyn Le Roy
Screenplay: Dalton Trumbo, based on the book by Ted W. Lawson and Robert Considine
Cast: Van Johnson, Phyllis Thaxter, Robert Walker, Tim Murdock, Robert Mitchum, Spencer Tracy, Don DeFore

A glitzy MGM recounting of the famous Jimmy Doolittle raid, the "counter punch" bombing of the Japanese mainland in revenge for Pearl Harbor, told through the real experiences of Captain Ted Lawson and the crew of their bomber, the "Ruptured Duck." It begins with the crews' selection and training, follows them on board the *USS Hornet*, and rides along on board the *Duck* as Lawson's crew bombs Tokyo. Because of their crash-landing off the China coast, all but one of the crew are badly injured, Lawson the worst. Eventually, he will lose his leg. But Chinese soldiers and civilians rescue them, heal their wounds, and guide them to safety. Intertwined in this is the love story between Johnson and Thaxter's characters. Tracy's portrayal of Jimmy Doolittle is spot-on.

Propaganda Appeals: Guilt, Satanism, Illusion of Victory, Biblical Typologies, Territoriality

THIS LAND IS MINE (1943, RKO)

Director: Jean Renoir
Screenplay: Dudley Nichols
Cast: Charles Laughton, Maureen O'Hara, George Sanders, Una O'Connor, Walter Slezak, Kent Smith, Philip Merivale, Thurston Hall

In a town in occupied France, a middle-aged, timid schoolteacher (Laughton) is too afraid of the Nazis to resist or to join the Resistance. But when his school's principal, a man he much admires, is taken hostage and shot, Laughton summons up all his courage and rises to the occasion. Falsely accused of murdering a collaborator, he nonetheless uses his defense speech in court to chide his fellow citizens for war profiteering and inaction. He urges them instead to make the sacrifices necessary to sabotage the German war machine however they can. Later, back at his school, before the Germans arrest him and take him away to be shot, he reads the Nazi-banned French *Declaration of the Rights of Men* to his class. To reinforce the propaganda statement that during Nazi occupation, when one resister is killed, another will rise to take his place, Renoir/Nichols conclude the film with O'Hara's character, also a schoolteacher, taking charge of the class and finishing the reading of the *Declaration*.

Propaganda Appeals: Guilt, Satanism, Illusion of Victory, Biblical Typologies, Territoriality

WAKE ISLAND (1942, PARAMOUNT)

Director: John Farrow
Screenplay: W. R. Burnett, Frank Butler
Cast: Brian Donlevy, William Bendix, Robert Preston, Albert Dekker, MacDonald Carey, Walter Abel

A dramatization of the heroic stand US Marines made against the invading Japanese on Wake Island at the outset of the war. Although heavily outgunned, outnumbered, and faced with an entire fleet of invading Japanese ships and carrier planes, the Marines, with four planes, a battalion of men, and a few artillery pieces, hold their position for over two weeks before finally being overrun.

Propaganda Appeals: Guilt (a heavy emphasis in this film), Satanism, Illusion of Victory, Apocalypticism and Biblical Typologies, Territoriality

A WALK IN THE SUN (1945, 20TH CENTURY FOX)

Director: Lewis Milestone
Screenplay: Robert Rossen, based on the book by Harry Brown
Cast: Dana Andrews, Richard Conte, Lloyd Bridges, John Ireland, Norman Lloyd, George Tyne, Sterling Holloway

A very personal account of one army platoon's experiences from the LST landing barge to the beachhead, to their journey inland to their final objective, an Italian farmhouse that they must take away from entrenched Germans. The two-hour film follows the patrol though this twelve-hour trek. Finally, the farmhouse is reached and a bloody final battle follows. The Americans win, and the platoon's survivors move on to other battles and other objectives. This film is significant for even-handed and sensitive treatment of the "battle fatigue" of one of its characters. Such treatments of battle fatigue (now known as post-traumatic stress disorder) were commonplace in postwar films, but this movie was produced during 1944 before the end of the war in Europe.

Propaganda Appeals: Satanism, Illusion of Victory, Biblical Typologies, Territoriality

WATCH ON THE RHINE (1943, WARNER BROS.)

Director: Herman Shumlin
Screenplay: Dashiell Hammett, Lillian Hellman, based on the play by Hellman
Cast: Bette Davis, Paul Lukas, Geraldine Fitzgerald, Lucile Watson, Beulah Bondi, George Coulouris

Story based on Hellman's stage play of the Muller family, a German-born engineer and his American wife and children, who have been living in Europe. Muller has been active in anti-Nazi operations and in 1940 manages to get to the United States and seeks asylum for himself and his family. Unfortunately, a houseguest where the family is staying is a German agent, who rifles through Muller's papers and identifies a resistance member in Germany, Muller's friend, who subsequently is arrested by the Gestapo. Muller kills the German agent and heads back to Germany to try to rescue his friend. The film concludes when, after a time in which the family hears nothing from Muller, his eldest son makes plans to seek his father back in Germany and carry on the fight.

Propaganda Appeals: Guilt, Satanism, Illusion of Victory, Biblical Typologies, Territoriality

WHAT PRICE GLORY (1926, FOX)

Director: Raoul Walsh
Screenplay: James T. O'Donohoe; Malcolm Stuart Boylan (titles); based on the play by Maxwell Anderson and Laurence Stallings

Cast: Victor McLaglen, Edmund Lowe, Dolores del Rio, William V. Mong, Phyllis Haver

US Marines Quirt and Flagg have had many postings together prior to World War I. Both seasoned veterans, now they find themselves in a world war, but with the same old baggage. They seem to delight in competing for the same women no matter what the duty. In this silent version of the story (in 1952 John Ford would remake it with James Cagney and Dan Dailey), while competing for a girl name Charmaine, they fight the war. All too used to the killing and maiming, these desensitized career soldiers both hate it and are attracted to it like moths to a flame. And at the end, it's not women but the next big push against the Germans that unites Quirt and Flagg, as together they head out to the front.

Propaganda Appeals: Illusion of Victory, Territoriality

BIBLIOGRAPHY

Agee, James. *Agee on Film: Essays and Reviews by James Agee*. New York: Grosset and Dunlap, 1969.

Andrews, James R. "They Chose the Sword: Appeals to War in Nineteenth-Century American Public Address." *Today's Speech* 17, September 1969.

Ardrey, Robert. *The Territorial Imperative: A Personal Inquiry into the Animal Origins of Property and Nations*. New York: Athenaeum Press, 1966.

Bandura, Albert. *Social Learning Theory*. New York: General Learning Press, 1977.

Basinger, Jeanine. *The World War II Combat Film: Anatomy of a Genre*. New York: Columbia University Press, 1986.

Bazin, André. *Jean Renoir*. New York: Dell, 1973.

Brokaw, Tom. *The Greatest Generation*. New York: Random House, 1997.

Burke, Kenneth. *Counter Statement*, 2nd. ed. Los Altos, CA: University of California Press, 1952.

Burke, Kenneth. *The Philosophy of Literary Form: Studies in Symbolic Action*. Los Angeles: University of California Press, 1973.

Center For Responsive Politics. "Overall Spending Inches Up in 2014: Megadonors Equip Outside Groups to Capture a Bigger Share of the Pie." https://www.opensecrets.org/news/2014/10/overall-spending-inches-up-in-2014-megadonors-equip-outside-groups-to-capture-a-bigger-share-of-the-pie/.

Clausewitz, Carl von. *On War*. Princeton, NJ: Princeton University Press, 1976.

Congressional Record. 65th Congress (Woodrow Wilson), vol. 55, April 2, 1917: 102–103.

Crowther, Bosley. *The Lion's Share*. New York: Dutton, 1957.

———. "The Ramparts We Watch." *New York Times*, September 20, 1940.

Davis, Jefferson. *Jefferson Davis, Constitutionalist*. New York: AMS Press, 1973.

Delahanty, Thornton. "Disney Studio at War." *Theatre Arts*, January 27, 1943: 31–39.

Dick, Bernard. *The Star-Spangled Screen: The American World War II Film*. Lexington: University of Kentucky Press, 1985.

Doob, Leonard. *Propaganda: Its Psychology and Technique*. New York: Holt, 1935.

Eisenstein, Sergei. *The Film Sense*. New York: Harcourt Brace, 1969.

Ellul, Jacques. *Propaganda: The Formation of Man's Attitudes*. New York: Vintage, 1973.

Frakes, Margaret. "Time Marches Back." *The Christian Century*, October 16, 1940.

Friedel, Frank. *The Splendid Little War*. Boston: Little, Brown and Co. 1958.

Grierson, John. *Grierson on Documentary*, edited by Forsyth Hardy. New York: Praeger, 1947.

Gussow, Mel. *Don't Say Yes Until I Finish Talking: A Biography of Darryl F. Zanuck*. Garden City, NY: Doubleday, 1971.

Harmon, Francis S. *The Command is Forward: Selections from Addresses on the Motion Picture Industry in War and Peace.* New York: Richard R. Smith, 1944.

Hays, Will H. *The Memoirs of Will H. Hays.* Garden City, NY: A. S. Barnes & Co., Inc., 1968.

Hellman, John. *American Myth and the Legacy of Vietnam.* New York: Columbia University Press, 1986.

Higham, Charles. *Warner Brothers.* New York: Scribners, 1975.

Higham, Charles, and Greenberg, Joel. *Hollywood in the Forties.* New York: A. S. Barnes & Co., 1968.

"Hollywood in Uniform." *Fortune,* April, 25, 1942.

Insdorf, Annette. *Indelible Shadows: Film and the Holocaust.* New York: Random House, 1983.

Ivie, Robert L. "Images of Savagery in American Justifications for War." *Communication Monographs* 47, no. 4 (November 1980): 279–94.

———. "The Metaphor of Force in Pro-war Discourse: The Case of 1812." *Quarterly Journal of Speech* 68 (1982): 240–53.

———. "Metaphor and the Rhetorical Invention of Cold War 'Idealists.'" *Communication Monographs* 54 (June 1987): 161–68.

Jensen, Oliver. "Too Much Success: Movies Made More Money Than Progress." *Life,* November 25, 1946.

Johnson, Lyndon B. "The President's News Conference of July 20, 1965." In *The Public Papers of the Presidents of the United States.* Washington, DC: Office of the Federal Register, National Archives and Records Service, 1965: 795.

Jones, Dorothy. "Is Hollywood Growing Up?" *The Nation,* February 3, 1945: 123.

———. "Hollywood Goes to War." *The Nation,* January 27, 1945: 93–95.

Jowett, Garth S., and Victoria O'Donnell. *Propaganda and Persuasion,* 4th ed. Thousand Oaks, CA: Sage Publications, 2006.

Koppes, Clayton R., and Gregory D. Black. *Hollywood Goes to War: How Politics, Profits and Propaganda Shaped World War II Movies.* New York: The Free Press, 1987.

Larson, Cedric. "The Domestic Motion Picture Work of the Office of War Information." *Hollywood Quarterly* 3, no. 4 (1948): 434–43.

Lasswell, Harold. *Propaganda Technique in World War I.* Boston: MIT Press, 1971.

———. "The Structure and Function of Communication in Society." In *The Communication of Ideas,* edited by Lyman Bryson, 215–28. New York: Harper, 1948.

Lazarsfeld, Paul, and Merton, Robert K. "Mass Communication, Popular Taste, and Organized Social Action." In *The Communication of Ideas,* edited by Lyman Bryson, 95–118. New York: Harper, 1948.

Look Magazine. *Movie Lot to Beachhead: The Motion Picture Goes to War and Prepares for the Future.* Garden City, NY: Doubleday, 1945.

Luther, Martin. "A Mighty Fortress Is Our God." In *The Hymnal, 1982, According to the Use of the Episcopal Church,* 682. New York: The Church Hymnal Corporation, 1985.

Mast, Gerald. *The Movies in Our Midst: Documents in the Cultural History of Film in America.* Chicago: University of Chicago Press, 1982.

Maynard, Richard A. *Propaganda on Film: A Nation at War.* Rochelle Park, NJ: Haydon-Books, 1975.

Meyers, Marvin, ed. *The Mind of the Founder: Sources of the Political Thought of James Madison.* Hanover & London: University Press of New England, 1981.

McBride, Joseph, ed. *Focus on Howard Hawks.* Englewood Cliffs, NJ: Prentice-Hall, 1972.

McKinley, William. *A Compilation of the Messages and Papers of the Presidents,* Vol. XIV. New York: Bureau of National Literature, 1965.

Morella, Joe, Edward Z. Epstein, and John Griggs. *The Films of World War II.* Secaucus, NJ: Citadel Press, 1973.

Murrow, Edward R. Speech from CBS television program *See It Now,* March 9, 1954.

Nugent, Frank S. "Confessions of a Nazi Spy." *New York Times,* May 24, 1939.

Osborn, Michael. "Archetypal Metaphors in Rhetoric: The Light-Dark Family." *Quarterly Journal of Speech* 53, no. 2 (1967): 115–26.

Pendo, Stephen. *Aviation in the Cinema*. Metuchen, NJ: Scarecrow Press, 1985.

"Propaganda or History?" *The Nation*, September 20, 1941: 241–42.

Reid, Ronald F. "Apocalypticism and Typology: Rhetorical Dimensions of a Symbolic Reality." *Quarterly Journal of Speech* 69, no. 3 (August 1983): 229–48.

———. "New England Rhetoric and the French War, 1754–1760: A Case Study in the Rhetoric of War." *Communication Monographs* 43, no. 4 (November, 1976): 259–86.

Richards, I. A. *The Philosophy of Rhetoric*. New York: Oxford University Press, 1965.

Roosevelt, Franklin D. *The Public Papers and Addresses of Franklin D. Roosevelt*, Vols. 1937, 1939, 1940, 1941. New York: MacMillan Co., 1941.

Rotha, Paul. *Documentary Film*. New York: Hastings House, 1952.

Rubin, Steven Jay. *Combat Films, 1945–1970*. Jefferson, NC: McFarland, 1961.

Rusk, Dean. "Laos and Vietnam: A Prescription for Peace." Address by Secretary Dean Rusk before the American Law Institute. *Department of State Bulletin*, June 8, 1961. Washington, DC: US Government Printing Office, 1961.

Santayana, George. *Reason in Common Sense*. New York, Scribners, 1920.

Schickel, Richard. *The Disney Version: The Life, Times, Art and Commerce of Walt Disney*. New York: Random House, 1976.

Selznick, David O., and Behlmer, Rudy, ed. *Memo from David O. Selznick*. New York: Viking, 1972.

Shain, Russell E. "An Analysis of Motion Pictures about War Released by the American Film Industry, 1939–1970." PhD diss., Urbana: University of Illinois at Urbana-Champaign, 1971.

Short, K. R. M. *Film and Radio Propaganda in World War II*. Knoxville: University of Tennessee Press, 1983.

Sklar, Robert. *Movie-Made America: A Cultural History of American Movies*. New York: Random House, 1975.

Soderbergh, Peter A. "The Grand Illusion: Hollywood and World War II, 1930–1945." *University of Dayton Review* 5, no. 3 (Winter 1968–1969): 113–22.

Taylor, Richard. *Film Propaganda: Soviet Russia and Nazi Germany*, 2nd. revised edition. London: I. B. Tauris, 1998.

Thomas, Bob. *King Cohn*. New York: G.P. Putnam's Sons, 1967.

Truman, Harry S. *Public Papers of the Presidents of the United States: Harry Truman, January 1 to December 31, 1950*. Washington, DC: US Government Printing Office, 1965.

Truffaut, Francois, with Helen G. Scott. *Hitchcock*. New York: Simon and Schuster, 1966.

Tyler, Moses C. *Patrick Henry*. New York: Fredrick Unger, 1966.

US Congress. *Investigation of the National Defense Program: Hearings before a Special Committee Investigating the National Defense Program*. US Senate, Seventy-Seventh Congress, First Session—Eightieth Congress, First Session, Part 37□. Washington: US Government Printing Office, 1947.

US Congress. *Propaganda in Moving Pictures: Hearings before a Subcommittee of the Committee on Interstate Commerce*. US Senate, Seventy-Seventh Congress, First Session. Washington: US Government Printing Office, 1942.

US Congressional Record, 65th Congress, Vol. 55, April 2, 1917.

US State Department Bulletin. "Laos and Vietnam—A Prescription for Peace." Address by Secretary Dean Rusk before the American Law Institute, Washington, DC. June 8, 1964.

"U.S. Total Media Ad Spend Inches Up, Pushed By Digital." eMarketer, August 22, 2013. http://www.emarketer.com/Article/US-Total-Media-Ad-Spend-Inches-Up-Pushed-by-Digital/1010154.

Wanger, Walter. "Hollywood and the Intellectuals." *Saturday Review of Literature*, December 5, 1942: 6–8.

———. "Movies with a Message." *Saturday Review of Literature*, March 7, 1942: 12.

———. "OWI and Motion Pictures." *Public Opinion Quarterly* 7, no. 1 (1943): 100–107.

———. "Walt Disney, Patriot." *Free World* magazine, III (1946): 445.

War Activities Committee of the Motion Picture Industry. *Movies at War: Reports of the WAC, 1942–1945*. New York: War Activities Committee, 1945.

Warner, Jack L. *My First Hundred Years in Hollywood.* New York: Random House, 1964.

Weaver, Richard M. *The Ethics of Rhetoric.* Chicago: Henry Regnery Co., 1953.

INDEX

ABOUT THE AUTHOR

Ralph Donald is professor emeritus of mass communications at Southern Illinois University Edwardsville. He taught broadcasting and journalism for forty years. Donald's professional credits include jobs as a newspaper editor, a television news producer, TV station production manager, and a writer-producer-director of commercials and documentaries on film and video. His research and publications include film and television propaganda, motion picture history, gender-related issues, American studies, and mass communications curriculum issues. Some of Donald's works include two coauthored books, both with Karen Mac-Donald: *Reel Men at War: Masculinity and the American War Film* (Scarecrow Press, 2011) and *Women in War Films: From Helpless Heroine to G.I. Jane* (Rowman & Littlefield, 2014). He lives with his wife, Karen, at the Lake of the Ozarks in mid-Missouri.

CPSIA information can be obtained
at www.ICGtesting.com
Printed in the USA
BVOW08*2321050417

480438BV00003B/8/P